SCORE MORE
FOR
DRESSAGE

SCORE MORE
FOR
DRESSAGE

A strategic approach for all-round improvement

WENDY JAGO

J.A. ALLEN · LONDON

© Wendy Jago 2006
First published in Great Britain 2006

ISBN-10: 0-85131-922-X
ISBN-13: 978-0-85131-922-3

J.A. Allen
Clerkenwell House
Clerkenwell Green
London EC1R 0HT

J.A. Allen is an imprint of Robert Hale Limited

The right of Wendy Jago to be identified as author
of this work has been asserted by her in accordance
with the Copyright, Designs and Patents Act 1988

A catalogue record for this book is available from the British Library

The author and publisher are grateful to the following individuals and organizations for their kind permission to reproduce material: HarperCollins Publishers Ltd for permission to quote from *Hare Brain, Tortoise Mind* by Guy Claxton and *The Inner Game of Tennis* by Timothy Gallwey; Meta Publications for permission to quote from *Changing Belief Systems* by Robert Dilts; Charles de Kunffy and Paul Belasik for permission to quote from their various works cited throughout; British Dressage for permission to reproduce dressage test material in Chapter 14; The German National Equestrian Federation for permission to quote from their *Handbook*.

Edited by Martin Diggle
Design and typesetting by Paul Saunders
Photographs by Leo Jago
Line diagrams by Rodney Paull
Line illustrations on page 54 by Maggie Raynor

Printed by New Era Printing Co. Limited, Hong Kong

For Kimberley Battleday, who introduced us to classical
dressage and changed our lives.

And in loving memory of Lolly, Loyal Knight,
for thirteen years our friend, teacher and partner.
Truly named and much missed.

Acknowledgements

Any author stands on the shoulders of many people, relying on their expertise, support and friendship. I am so grateful to you all – and it has been such fun working with you. If I have wobbled, that's my responsibility, not yours.

The warmest of thank-yous to all the following:

The team at J.A. Allen's:
Caroline Burt and Cassandra Campbell, who commissioned and nurtured the project.

Martin Diggle, probably the best editor I could ever have.

Paul Saunders, who turns my raw typescripts into things of delight and beauty.

The centaurs, who worked and played with me so willingly and so splendidly:
Roy Brown and Cori.
Shane Petkovic and Ted.
Carolyn Peers and Ambrose.
Annie Rowland and Red.

My friend Nikki Green, who often explores riding with me and makes loose-schooling with her horses both a conversation and an art form.

The TTT, the inspired foundation of Tom and the late Jennifer Sewell, where I have learnt so much over the years and where, as Paul Belasik shows us, we are always beginning.

Ali Cookson, whose ability to ride it wrong (to order) is as amazing as her ability to ride it right; who, with the help of Jay and Wattie, demonstrated both so outstandingly; and who hones and stretches my own riding with fun as well as finesse.

Those great masters, Charles de Kunffy and Erik Herbermann, whose teaching I have watched and whose books I have read with such a sense of inspiration, and who help me continue to further my own journey of apprenticeship.

And finally, my husband Leo, whose project this has been as much as mine, and whose photographs say it all so eloquently for me.

How privileged I have been to be in such company.

Contents

Section one **New keys to improvement** 11

Maxim: the goal is within you, not outside you

1 Starting points 12
Underlying themes 15

2 What's the point of dressage? 22
Dressage and Classical Riding 24
Why you should do dressage 28

3 The diagnostic horse – what your horse is telling you 34
What you get is what you asked for 36
Your horse as your mirror 42

Section two **Pathways to performance: the physical skills** 49

Maxim: begin with yourself

4 Let's talk about outline 50
Getting the horse on the bit 50
How the classical position works 52
Making changes 55
Earning a more advanced outline 56
Trouble-shooting 58

5 The training spiral 60
Rhythm 63
Suppleness (Losgelassenheit) 65
Contact 67
Impulsion with elasticity (Schwung) 69
Straightness 70
Collection 72

6 Working up the spiral and the competition levels 74
   The competition levels 75
   Tips for trainers 86

7 Decoding your test sheets 88
   Reading your sheets right 88
   Decoding specific comments 91

8 No arena, no problem 108
   Schooling without an arena: the guiding principle 109
   Schooling 'outside the box' 112
   Making the most of what you've got 114

Section three **Pathways to performance: the mental skills** 123
Maxim: how you think shapes what you do

9 Is your mind on the job? 124
   The mind-body connection 125
   Using your mind bank 130

10 Paying the right kind of attention 136
   Just how are you paying attention? 136
   Bubbles of concentration – helpful or unhelpful? 137
   Broad beam or narrow focus – your choice 141
   What's in it for your horse? 146
   Tips for trainers 146

11 Where do your assumptions get you? 148
   Assumptions about physical problems 150
   Assumptions about what horses think and feel 154
   Thinking differently 157
   Tips for trainers 162

12 Self-belief, self-talk and rehearsal 163
   Self-belief 164
   Self-talk 168
   Rehearsal 173
   Tips for trainers 176

Section four **Pathways to performance: the strategic skills** 179

Maxim: there are always alternatives

13 Strategies for managing competition nerves 180
What nerves mean 180
How you can change things around 184
A strategy for effective self-management 188

14 'Reading' and choosing tests 194
Learning to 'read' the tests 195
Taking the test from your horse's perspective 196
Thinking ahead 215
Choosing the right tests – a strategic approach 216
Showing your horse at his best 218

Section five **Working together** 220

Maxim: you've got what it takes

15 Are you on target? 222
The need for mental strategy in riding 223
Exploring the neuroLogical levels model 224
Learning and change – don't stop too soon! 229
Tips for trainers 233

16 Coaching centaurs 236
Annie and Red 238
Carolyn and Ambrose 246
Shane and Ted 254
Roy and Cori 263
How we worked together 272

References 279
Useful reading 281
Useful contacts 283
Index 284

We should ride to do something good for the horse's sake so that he can be beautiful and display himself by his own will to his own advantage. We should not manipulate horses to make them our competition vehicles for winning ribbons. I think it is very important that we raise a generation of riders who understand how competition can be rewarding, but should not become the ultimate goal of horsemanship…

…and I think that when a very good rider on a very well-trained horse appears in front of an expert judge, he will inevitably be victorious.

Charles de Kunffy, *The Ethics and Passions of Dressage*[1]

section one

New keys to improvement

Starting points	12
What's the point of dressage?	22
The diagnostic horse – what your horse is telling you	34

1 Starting points

> Always, you start with the rider.
> **Charles de Kunffy,** comment in training

The good news is that improving your dressage scores starts with you. If there is any corresponding 'bad news' in this, it's just that this offers you the demanding, but often exciting, challenge of regearing your thinking as well as retraining your body.

To continue the good news: when you change the way you use your body and your mind, your horse will change too. He can't do other than this, because you will be giving him different messages to respond to. Think of relationships between people, where the same thing happens. If one person in a relationship makes even a small change in the existing pattern of interaction between the two of them and behaves in a new or different way, they are cueing their partner towards responding differently as well. Riding is built on communication; deliberate aiding is one form of signalling, but so too are our mental assumptions and accidental or unintentional body signals. Horses receive and respond to both.

I've been a rider since I was 10 years old, and a dressage judge for many years. Through these experiences, and through riders' responses to my previous books, *Schooling Problems Solved with NLP* and *Solo Schooling*, and working with them in my 'Make a Difference' clinics, I've realized very clearly that improving your dressage score isn't simply a matter of technique. You will certainly find plenty of technical information and tips in this book, and photos that show you clearly the 'how-tos' and 'how-not-tos'. But in addition to (1) telling you how to develop your competition strategies, it will also show you (2) how to achieve more effective control of your body and its messages to your horse and (3) how to recognize the way your feelings affect your riding, so that you feel more in charge of yourself,

Maxim | the goal is within you, not outside you

both in schooling and in competition. So it will give you a three-pronged approach to the question: *'How can I get higher marks?'*

My intention in this book is to offer you a much richer range of strategies for improvement than simply expanding your technical know-how. Test-riding is your benchmark for your current way of working: when you change that in this rich range of ways, you open up the possibility of improving your technique on a different basis. As a result you may find that you can increase your score just a small amount in one area, perhaps not at all *yet* in another, and by several points somewhere else – just because you will be achieving greater mastery of yourself and your horse in a whole range of ways.

Improvement on this rich basis doesn't stop or even stall, because it continually opens up the way to further understanding, further subtleties and further achievements. And there will be other benefits, too.

Often, riders tell me that they feel they are letting their horse down in some way. We love our horses and admire their good qualities, even when we're fully aware of their limitations; most of us are aware of *our* limitations, too, and hate the feeling that we're not worthy of that talent underneath us. Most riders want to be able to show their horse at his best: this book will help you to do that. In the process, you're likely to discover more about your own body and, as you work to develop more fine control over it, you'll find more pleasure not just in your riding but in being yourself in your own skin, whatever situation you're in. And as you pinpoint just what assumptions or limiting beliefs may be getting in your way and learn how to reroute the power of your mind into more productive patterns, you'll find not just your riding but your whole self-confidence blossoming.

How do I know that this can happen? When I'm not writing books I work as a coach, helping people manage themselves more effectively at home and at work. Every one of us has individual strengths and limitations: once we identify what these are and learn some skills for managing them, we can become more at ease with ourselves in every area of our lives. The secret of self-management – in riding as in anything else – is to suspend not observation, not understanding, but positive or negative judgement. Labels like 'good' and 'bad' get our feelings involved and usually get in the way of clear sight and objective judgement. The key question is always: *what results?* An apparently 'good' personal quality such as determination may not be appropriate, or indeed effective, in every situation – for example, when it involves someone losing their temper with a horse, overfacing him, or ignoring his signals of confusion, discomfort or distress. On the other hand, an unwanted quality in yourself, like nervousness, may not only keep you and your horse out of danger but, with this new, rich approach, be your signal for new understanding and new learning that can not only improve your riding, but may cascade into and transform other areas of your life.

Maxim | the goal is within you, not outside you

Another way of looking at this is to think of your actions – what you *do* – as only one layer of the onion – and an outer one at that. Some actions in riding are *inexcusable*, for example, using violence when your horse doesn't do what you want. But even something like this can be *understandable*, because physical violence is always a sign that someone has run out of other options. By going deeper into the onion and asking yourself what was going on in you, in terms of thoughts and feelings, and what kind of a blockage in communication resulted between you and your horse, you can begin to open up a much more fruitful conversation, first with yourself and then with him. And your interaction will change as a result. You will have become more resourceful inside, and what you do on the outside will be more effective.

The same is true for qualities you'd be more likely to consider 'good'. For example, I'm really skilled at building rapport with people, encouraging them to accept themselves and allowing them to take their time to work on their problems or limitations. This doesn't work nearly so well when I need to assert myself or put my foot down – and it doesn't work all that well with horses, who need to have the confidence of clear instructions and clear boundaries. So one of my ongoing tasks as a rider is to get clearer and quicker in telling my horse what I want.

Here's another for-instance. Carolyn, one of my case-study riders, is very talented, but such a perfectionist! This is great at work and helps her to be a good parent and a conscientious and skilled rider; but it also means that she often isn't satisfied with herself when she really has the right to be. Shortly before I wrote this she competed in the National Riding Clubs' Pairs Dressage, which she and her partner had won the previous year. This time, they had a couple of lowish marks and 'only came second'. Carolyn feared that she had let her partner down. But what had been the build-up to this competition? A few weeks before the competition Carolyn's usual pairs partner suffered a sudden and serious brain haemorrhage, so on the day she rode with her friend's daughter instead. Because of accidents on the motorway their journey to the venue took over six hours. When they got there Carolyn's (large) horse banged his head in his (small) box. Furthermore, on the day of the competition it was windy and pouring with rain, so their horses didn't halt straight but with their quarters into the wind – earning them a double set of disappointingly low marks. Was their disappointing second place really a 'failure' – or couldn't it actually be seen as an amazing achievement in really difficult circumstances? Part of my case-study work with Carolyn involved helping her become more generous in the way she thinks about herself.

The case-studies are an important part of this book. I wanted to work with a number of riders over a reasonable length of time, to show how much difference can be made by working with more layers of the onion. I saw each of them once a month for a three-quarter hour session. In between they worked alone or with

Maxim | the goal is within you, not outside you

their regular instructor. Shane and Annie are primarily eventers; Roy and Carolyn focus on dressage. In writing up our work I have used notes which my husband Leo made during the actual working sessions – in between taking the photographs – and I have also used notes made by the riders. Throughout the book you'll find photographs from their sessions used as examples of the issues, approaches, techniques and strategies I'm talking about. I owe the riders and their lovely horses an enormous amount. They achieved a great deal in a shortish time because they were willing not only to put time and effort into the project but also – and perhaps even more importantly – because they were willing to experiment, to see things and do things differently. They worked hard, and asked a lot of themselves and their horses. Yet we also had a lot of laughs together and plenty of playtime, which I believe is how true learning happens.

I hope that, as you read, you will keep these four riders' achievement in mind, and tell yourself that you, too, can take your riding forward within a similarly realistic time-frame. Riding is, of course, never finished, never a 'done deal' – that's its frustration and its excitement. But even if each achievement seems to open up yet further challenges, even if each refinement leads to the possibility of further subtleties as yet unattained, I hope you'll also receive the message that enjoyment and celebration are essential factors in taking your learning forward.

Another important benefit is that taking this approach also gives such an important message to your horse: working together, even when you are really serious and really committed, can and should be enjoyable and even playful for you both. And a happy partnership doing good dressage will score more than one that's feeling grim with determination or sour with endless drilling. Dressage is not just an arbitrary load of exercises to impose on the horse, but rather a process of discovery/learning that explains to him how he can move better and enjoy being active and in partnership with a kindly friend and mentor.

Underlying themes

There are hundreds of books on riding, and there cannot be any new technical advice to give. I hope, though, that you'll find this book offers you a different take on what it can mean on a daily basis. Let's look at the underlying themes I'm going to explore, and begin to unpack how, taken together, they can give you a new way forward.

Maxim | the goal is within you, not outside you

Riding begins with you

It's within your power to make it so much better and at the same time so much more enjoyable, whatever degree of experience you have and whatever level of skill your horse has reached. That's the first premise on which this book is based. This means noticing just how often you and other horsy people blame – or praise – the horse for what he does as though it's as much part of him as the colour of his coat. It isn't. As soon as you begin to believe that the power and responsibility for his actions lie with you, you begin to empower yourself. For you can change *you* – and in so doing begin to change him. This is a really key point, and I'll explore it further later on.

Recognize your assumptions and where they may get you

There are lots of assumptions in the horse world about what horses 'are like'. Some of them empower riders, and some disempower them. Some lead them to take certain kinds of actions or set up certain kinds of training patterns, rather than others. For example, if you believe that 'horses are naturally lazy' you will be expecting them to 'resist' or 'evade' your attempts to 'make them work'. The ideas go in a cluster, don't they? And where do they lead your feelings and your actions? Do you 'have to practise', 'try to get it right', get cross or frustrated when you 'get it wrong'? Does going *in* the school feel a bit like the worst bits of *being at* school?

I want to invite you to assume instead that horses are natural learners, and that it's up to you to help them find ways to learn things that are ultimately as much for their long-term benefit as for your greater ease and comfort. Better scores, at dressage or any other discipline, will surely come almost as a by-product of learning enjoyably and with a varied mixture of activity rather than through routine, drilling or numbing seriousness. Was that the way you learnt best as a child? Is it the way you learn best now?

The children's writer Arthur Ransome was a great learner of languages – going to Russia as a journalist just before the Revolution and needing to learn the language, he bought as many children's books as he could and started from there. Clear, simple language; easy and enjoyable content. Can you make your dressage like that? With the reward, of course, of finding that you are understood and responded to, first at a simple level then with increasing complexity and subtlety.

Learning is a matter of patience: it takes time. That picture you have in your mind of you and your horse performing at the highest level you can achieve can be a harsh taskmaster if you beat yourself up every day for not having got there yet. On the other hand, it can be a true inspiration on those cold, wet, dispiriting days when things don't seem to be going right – if you remember that true learning

Maxim | the goal is within you, not outside you

often involves backward and sideways steps and many less-than-perfect approximations to your ideal and that each of these is, in its own way, an inevitable and therefore valuable part of your progression.

Assume that whatever your horse does or doesn't do, and how he does it, tells you precisely what he thinks you wanted

This is a hard and humbling one – but it's also an eye-opener that gives you real, precise and invaluable feedback. Feedback is a word that's widely assumed to mean 'comment on how you're doing – mainly negative'. In systems theory, where it comes from, it means simply 'what happens as a result of your actions'. If the result you get isn't the one you wanted, it tells you your message didn't get through. If you're prepared to set aside the assumption that this was because your horse is lazy or difficult, what other explanations could there be?

- He didn't understand what you wanted.
- You didn't explain it clearly enough.
- You actually gave him a different instruction from the one you intended, and he did what you actually asked for.
- He found it too difficult.
- He was distracted.
- You were distracted.

Which seems most likely in the circumstances – and what can you now do that's different?

Different is an important watchword. Doing the same thing again is only worthwhile if your horse's behaviour tells you he has understood what's wanted but hasn't got it quite right. If he's not understood, or is distracted or fearful, attempting the same again without first changing your explanation or how he feels is just like shouting louder at foreigners when they don't understand: you make a lot of noise and everyone gets hot and bothered. That's all. So if you can train yourself to ask yourself questions like: 'What did I do to give him the impression I wanted that?', or 'How else could I explain this?' every time you get a response that differs from what you want, you will save yourself and your horse a great deal of frustration, and go further towards solving the problem, improving the situation and maintaining harmony in your relationship.

Maxim | the goal is within you, not outside you

You actually gave him a different instruction from the one you intended. In the first picture (*above left*) Ali's collapsed left hip and drawn-back left leg are allowing Wattie to understand that she wants angle – but not the bend she also intends. In the second picture (*above right*) her upright posture and deeper, closer leg position help him understand that she wants bend, engagement and 'throughness' – so that's what he gives her!

A good example here is what can happen when you ride a horse who's new to you. Often, the signals that worked with your old horse just don't seem to get the same result! I remember years ago when a little Danish Warmblood came to our yard. He was extremely well trained – but for a while none of us could find the 'canter button'. It just wasn't in the place we were used to. From his viewpoint, of course, we weren't making any sense! Those of you who have read my other books will have seen pictures of our old horse, Lolly, who had a pronounced sway back and a rib-cage that just dropped away under you. In the thirteen years we had him, my husband Leo and I got used to riding him and found him very light to the leg. When we got our next horse, Bertie, we had to learn all over again. 'Bertie's not off the leg' and 'Bertie's not quick on upward transitions' were the kind of judgements

Maxim | the goal is within you, not outside you

that came to mind. But actually the truth is more like: 'Bertie's a different shape from Lolly (as well as a different individual), so we need to talk to him differently if he and we are to understand and enjoy being with each other.'

Building on the horse's responses

Once you have asked yourself the fundamental question about why your horse did what he did, then you can ask yourself what kind of information would help him deliver what you really want instead. There will be lots of instances throughout the book, but as a start let's take some very common examples that I see almost every time I'm judging, and unpack them in some detail.

1. Lengthened strides that are fast and flat

- The sort of comments you're likely to get for this could be: *'hurried'*, *'needs to be more uphill'*, *'pushing not lifting'*, *'rushing'*, *'falling onto forehand'*, *'not through the back'*, *'losing rhythm'*.

- What might you have been doing to give your horse the impression that this was what you wanted? Probably you came round the corner from a working/collected trot or canter, put both your legs on and hoped for the best. Both legs on actually tells your horse 'go faster', so you're getting what you asked for!

- What's the missing ingredient? Almost certainly, a half-halt (using your legs, seat and shoulders but keeping your hands passive and soft) before the corner or the marker to ask him to step under and rebalance. Only from that position of 'sitting' more (greater engagement) can he respond to your legs-on-forward aid and use the powerful leverage of his hind legs correctly to lift his forehand and deliver power through his back to cover more ground with each step.

- What can you do in training to help him learn this? Get him to make plenty of active, forward transitions between and within the gaits, because each time he does you have to use your legs to ask him to step under and sit more. Ask for a few lengthened strides from this 'tucked' position – but return to working length strides again before he has had the chance to lose balance, swing or rhythm. From a couple of bigger strides two or three times down the long side you will be able to progress to three or four as he builds the habit, the muscle and the strength. Eventually, he'll be able to sustain this 'uphill balance' and stay soft and 'through' for a whole long side or diagonal. There is no short route to muscle-building – but lots of practice, both in the school and out hacking, will help you get there!

Maxim | the goal is within you, not outside you

'Through' and 'uphill'. By giving her hands forward Ali is confirming that Jay is truly in self-carriage in this lovely rounded, balanced canter.

2. Corners/turns/circles that lack bend

- My most frequent comment in judging? *'Needs more bend.'* Why? Because bending along the line of the curve means that the horse delivers hind leg power along the line of the curve too, rather than pushing out through the shoulder or falling in like a motor bike. It means balance and control. It's an essential ingredient of that magical thing, self-carriage.

- Why does this matter? Not just for the look of it, but because a horse who's bent on curves as well as straight on straight lines is using his body economically and elastically – and that ultimately means less stiffness and less wear and tear. The bottom line is: it means a longer life and a more comfortable old age – just as it does for you!

- What can you do? Teach yourself and your horse that, whereas two legs on means 'forward', one leg on means 'use the same-side hind leg more actively'. Give him time to go through corners slowly enough to pick that inside hind leg up and step under with it at every stride, so that every stride is energetic but not hurried. Teach yourself to guard his quarters with your outside leg so that they don't swing out, and to keep your outside elbow in, rather than straightening it and pushing that hand forward (which encourages him to slip outwards). For the same reason, make sure you are not kinking inwards at the

Maxim | the goal is within you, not outside you

waist. Then you will keep control of his outside shoulder and help him to carry himself round the corner in balance rather than pulling him round with the inside hand or allowing him to push outwards.

- Where and when to do it? All the time, every day, everywhere, in every corner! It needs to become as basic as 'go' or 'stop'.

Does this sound complicated? It's not really: even as a baby and toddler you learnt far more complex things about controlling your body! There are two important differences now: (1) in riding, you're using your body to tell your horse what to do with his; (2) he is helping you to know how effective you are at this through the way he responds. His behaviour is the best mirror you could get!

There is another difference of course: when you were little, you learnt by *doing* but without *consciously monitoring* your own learning. Now, I'm asking you to experiment in just the same way as you did before – but to observe consciously and evaluate what gets you what. Repeat what works, change what doesn't and try again. Use the feedback from your horse, as well as essential technical information from books or videos and the knowledgeable comments of friends and teachers, to help you investigate and refine as you go. For a while, this process may feel strange, even lumbering. But the more you do it, the easier and more automatic it will become. This is a prime example of how conscious learning turns into unconscious competence, a process that I discuss further in Chapter 9.

Above all, remember that you and your horse will have greatest pleasure in your time together, you will develop your shared skills most easily and rapidly, and your competition results will improve almost as a by-product, if you work together in a spirit of playful experimentation and shared discovery rather than one of dogged determination or rigid drilling. That's what this book is all about.

Maxim | the goal is within you, not outside you

2 What's the point of dressage?

> The goal of all riding should be the development of the horse's athletic talent beyond what he would voluntarily do, and in such a way as to accommodate his carrying the added weight of his rider. In order to carry his rider, the horse has to be maintained in near-perfect balance in motion. In order to develop his athletic potential, we have to develop his strength and skills knowledgeably with these goals in mind.
>
> **Charles de Kunffy,** *Dressage Principles Illuminated*[1]

When you find yourself frustrated and wondering 'what's the point?', it's worth remembering these words of Charles de Kunffy's. Embedded in them is a clear line of thought, which emphasizes that the goal of classical riding is that *it helps the horse carry the weight of the rider.*

I find this a fascinating and beautiful circularity: we ride in this way to assist the horse in helping us to ride with the most elegance and least harm to his physical structure. It means that the process is its own goal, if we approach it right. Where horse and rider develop a true partnership of respect and physical harmony, there's no need to think of riding as steps on the way to somewhere else: it can be enough in itself. If you take this stance, you don't seek to perfect shoulder-in, or halts, or advanced movements like piaffe and passage as achievements in their own right but, instead, as ongoing ways to contribute to something else – which can be happening every day, right now, each time you get on the horse's back. If you can honestly say at the end of a ride, '*What I did today helped him carry my weight better*', or '*helped him become more athletic*' or, perhaps even better, '*helped him express his own best way of being and moving more fully*' you have achieved – for today – the goals of all riding. Of course your achievement is relative: it relates to what is possible for the two of you *today*. But it is important

Maxim | the goal is within you, not outside you

that you know you can celebrate it for what it is, in however private a moment between the two of you as you walk back towards the box or the field.

What will help the horse in achieving this goal? *Being in almost-perfect balance under the rider as they move together*. What does this require? Long-term, the development of the horse's strength and abilities. But here and now, awareness, working within what is currently possible ('almost perfect') and at the same time seeking to extend it. Balance is a fluid thing. If you stand on one foot you will immediately feel just how fluid it is, and how full of tiny adjustments. Yet you can walk, run and stand on a bus or train with relative ease. The test of balance is whether you still keep standing. Good balance, excellent balance, are developments from this, in the same way as the near-perfection of the Olympic athlete upon the balance beam is a development from the toddler's first few seconds of independence.

What you're working towards with your horse is relative ease in relation to his movement carrying your weight. He already knows how to balance himself – but he needs your help in carrying you. The baseline test of balance with a rider is whether the two of you can stand up as you move together. When I was about 15 I used to ride at a stable on the outskirts of London, and one day I was allowed to ride the instructor's well-bred Arab – the horse he normally sat on when he taught us. I remember starting to canter around the short end of the indoor school – and then we both fell inwards to the ground. As the little mare got to her feet again her expression was one of surprise, outrage and shock. I can see it today. I suppose I must have tipped to the inside and caused her to lose her balance. Her expression said it all: *'How could you do that to me?'* The pirouette, the piaffe, the airs above the ground, all have their foundation in something as simple as *not* falling over when you go round a corner.

Balance in the horse/rider partnership is achieved and refined through the development of the rider's understanding of how to communicate effectively to the horse, so that they can develop the strength and skills they need at each stage. You begin, again, with yourself. You begin with discovering how to carry yourself in balance, and progress to doing it in such a way that you help your horse to carry himself and you in balance too. You begin with your posture and your aiding, as I'll explain more fully in Section Two. You seek to clean up the unintentional messages that poor posture and approximate or incorrect aiding can give, and to develop the knowledge and skill to give precise, clear and economical messages about what you want. As you progress, you keep needing to refine your balancing abilities as a basis for everything else you do. You begin and end with dressage – not as a competitive skill but as a way of riding that's been handed down for centuries. You begin by riding classically.

Maxim | the goal is within you, not outside you

Dressage and classical riding

If you ensure that everything you do as a rider helps your horse carry you with minimal stress and in balance, whatever you are doing, you will also be working towards the age-old goals of classical riding. You will be doing dressage, whether or not you choose to compete. Indirectly, reading a book like this for the short-term purpose of improving your dressage scores can be the means towards helping you enjoy more pleasant riding and giving your horse a longer life. Worth it? – I know so.

So the most basic of all reasons for getting involved in dressage is to make the horse's life easier and less uncomfortable. His back is a mechanically weak part of his physical structure, and wasn't designed to carry your weight. It was designed in nature as a flexible bridge between his forehand and hindquarters, transmitting energy and thrust from the powerful hind end to the controlling, direction-finding front end. When a judge comments that a horse is '*flat*' or '*hollow*', that tells you that his abdominal muscles aren't lifting his back and his long back muscles aren't carrying: maybe that's temporary, as when he loses balance or engagement in a tight turn or difficult movement; maybe it's how he normally goes because those muscles have not learned to flex correctly or haven't developed enough strength to do it consistently.

Just like in the song, the hip-bone is connected to the thigh-bone, so when the back isn't lifted the legs often aren't bending and stepping under the horse's body but instead jarring and pushing out behind, so his joints are taking a hammering. We are then talking about a whole physical system that's not helping the work it's being asked to do. And that's our responsibility as riders. A horse's natural way of accepting a foreign weight is to hollow and push – but that's the worst possible way in the long term. He needs you to teach him to round and step under and lift, to put his raised muscles as a cushion under you and to use his strength to carry rather than simply propel himself under you. He can do this from time to time as a natural reaction to what's going on around and within him, but it isn't his natural habit. He needs you to make it so.

If you look at equitation like this, you could say it's our moral duty to ride classically. Sounds a heavy responsibility? Yes – but one we can learn to carry out by following the well-tried systems of maintenance and development that the masters have formulated for us through centuries of experimentation and refinement. *Dressage* is simply the French word for this approach and these systems. In this sense it is essential whether we plan to compete or not, and whether we want to work in the school, over jumps or over open country. Dressage in this sense, meaning 'correct training', is not just about flatwork, though many people think

Maxim | the goal is within you, not outside you

In the top picture, Ali and Jay are demonstrating the pose of a horse who is hollow and out behind – Jay is dropping her back and not stepping under. Her neck has contracted and she is not truly on the bit.

In the picture below Jay is rounding and lifting her back, stepping well under her body and working into the contact.

that's what it refers to. Take a broader view. Do you know anyone who has run a marathon – or even a fun-run? If they had any sense they will have built up gradually through regular, progressively longer and more taxing training sessions. They will also have thought about eating the kind of food that helps deliver the energy they need when they need it. They will have thought about rest, and appropriate clothing. They may have run with friends, joined a club or worked with a

Maxim | the goal is within you, not outside you

trainer. All this makes sense, doesn't it? They have given themselves the best chance they can. They have been doing dressage. We owe the same to our horses because they can't do it for themselves.

If you are already a 'dressage specialist' all this may just reinforce what you know already; and as for so-called 'recreational' riding, what hack isn't safer, more comfortable and more enjoyable on a well-schooled horse? I hope that you will find as I do that stopping from time to time to take this longer view helps to put the everyday frustrations and difficulties of educational riding in a wider perspective. This reminds us why it's worth doing even on a blustery day, after dark, in the winter...

Unless either you or your horse is unwell, or for some good reason cannot really give your minds to each other, you can and should perform classically together because it reinforces and develops a whole way of being with each other. There will be times, of course, when you have to decide whether to change or even abort what you had planned – but the reason should be that riding would, on this occasion, in those circumstances, damage your partnership rather than enhance it.

If you are angry for reasons that have nothing to do with your horse, can you put that anger aside for the time being? If not, why burden him with it? He will feel the difference in you, even though he won't understand it. If you are angry with him, are you self-aware enough and generous enough to ask yourself what you may have done – or not done – that's contributing to his behaviour? (More on this in the next chapter.) If there are distractions around you, can you work through them – or is it fairer to put him back in his box, or in the field? I can remember having a very useful lesson one Guy Fawkes evening, with a huge bonfire only a short distance away and fireworks going off frequently: my horse Vals wasn't that scared (though he was on his toes!) and we really improved our concentration and our ability to focus on each other. On the other hand, I would never ride our old horse Lolly in high winds – he was really frightened by them, so what would be the point?

Competitive dressage riding is not necessarily the same as classical riding. In fact, the struggle to 'do the movements' and get better marks can mean that riders get seduced by technique and short-term, performance-related achievements, to the detriment of ongoing and long-term development.

In *The Ethics and Passions of Dressage,* Charles de Kunffy writes: 'No serious riders ever believed the training goal was to compete. They believed that you rode a horse to unfold his natural potential until it was fulfilled and the horse could offer no more physically because he had no more genetically defined talents to display.'[2] In this book I want to invite you to think of dressage and classical riding together, and to believe that better results in competition will come to you as a welcome by-product rather than as your main aim. So when I use the word

Maxim | the goal is within you, not outside you

'dressage', it's as shorthand for this whole way of thinking about equitation and as a reminder of all that it means. (If I'm talking about competition, I'll add the word 'competitive'.) I want you to put your personal goals for competition into the broader context of riding within a classical framework.

'The longest journey begins with a single step.' Every step you take that's rooted in this wider classical understanding will help you along that longer journey. On the way, you'll find yourself arriving at Novice, Elementary, Medium and the rest of the familiar way-stations. If you start from the other end, with the limited and limiting goals of simply improving your technique, you can lose the enjoyment, you can lose the expressiveness, you can – ultimately – lose the soul of the relationship between yourself and your horse.

In his book, *Exploring Dressage Technique*, Paul Belasik says: 'For the rider, getting stuck in the land of technical bravura can be the end of his advance on the journey of horsemastership.'[3] By contrast, the same writer tells us in *Riding Towards the Light* that: 'In classical dressage the creative focus is in exploring the personality of a particular horse's movements, within the structure of the art….'.[4] In other words, the rider's task is to help the horse discover his own best individual version of any gait or specific movement.

This raises a really exciting possibility for each of us: for in suggesting that part of our essential business in riding is to discover what is special to our horse as an individual, and to us as a unique partnership, it offers us a much more achievable goal. It asks us to collaborate with our horse in discovering not only something that is far off, perhaps even unattainable, like his piaffe and other school movements, but also the very basics of his way of going: his individual trot, his walk, his canter. We can achieve this, not only in the future, but here and now, because his best individual trot *now* will not be the same as his best individual trot next month, or next year. I think this gives us a whole new meaning – and a whole new excitement – to thinking about 'moving up the levels' in competition. How would it be to regard a new level of competition as a benchmark for a newly acquired level of balance, expressiveness, and individuality in partnership?

That's what I'm referring to when I make judging comments like *'hurried out of his natural rhythm'*; I've begun to know when a horse isn't being true to himself. I've heard great teachers like Charles de Kunffy point out that each horse has his own 'signature rhythm'. That's one aspect of it – but we can also learn to recognize, respect and celebrate his way of moving and way of being. Among our horses, Lolly was a light and limber enthusiast, our huge Hawk was magnificent in his lightness, Bertie is compact, forward-thinking yet a little dogged. The natural movement embodies the character. It's up to us all, as riders, trainers and judges, to find this and enable it to be its best.

Maxim | the goal is within you, not outside you

Why you should do dressage

There is nothing more enabling, nothing more curative, and nothing more individual than dressage, provided you look at it from this standpoint. It's the one true way – which is broad enough to include the most novice rider and the most ordinary pony as well as the greatest expert and the grandest, most athletic horse. Envisage it as a way of thinking and being, which gives meaning and purpose to all the things you actually do with your horse. How does it achieve this?

Dressage is about self-control, so it's a goal we can all achieve every time we ride

True dressage involves a command of ourselves that makes our bodies a 'clean' means of communication with our horses. If you look at the equestrian pictures you find inspirational, my guess is that a fair number of them will show riders with an inwardness and absorption, and horses with the 'sideways' ears and calm eyes of true attentiveness. A sense of rapport, focus and concentration will reach up off the page. When I showed the picture of Roy and Cori on page 267 to friends and colleagues who knew nothing about horses, that was what struck them. They knew they were looking at a truly special moment, in which horse and rider had become a creature that *was* neither but *expressed* the best of both. This is the centaur of classical legend.

Not every ride looks like this to outsiders; but virtually every ride can have a moment when your body is as balanced as you can make it, so your aiding comes through sweet and clear and your horse virtually breathes a sigh of relief. Don't dismiss this as being out of your reach because 'I'm not that good' or, worse, because 'I'll never be that good'. Think about these moments of poise, balance and control within the context of how you are now – the peak of where you are at the moment – not in comparison with 'better' riders or those you idolize. Think about the last time you rode – about every moment of it. Was your horse truly still when you got on? Did he move off – or slow down, or stop, just as you had the thought? In one of our sessions I asked Shane, who often doubts herself, to 'try what happens if you just *think* a halt on a long rein'. 'We do that all the time,' she replied – as if it were nothing special! – and they did it again just for fun to show me.

What was your special moment? Did you take time to appreciate it? Start collecting them – they are your Brownie points and gold stars along the way.

Maxim | the goal is within you, not outside you

Dressage opens every riding door

Years ago, you could tell Continental showjumpers from English ones because European horses looked to the inside of the bend as they went around the arena, and were able to view their fences as they approached them. Non-continentals looked to the outside and motor-biked round the corners. Usually, they also had their heads in the air. I suspect that the fences often came as a surprise to them. Nowadays, this has changed – in large part, I think, because the Continental training gave an edge that others lacked. Years ago, many event horses were stiff and unbalanced in the dressage arena. They often needed their studs to get round without skidding! Nowadays, when I judge eventing dressage, I know I am looking at the same thing as when I judge 'pure' dressage. Eventing dressage is speaking the same language. And the reason is that eventers are athletes who have to be versatile and flexible and balanced and obedient. The best ones probably always were; nowadays they all have to be. I've judged world-class riders like Mark Todd and Matt Ryan. Their subtlety and skill in dressage helps them support and manage bold, forward-thinking horses across the most taxing cross-country courses and over the contrastingly flimsy showjumps. They are great riders whatever they are doing.

Putting yourself in a dressage frame of mind and becoming fluent as a partnership in this way of working will take you further in showjumping or eventing – or give you greater pleasure and safety in hacking.

Dressage is the key to economical, effective and elegant movement

It seems to be the case that in every field 'less is more'. There's a simplicity about real skill, whether it's in music, athletics, the written word or even in human relationships. What's there is what's needed, no more. This isn't just about volume or the amount of detail: it's also about what's needed to do the job, and about paring away what isn't. Kimberley, our first dressage teacher, sometimes used to say, 'You're working too hard'. When I'm judging I quite often comment *'rider's legs too busy'*. To take an example from a different sport, there's a stillness at the heart of good sprinting, which is why the commentators often say of a competitor that 'he was relaxed'. Of course the winning sprinter wasn't physically relaxed – his muscles were working really hard. In all sports, athletes need *tone* in their muscles. The 'relaxation' which people noticed was about something else: maybe it was mental, maybe it was the absence of tension, so that there were no blocks or other unwanted knock-on effects within the mind-body system as a whole. What became visible was a oneness of the person with the task.

Maxim | the goal is within you, not outside you

This is something that results from physical discipline and exertion when it has gone through technique and out the other side. So of course it can be available to us, even when our technique comes and goes. In this book I want to show you how you can achieve more of that oneness.

Dressage opens the way to two-way communication with another species

Years ago, I went to watch a performance of the Spanish Riding School. As they rode their intricate patterns to their characteristic baroque music I was surprised to find tears coming to my eyes, and to see them on many other faces in the audience around me. Earlier this year I judged a Rural Riders' competition, in which six riders rode a test pattern together, following and leading, forming and reforming the patterns of dressage. I felt just the same, in a silent field in Surrey. Here was the miracle of real communication and harmony between such different species – times six. But here was a unified entity that also went far beyond $1+1 \times 6$. I had tears there, too. How can you judge a miracle? I am sure that this is one of the fundamental reasons why we ride, and one of the best reasons of all why we should strive to cherish that communication and get it right.

The benefits of dressage to the horse

Let's just summarize these.

1. Physical

- He builds his muscles and develops a way of moving that helps him carry his rider's weight with less effort. He lifts his rib-cage and raises his back. He learns to take weight further back towards his hindquarters.

- He learns to use his joints actively and with less jarring, so they suffer less damage and last longer, with minimal wear and tear. He does this by learning to flex his joints rather than just swinging them, and by stepping under rather than pushing out behind.

- He becomes fitter and can enjoy the demands of his work with less effort.

- If he has less-than-ideal conformation, the increased strength, suppleness, flexibility and balance that classical training gives him will lessen the problems that go with his particular limitations.

Maxim | the goal is within you, not outside you

- It can give him a greater pleasure in his natural movement – in being in his own skin and using his own power. Often, you can see this pleasure on his face.

2. Mental/emotional

- The increased clarity of understanding between him and his rider helps him get a much clearer idea of what's wanted, with less confusion, so he's more able to please and more likely to be praised.

- Because classical training is systematic and progressive, he will not be alarmed or overfaced by being confronted with tasks that are too advanced for his current level of ability.

- Because it is based on the principle of cooperation, he will not be punished – when he can't or won't do something he is likely to be given the benefit of the doubt and offered other opportunities to understand and to learn.

- Because classical riding rests on a well-developed and well-tested system of communication (aiding) and training, it can make his relationship with his rider more enjoyable as well as freer of misunderstandings and conflicts.

The benefits of dressage to the rider

1. Physical

- You find riding is more comfortable because your horse is more elastic and supple. No more bouncing and jarring, much more swinging and 'surfing'.

- You become fitter and more in control of your own body. There is nothing like dressage to teach you about your body! Once you start taking your horse's behaviour as feedback about your own, you really want to clean up and streamline! And that means developing control over yourself. That's what 'independent hands' and 'an independent seat' mean. They mean that you can control them independently of each other and of any other part of yourself – as well as independently of what your horse is doing. Independence indeed! For this, you need muscle tone and flexibility as well as strength. You need breath control. You need thought-to-action speed. You need to build the right habits.

- You know that both you and your horse have the basic training, strength, balance and flexibility you need for any of the disciplines. This is so because if you and your horse are to enjoy your riding rather than becoming imprisoned

Maxim | The goal is within you, not outside you

by it, you're going to need to do more than schoolwork. You're going to need to become versatile. As you become more versatile, you'll build the mental and physical repertoire you need to enjoy being yourselves – and, by the way, achieving more in your chosen discipline.

2. Mental/emotional

- You feel safer because your horse understands and obeys you more readily. Safety needs to come first in riding. Safety comes from two things – trust and obedience. And both of these arise out of taking the time to build a relationship of two-way respect and clear communication. If you respect him, you have a right to ask for respect in return – and you're more likely to get it. If you listen to what he's telling you, you'll be clearer in what you tell him, and you'll know when he has or hasn't understood. It all begins with you. Start there.

- You become less anxious about 'what if...?' and 'what might happen...?' The better the communication between you and your horse, the less likely you are to be taken by surprise. Just as important is learning how to recognize and work with your own patterns of thinking and feeling: it is the first step to building a better alliance with yourself. If you can be grateful for that anxious part of you and recognize how it's trying to protect you, you can stop arguing with yourself and feeling that you're stupid. Recognizing the substance of your fears can help you to sort out what's realistic and do something practical about it, and learn imaginative ways to turn what's purely imaginary around. (You'll find more about this in my other books as well.) When I first started working with Carolyn, she was very anxious about cantering – because she and Ambrose had once slipped badly while cantering and skidded along the grass. It wasn't a good experience, and the memory fed forward and made her reluctant to canter. But in one of our early sessions, respecting the fear, she bravely had a go at cantering large numbers of circles instead of her usual one or two. Riding on a long rein so that she and Ambrose both knew that he was able to take care of his own balance, she began to change things around and by the time we got to the end of our sessions they were cantering happily at home, out hacking and in competition (see Carolyn and Ambrose in Chapter 16.)

- You enjoy riding more because your partner is more willing. It goes without saying that willing partners enjoy being together more, even when they're working with serious commitment. In fact, why not turn the whole thing around: start with enjoyment – and then work towards refinement. Begin to find your lengthened strides out hacking, or over poles, where they come naturally. Use shoulder-in to get you past those dragons hidden in hay-bales.

Maxim | the goal is within you, not outside you

Practise halts and lateral obedience opening gates (see 'A hack with Roy and Cori' in Chapter 8). Get your horse going forward and rounding through his back over jumps. There are endless opportunities, every time you ride.

- You become more confident in your ability to give the signals you want when you want to, and know that they will be understood and responded to appropriately. Good signalling comes from two things: good body control and the ability to understand how your signals come across to your partner. Classical riding takes the experience of many great horsemen over the centuries, working with many thousands of different horses, and distils it into a body of wisdom that saves you reinventing the wheel. But you still need to customize how you can apply these principles and make them come alive for yourself, your partner and the situations unique to you. You need to develop your own body of expertise, as you do in building any good relationship. This book both gives you access to the classical tradition and shows you ways to customize it for yourself and your equine partner.

- As your partnership develops and your skill increases, you and your horse make the most of each other in little things as well as big ones, enjoying more and more often those moments of harmony, lightness and mutual understanding that make riding such a special and unique experience. Why did you take up riding in the first place? Have you lost sight of any aspects of what attracted you? Riding is always a here-and-now, in-the-moment experience. If you wait until you get to Grand Prix to let yourself enjoy it, I can promise you that you won't. And you'll have given up so much along the way – only to find that you were cheating yourself of the marvels that were within your daily grasp.

The marvels that were within your daily grasp. The author and Lolly enjoying an evening hack together.

Maxim | the goal is within you, not outside you

3 The diagnostic horse – what your horse is telling you

> Horses don't care about your words: they care about and respond to your actions.
>
> **Paul Belasik,** *Dressage for the 21st Century*[1]

Riding effectively is essentially about good communication, with the exciting difference that it is about communication between two different species. In my book *Schooling Problems Solved with NLP* I tried to show how many of the strategies that help us in human communication can also benefit us and our horses. Communication, of course, takes place not just between us and others but also *within us*, as when we think, picture, feel and talk to ourselves.

NLP (Neuro-Linguistic Programming) gives us tools to understand both kinds of communication, because it explores the *'how?'* questions in life. How does someone who is excellent in any field behave, and think? Just how do they go about what they do? Just how do *you* think – and how is that different from the way *I* think? How does thinking affect emotion – and emotion affect thinking? How does the mind affect the body, and the body reflect the mind? How can we get an idea of what our communication actually means to someone on the receiving end? How might that be different from what we intended them to understand – and how could we make our communication with them work better? Asking and then beginning to answer these questions gives us our own step-by-step recipes for what works for us and what doesn't, in riding as in every other sphere of life.

The classical tradition in riding is based on physical communication methods that work. If we follow it we will certainly be on the right track for greater effectiveness, greater harmony, and almost certainly better performance. There are many books that can help you to know what the classical position looks like and good trainers who can help you achieve it. In this chapter I want to add the extra dimension that NLP gives us with its 'how?' questions. Not just *what* you should

Maxim | the goal is within you, not outside you

do, but *how* and *why* it makes sense to your horse. With this additional take on equitation you will be better placed to understand some of the things that frustrate and puzzle you as a rider even when you are trying to follow the classical path. And you will be better able to understand how, even with the best will in the world, you could be contributing to or actively encouraging the very things you don't want. I want to share this viewpoint and this body of understanding with you because I have found it so helpful in my own riding and that of people I have worked with.

For example, I find this approach can really help with frequently asked questions like these: Why does my horse sometimes misunderstand what I want? Why is he 'difficult' some days, or in some circumstances? Why do I get scared even though I know I have a fair amount of skill? Why does something come easily one day – but not the next time I try it? I know that most riders ask themselves these questions more often than they would like to.

In this chapter I want to open up some of these knotty areas with a really useful NLP key. And the key is this: *the meaning of your communication is the message that is received.*

This is quite a humbling proposition to take on board, because it means that intent – even good intent – is not enough. Whether our message is aimed at another human being or an animal, we have to take their perspective and their understanding into account. (Preferably, we take it into account before we start sending messages!) Fortunately, though, we can find out what the receiver thought our message meant by paying close attention to how they respond. Even when we don't like what we get, if we take that response for the valuable information it is, rather than dismissing it as 'misunderstanding', 'resistance', 'evasion' or good old stupidity or cussedness, we can begin to learn more about ourselves as we are seen by others. While human beings can deliberately misunderstand or misinterpret each other's communications, it is still wise to start with the assumption that maybe, just maybe, you could make your message clearer. In the case of horses, a much greater transparency prevails. Even though they may sometimes ignore or disobey a message, horses don't wilfully misinterpret. If we take the response we get as a direct reflection of the message the receiver got, we can refine our messaging, and stand a much better chance of getting through to our equine partner more successfully.

What your horse does is a really good source of information about how you come across to him. I've called this chapter 'The Diagnostic Horse' because, when you start from here, you find that his reactions and behaviour give you a diagnosis of how you are *now*. In exchange for your readiness to take him seriously he will offer you a neatly tailored recipe for what you need to do next. In itself, this should encourage you to sigh with relief. Although 'getting it right' remains a long-term

Maxim | the goal is within you, not outside you

aim of both communication and training, the day-to-day consideration, which will help you immensely, becomes 'are we understanding each other?' Let's look at this in a bit more detail.

What you get is what you asked for

Would it change what you felt if you read things like *'on forehand'*, *'not forward enough'*, *'against the hand'*, or *'hollow'*, on your test sheet and thought, 'I was responsible for that'? And how different might you feel reading *'calm and attentive'*, *'expressive'*, *'well-balanced'*, *'lovely attitude'* and thinking, 'I helped him be like that!'?

You and your horse are a partnership – but you're the one shaping his energy and helping him make the most of himself. When I watched Charles de Kunffy teaching on one occasion, one horse was producing lengthened strides that were fast and flat. Charles said to the rider: *'Your legs told him this.'*

What you get is what you asked for. In the left-hand picture, Ali has collapsed her waist and allowed her legs to become flaccid and without tone, so Wattie has dropped his back and become hollow. In the right-hand picture, Ali has become taller in her body, deepening her heels and becoming more toned and connected, so Wattie is following suit by connecting through himself, making a continuous flow of energy from hind leg to bridle.

Maxim | the goal is within you, not outside you

> Look at your old test sheets from this viewpoint. What themes recur? What is really working already – and do you know how you achieved this? What would help you and your partner do more of what works and make some progress towards changing what doesn't?

Let's take some common comments from dressage sheets and see how your horse can help you diagnose your riding issues:

What did the horse do?	How did the rider 'ask' for that?
Transition too progressive	Aid not clear enough, not crisp enough, or too abrupt (poorly prepared)
Transition on the forehand	No warning half-halt, so horse unable to rebalance in time
Downward transition not forward	Over-reliant on hand, so forward momentum blocked
Hollowed in transition	Over-used hand, or stiffened back
Moved in halt	Took legs off, leg pressure unequal, or horse was stopped with hand, rather than engaged and held with the seat
Came against the hand	Hand not soft enough, or pulled backward
Not enough bend	Not enough inside leg, not enough outside leg
Falling out through shoulder	Too much inside rein, not enough outside rein, rider's outside elbow straightening and hand giving forward, rider tipping to inside
Quarters swinging	Not enough outside leg, or not enough 'framing' between the legs
Overshot marker	Lacking preparation – aiding given too late
Lengthened strides fast and flat	Rider kicking repeatedly
	No half-halt to help horse step under, engage and lift

Maxim | the goal is within you, not outside you

Falling out through the shoulder. In the left-hand picture, Ali has effectively 'asked' Wattie to fall out by tipping her body to the inside and her weight to the outside (you can see that she is pressing down into her left stirrup). Her left arm has straightened, so she is no longer supporting Wattie's left shoulder, and her left leg has come forward so she is allowing him to overbend to the right and bulge out to the left. In the right-hand picture, though Wattie is showing only a slight bend, he is connecting 'through' while producing quite a deep crossing with his hind legs. Ali is supporting him with bent, flexible elbows, closed, quiet legs, an even balance and a turning of her own body which mirrors the angle of his shoulders.

Maxim | the goal is within you, not outside you

Here is some space for other comments you may have received: what was your horse's behaviour telling you?

_____

_____

_____

_____

_____

_____

_____

> Do you see any patterns emerging? Which of your personal 'communication tools' seem to be most implicated?

Your horse's behaviour tells you how you rode

The comments you get in a test can point you, via your diagnostic horse, in the direction of two kinds of remedy. You may need to improve your specific test-riding strategies (see Chapter 14) or you may need to work on the underlying skills and patterns of your ongoing schooling. Though this large, latter view can seem more daunting, in fact when we work on our partnership's whole way of going the details often look after themselves. For example, a horse on the forehand is one who is unbalanced in terms of his ability to carry himself and you with ease. Building the kind of regular training patterns that help him progressively to take more weight behind, whilst remaining soft and connected through his back and neck, will mean that you both get used to frequent rebalancing, so in a test it will tend to come automatically. Your part in this is to get your habitual posture as classical as you can – because this is what will help your horse. '*The horse will want to communicate with you through your seat*', says Paul Belasik.[2] What is your horse telling you? If you sit upright with a tall neck rather than hunching and looking

Maxim | the goal is within you, not outside you

down, your weight will be transmitting directly downwards and helping you to deepen your seat, rather than unintentionally telling your horse to drop onto his forehand or weighting him to fall in, or out. If you have a good, upright posture, your seat becomes automatically more effective, so you are less tempted to give crude 'driving' aids that can unbalance the horse and cause him to hollow.

Take another example. A horse who hollows or comes against the hand in transitions is telling you that you need to sort out your contact. A longer rein may be one answer: horses don't build top-line muscle by being held into a short frame, but by the work they do behind. (See the photos on page 260) of Shane with her sister's horse at the beginning and end of their session.) Your horse may need a longer rein than you are currently giving him while he builds the big neck muscles that will naturally result in a higher and rounder outline: a good rule of thumb is that the muscle has to grow before the outline, otherwise the outline is only cosmetic. A horse against your hand probably means your hand is against your horse. Bending your elbows and keeping them close to your sides, yet still flexible, will stabilize your rein contact and encourage your horse to work into it rather than hollowing or tilting, or alternatively boring down and dropping behind the vertical. I have heard those two masters of classical equitation, Charles de Kunffy and Erik Herbermann, tell their pupils: '*Without elbows there is no riding.*'

Hollowing and resisting are not the only symptoms of hand issues. Restriction and freedom in the rein also affect the effectiveness of the signals from the rider's legs. When a horse is not using his hind legs actively, Charles de Kunffy will say: '*His hind leg tells me what your hand is doing.*' Paul Belasik uses the wonderful phrase 'power wave' to describe: '*…a wave of energy* [that] *is thrust right up the horse's spine towards the head, lifting the horse's centre of mass and lightening the forehand. The horse's whole back swings and the shoulder reaches out…*'[3]

This is what is often described as 'engagement' on your sheets: a stepping under, a commitment, and a connection throughout the whole body in movement. This is what we feel in our most fortunate and memorable moments as riders – a connection that we may, for a while, be blessed to be part of. It's all too easy to interrupt that power wave, but everything that you do to improve *yourself* helps you be a better custodian of your horse's inherent ability to power through in his own unique way.

Your horse's response is filtered through his understanding of your messaging

Let's go back to Shane and Ted and their ability to halt just by thinking about it, even on a long rein. What is really going on here? Ted was a very spooky and at times difficult youngster, and often resistant to the rein. Yet with no rein contact at

Hunching and looking down. In the top picture, though Jay is producing an expressive and well-connected medium trot, Ali has slightly weakened her own position by looking down, which in turn has rounded her shoulders, so Jay is beginning to run onto her forehand and propel herself rather than being truly in self-carriage. In the picture below, the trot is expressive, with much the same free reaching out from the shoulder, but Jay is better balanced because Ali is 'all of a piece' herself.

Maxim | The goal is within you, not outside you

all he would halt willingly. Clearly, Shane's thinking is somehow getting through to him. In the same way that your face and body reflect your feelings when you are confused, embarrassed or delighted, your mere intention to do something in riding can be translated to your horse through minute changes in your weight and the way you move.

Think about the centaur again: half man and half horse; the mythical centaur moved as one entity because it was one. I'm sure, though, that this ancient classical image arose from the way real riders and real horses seemed when they were moving together in effortless unity. No visible aiding; mutual concentration and instant responsiveness; one being, not two. We can all achieve moments like this – and one way to begin is by thinking very carefully about them and seeking to understand what subtle signals your horse is responding to, even when you think you aren't giving any.

Centaur signals aren't always those you want to give, of course. When your horse stops before a big fence, or hesitates going through a field with sheep or pigs in it, or spins round on the road when a lorry or a tractor comes towards him, is he acting entirely on his own initiative or is he responding to one of those 'what if...?' thoughts running through your mind? Was your body passing on your doubt? When your teacher tells you to *'throw your heart over the fence and your horse will follow'*, that's what she's talking about. Is your horse really reluctant to take a different path out hacking, or are you wondering what you might encounter in unknown territory?

Of course you are not responsible for everything your horse does: he's a prey animal with prey instincts. He's also a herd animal, preferring company to solitude. But in my experience it really pays to question yourself, and consider your possible contribution, before blaming him or feeling there is not much you can do. There is usually a lot you can do – with yourself!

Your horse as your mirror

I am talking here of the 'mirror' your horse holds up to you by his responses to your messages. Here are some common 'mirror effects' in rider-horse pairs. For our purposes, I want you to focus on correcting yourself *even when you believe the issue originates with your horse*. For example, one horse we had was rather on the forehand, partly because he was built slightly croup-high and partly because he was at a relatively early stage in his schooling. Nonetheless, the way he was ridden could make a substantial difference to his ability to carry himself in balance.

For this reason, the first bullet point below is illustrated by photos of Ali, who is a very experienced rider, working with a well-educated horse, and both photos

Maxim | the goal is within you, not outside you

THE DIAGNOSTIC HORSE – WHAT YOUR HORSE IS TELLING YOU • 43

were taken in the same session, often within minutes of each other. When Ali changed how she carried herself, her horse immediately mirrored her and gave her what her body was 'asking for'.

- A horse who's on the forehand can be made worse by a rider who's collapsed in the waist or who's looking down. He can be helped by a rider whose weight is centrally balanced and whose head is carried upright and aligned with her spine.

A horse who's on the forehand can be made worse by a rider who's collapsed at the waist or looking down…

…he can be helped by a rider whose weight is centrally balanced and whose head is carried upright and aligned with her spine.

Maxim | the goal is within you, not outside you

- A horse who lacks longitudinal (head to tail) suppleness through the back can be made worse by a rider who isn't flexible in her own waist and lower back. (Similarly, I have often seen horses 'drifting' to the side to which their rider was leaning, and facing 'out' when their rider's shoulders were unconsciously turned that way rather than being straight.) He can be helped by a rider who 'gives' in these areas.

- A horse who isn't laterally supple (doesn't bend, or finds it harder to bend one way than the other) can be made worse by a rider who isn't flexible in the use of her waist, shoulder and hip joints (as well as her lower legs) to shape him through turns, corners and lateral movements. He can be helped by a rider who can use these parts of herself flexibly and accurately to give him refined weight and directional aids.

- A horse who doesn't collect or extend easily can be made stiffer and flatter by a rider who isn't soft in her own back, or who isn't sitting correctly in balance. He can be helped by a rider who uses her weight and posture as aids to help him rebalance, and who is flexible enough in her lower back to 'surf' his movement rather than deadening or flattening it.

- A horse who is spooky or 'doesn't concentrate' can be made worse by a rider who is distracted by looking out for the things that may distract him, or by what's going on her own mind (both of these tend to happen a lot when riding-in at competitions!). He can be helped by a rider who matches his short concentration span by providing variety in what she asks him to do, keeps his attention by minute-to-minute (or even second-by-second) responses and adjustments to what he is doing and remains very focused herself. (This is also very relevant when riding a spooky horse out hacking, in challenging circumstances. Things like asking for a little lateral bend one way then the other not only give the horse something else to think about; they also put him on the aids in postures from which it is harder for him to buck, shy, spin round, etc.)

- A horse who is timid or fearful can be made worse by a rider who is hurried or over-dominant, who may add to his anxieties and rush him out of his natural pace for assessing his surroundings – and perhaps deciding in his own time that he can manage them. He may be helped by sympathetic firmness, as, for example, when an experienced rider lets a youngster stop and investigate some new object, so that he can gain his own confidence, rather than pushing him forcefully past – which might achieve the immediate objective of getting him past but at the expense of leaving him fearful, or having a battle of wills.

- A horse who is difficult, or challenging, usually has a reason for being that way that makes sense to him. He can be made worse by a rider who simply gets into

Maxim | the goal is within you, not outside you

a conflict over his behaviour. He can be made better by a rider who seeks to understand what is affecting him and consequently what response from her would make sense in his terms and allow him to do what she wants with a better grace. (If he is always difficult, it's worth considering that perhaps what he is mirroring to you is that a different partner would make both of you happier.)

I'm not saying here, *'If you have a problem in your riding it's all your own fault.'* What I am saying is that it is always worth asking yourself what contribution you are making to your horse's behaviour – 'good' as well as 'bad'.

What is your horse mirroring to you?

Unwanted effects: _____

_____

_____

_____

Desired effects: _____

_____

_____

_____

Looking at our riding like this can open up some very useful ways forward. In the other sections of this book, I'm going to focus on three kinds of skill that you can develop in yourself which will help you and your horse achieve more – not just in competition but in the whole of your partnership together. For convenience, the following sections deal with physical, mental and strategic skills as though they were separate – but of course they are not. You can understand them better when you examine them separately, but the art of effectiveness is putting them together.

Maxim | the goal is within you, not outside you

Your hip-bone is connected to your thigh-bone. Your mind is connected to your body. Your mind and your body are connected to your horse. That's the way it works. And that's the way you can make it work better yet.

'Good' is relative in riding. We can all admire outstanding performances, marvelling at great conformation, elevated gaits, unobtrusive aiding and apparently effortless achievement. But that's only one end of the scale. Relative good is about what you and I can work towards always and achieve sometimes – but more often than we had expected if only we learn to recognize 'good' as being the best we can do today, now, this minute.

Remember, you have all it takes

- **Four limbs give you four legs.** When you learn to control your four limbs, you gain control of your horse's four legs.

- **What you model, you get in return.** Horses learn by doing. If you do it right, he will do it right. You are the model he reflects.

- **Balance brings balance.** When you get in balance, you help your horse find the balance he needs with you on his back.

- **Weighting works better than pushing.** You can't push half a ton of horse anywhere unless he lets you. But you can shift your weight to give him invitations to move where you want. You can make it easy for him.

- **Joints give you independence, elbows are an integral part of your seat.** Good riding is about *interdependence*, and for that you need *independence*. You need control of each part of your body so that you can use it independently of the rest of you, and independently of your horse's movement, even while you are following it appropriately and without interference. To achieve this, your elbows need to have a 'default position' close to your upper body, rather than waving around as your horse moves. When they are stabilized like this, your hands can work independently without randomly yielding or jerking. Making the classical position your habit means that you'll achieve this more and more, until it becomes automatic.

- **Schooling patterns set up successful experiences and make learning easier.** One of the great arts is to make it easy, or even inevitable, that your partner should do what you want. Whatever you suggest needs to make sense in his terms. You have the advantage in that you can set up situations so that he just finds himself doing what you want – then you can praise him for it. The classical example is asking young horses to go into canter from an energetic trot on

Maxim | the goal is within you, not outside you

a corner, when the change of balance will make it natural to pick up the correct lead. Using the correct aids and giving the verbal command 'canter' at the same time helps them associate the action with the aid and with the command. Once they have made the association, the rider can trigger the behaviour by the physical aid, or by saying the word. Our old horse, Lolly, used to go from walk to trot and trot to canter out hacking when I said, 'Shall we?', because he had learnt to associate the verbal invitation with an upward transition! (Riders can also inadvertently teach 'triggers' they don't want – do you and your horse share any of those?)

You can use the schooling patterns in much the same way. You will find many effective strategies to help you develop collection, extension and lateral movements within Charles de Kunffy's *Training Strategies for Dressage Riders* (see Useful Reading). By choosing whereabouts in the school you ask for certain responses, or by combining different patterns with each other, you can make it easy for your horse to find himself having the experience of collecting, or doing shoulder-in, or whatever it is that you want him to learn. You will have to be careful that such triggers ('we always do that in this place') don't become so automatic that he anticipates and stops listening for your aiding – habits are double-edged!

- **Less gives you more.** Finally, ask yourself if you are doing too much. If your horse is a receiving instrument, is he getting too many signals at once? How does he know what you would really like him to tune into?

    1. You may be confusing him with your emotional 'white noise' – poorly controlled emotions or distracting thoughts which will certainly reach him even though he won't understand them. This is why the classical tradition emphasizes a calm and focused mind as well as a controlled and harmonious body.

    2. You may be confusing him with repetitive aiding. As I mentioned earlier, when I judge I often comment *'rider's legs too busy'*. This isn't just an aesthetic comment (though flapping legs and nagging heels certainly don't look attractive): it's meant to draw the rider's attention to the fact that, when endlessly repeated, aiding becomes less and less, not more and more, effective. If he doesn't respond to a clear leg aid, try a single big thump, or a tap with the whip behind the leg. As Stephen Clarke, one of our Olympic judges, says, *'Get a reaction!'* When you get a reaction, stop the signal. That way, the very *absence* of signal tells your horse he's doing what you want.

    3. You may be asking him (and yourself) to do too many things in one riding session, with the danger that neither of you has time to learn and improve.

Maxim | the goal is within you, not outside you

This doesn't mean that you should repeat, repeat, repeat, but rather that it's usually more effective to do a lot of what you both know and only a little of what's new or what needs improving. Then the latter will stand out, and your mental and physical energies can really be applied where they're needed. Why not do a shortened period of schooling with a hack before or after, to warm up or cool down, or as a reward? Why not do a few jumps or trotting poles, as a freshener? Why not do some school movements, like transitions or leg-yields, on a hack? Be inventive.

And above all, let your horse tell you how, as well as what, you are doing.

Maxim | the goal is within you, not outside you

section two

Pathways to performance: the physical skills

Let's talk about outline	**50**
The training spiral	**60**
Working up the spiral and the competition levels	**74**
Decoding your test sheets	**88**
No arena, no problem	**108**

4 Let's talk about outline

> Cramped necks and hollow backs are common, but true collection will be a function of true engagement, which in turn is a function of true extension over the top line. This means that a horse must be encouraged to seek the rider's hands, and its hind legs must carry and push up into a higher bascule. The rider must not pull the horse back onto the hind legs.
>
> **Paul Belasik,** *Dressage for the 21st Century*[1]

Getting the horse on the bit

Most of us have had the experience of finding the comment *'above the bit'* on our dressage sheet. Or perhaps, *'not on the bit'*, *'against the hand'*, *'resisting'*, or *'not through the neck'*. Being on the bit is a basic goal for dressage. And it's a goal that often leads us into committing a variety of crimes – against our horses, against our better natures when it makes us struggle with them, and against the true principles of classical equitation.

A while ago I was judging a championship show at a prestigious venue. Walking through a livery yard on the way to the showground I saw a horse all kitted up for lungeing with a popular 'training aid' aimed at getting him to work in a rounded outline. This involved a complex system of ropes affecting hocks, poll and mouth. I found myself wondering why I was judging – not just there, but at all – if by doing so I was seeming to sanction such artificial ways of producing a 'correct outline'. I felt really depressed. Some days later, teaching a clinic, I heard of a horse whose ligaments had been permanently damaged by being 'winched in' by a training gadget. That made me feel even worse. I always prefer to make the assumption that riders love their horses and wish them well: how tragic that anyone should unintentionally sacrifice a horse's comfort or damage his physique in order to get a desired outline or way of going.

Training in any field involves repetition; building up knowledge and habits until they become automatic. Physical training involves developing the strength and suppleness that are appropriate to the activity. We don't expect novice athletes to run marathons, to achieve world-class sprinting times, lift heavy weights or complete the Tour de France. But some riders do aim to have their heavy cob, their Thoroughbred cross, their Irish coloured or their Pony Club all-rounder miraculously develop the high, rounded profile of a Grand Prix horse. If only they could find the magic way to persuade him. That's what 'dressage' too often seems to involve. And it can lead us to blocking hands, draw-reins and other unfriendly methods.

There are two key issues here. One is the issue of *time*. It really does take time for any athlete to develop muscle build and tone, so the Grand Prix outline will never come rapidly. Buying horses who are already 'built uphill' seems to offer a start – but actually disguises the fact that, even with a good basic structure, muscle-building takes time. The other issue is that of *persuasion*. Why would a horse, naturally constructed to amble and graze with his head lowered, or on occasion to propel himself out of danger as fast as he can, wish to step under his body, lift his back and round his neck and carry a rider at the same time?

For some people, gadgets seem to fit the bill nicely. They offer the temptation of creating a 'correct' outline easily, even automatically. Once the horse gets used to this, the implication is, he will maintain the position without the artificial aid. Failing gadgets, the rider's hands will have to do: let's shorten the reins and brace the back and teach him that way. When I judge, I can easily spot horses who have suffered these kinds of 'training'. They have indeed learnt – learnt to drop their polls even when in a so-called 'free walk' or when the rein is released; they have often learnt to stiffen their backs and brace their necks. All this makes me very unhappy – the more so because there is another way.

This other way, strangely enough, doesn't have to take an age, and it doesn't involve external pulleys, levers or coercion by the rider. It involves, instead, arranging things so that the horse puts himself in the right frame – *because it seems natural and comfortable for him to do so*. Although I made the point that, in the wild, horses spend much of their time ambling around grazing, it is also true that virtually every posture in dressage has its counterpart in nature, exhibited at times when the horse is full of energy and delight in being alive, stepping under himself with active hind legs and a lowered croup. When his back is lifted; when he is confident and joyous.

This can happen in an instant – and even an unfit horse can carry himself like this (albeit for only a short time) if given enough prompting by how he feels about what's going on around him. A mare or gelding won't have the neck muscles of a stallion, but they do have the muscles and ligaments that produce the beginnings of the 'bow before and the bow behind', as expounded by Üdo Burger: '…by elastically bracing the top of the horse's neck (the bow in front of the hand), we also brace elastically the loins (the bow behind the hand) and thus engage the hocks.'[2] That's what we're after, not just because it looks beautiful but because, as I've explained earlier, it helps horses carry their riders with more comfort and less wear and tear.

If gadgets are out, and physical coercion is out, what can we do? We can begin with ourselves and, in doing so, we need to remember that essential concept, elasticity.

How the classical position works

In the previous chapter, I mentioned the axiom: *'Without elbows, there is no riding'*. As the classical riding masters knew from experience, there's an intimate connection between the classical outline in the horse and an equally classical outline in the rider.

- The toned yet flexible, upright stance of the rider, with a 'long front line', produces a vertical balance that causes minimal disturbance to the horse in movement.

- Vertical upper arms, kept close to the rider's sides, mean that the hands and forearms are more stable, rather than being tossed about as the horse moves his head.

- Bent elbows mean that the rider's hands are positioned rather as though carrying a tray, absorbing movement in the elbows while at the same time the hands and forearms can stay soft while subtly influencing the horse's forehand. The hands will neither 'hold the horse up' nor be pulled backwards and forwards by the natural movement of the horse's head within the different gaits.

- A soft lower back allows the rider to absorb the horse's movement in three planes – lengthwise, up-and-down and sideways – staying close to the saddle and 'surfing the wave' rather than either flopping about loosely or thumping stiffly.

- Legs that are stretched down vertically, with the lifted toes that produce toned and effective calf muscles, can give quiet aids to the horse's sides, suggesting just how the horse's hind legs should move – for example, whether with more forward activity or more sideways reach.

We can begin with ourselves. Carolyn's correct, yet soft, self-positioning is making it easy for Ambrose to lift his back and connect through his top-line. Ideally, her heel could be lower, which would stretch her calf muscles more.

When Roy and I started working together, he had many of these elements already in place. But he was not fully vertical, and his over-lengthened stirrup leathers meant that his heels were often raised, so that his calf muscles were slack and ineffective. Shortening his leathers a hole and focusing with his inward eye on the posture of the Spanish riders he had recently seen on holiday provided Roy with a different inner template – and resulted in a truly classical posture which improved his riding and, with it, Cori's way of going. You can see this contrast illustrated clearly in the photos on pages 269.

Riders who really want to make a difference can easily take the initial steps that will lead to extensive improvements. A while ago, I judged at a competition, and the following day gave a clinic. Two riders got rather poor scores in the competition, because their horses were hollowing and not accepting the bit. This also had a knock-on effect on the way they moved, making them lose rhythm and go rather flat. I heard afterwards that the riders were disappointed, saying that I 'didn't like' their horses. They were also dismayed because they had booked lessons on my clinic the following day! When it came to the clinic, we focused on what each rider could do to help her horse find it easy to soften through his back and drop naturally onto the bit. Different though the horses were, the remedy was much the same. It involved the riders bending their elbows and keeping them closer to their sides, and lengthening their reins to make up the distance they'd moved their

Maxim | begin with yourself

elbows back (see the drawings below). To them, the reins felt considerably longer – but to the horses, the contact didn't feel any lighter. Nor, as the riders sometimes feared, did a longer rein inevitably mean a 'flappy' or intermittent contact. In fact, it felt more consistent because now the rider's hands were much more stable; there was less accidental messaging from waving about, less discomfort

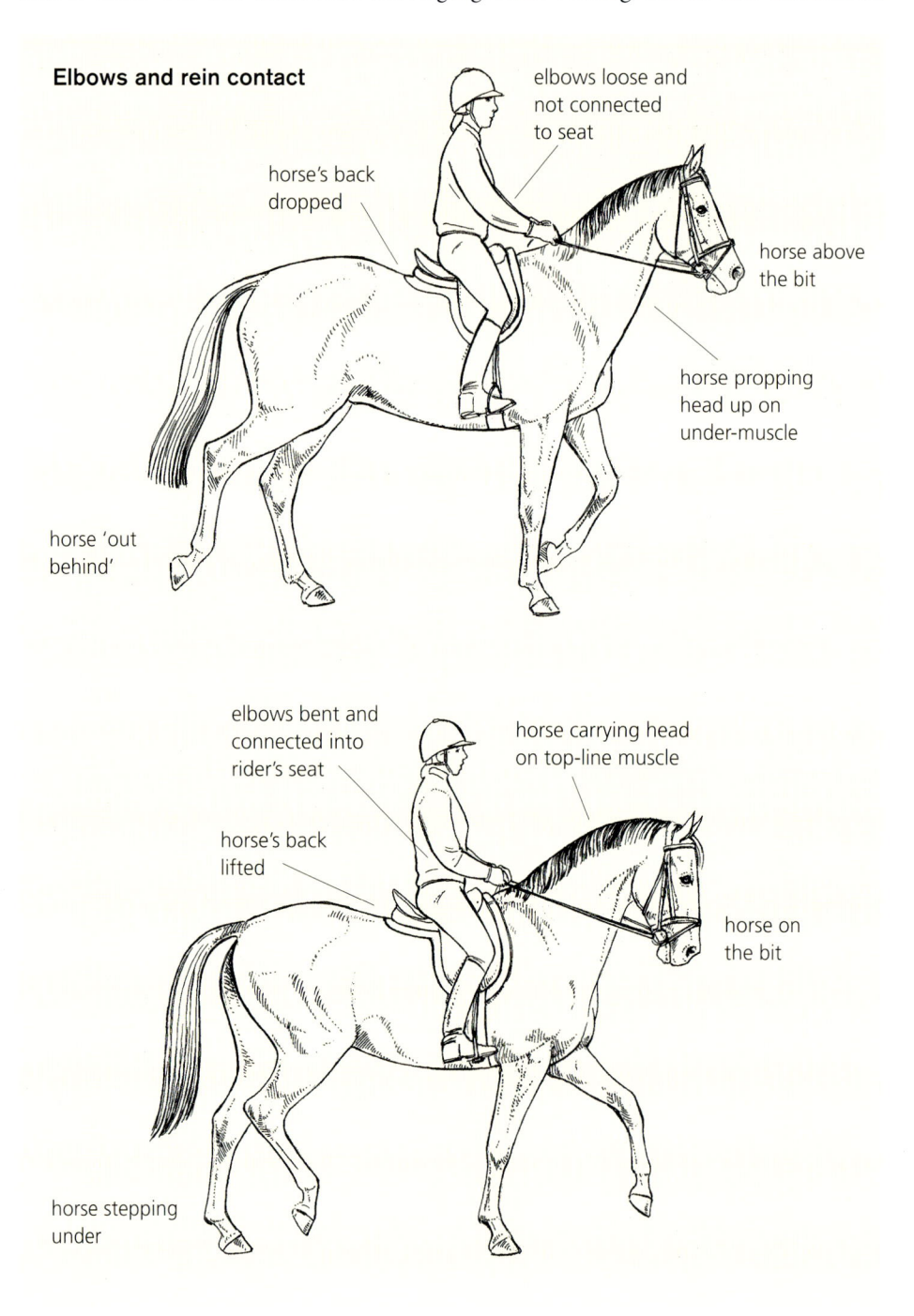

Elbows and rein contact

elbows loose and not connected to seat

horse's back dropped

horse above the bit

horse propping head up on under-muscle

horse 'out behind'

elbows bent and connected into rider's seat

horse carrying head on top-line muscle

horse's back lifted

horse on the bit

horse stepping under

from inadvertent jerking at the bit. Within a few minutes, both horses started to lift their backs and, as a result, offered much improved outlines. There was no more hollowing, no more resistance, but even, flowing, forward strides. A real visible connection over the top-line with energy from the hind legs swinging through the back, vibrating the softened neck with each stride and arriving without any block in a soft, wet contact. This is what is meant by 'submission' on your sheets – but it's a very different submission from giving in, or yielding to pressure. Or, for that matter, giving up, resulting in a more or less polite but deadened obedience. What we are really aiming for is the kind of giving that happens between good friends. It's two-way. It's mutually attentive. It's lovely to feel and lovely to watch.

Each of these horses showed that their way of going depended to a very large extent upon their rider: the upper picture of Ali and Jay on page 25 shows how, given a dictating frame in front, a horse will hollow and leave his hind legs out behind. When this happens, the horse can't maintain rhythm because his energy is being blocked. Although the riders on my clinic had the best of intentions, in their tests they were inhibiting, not encouraging, performance. But when, in their lessons, they took the apparent risk of riding with a length of rein that more nearly matched their horses' current muscular development, and made their hands more stable and their elbows more part of their seats, then each horse was able to show much more of his true potential. 'I could go on all day like this', one of these riders said. My guess is that her horse was enjoying it, too. His superb rhythm, active steps, swinging back, attentive ears, calm eyes and soft mouth were his way of telling us so. If they had produced work of this quality in the competition, each movement would have earned one, perhaps in some cases two, more marks. Only one day later, but a world of difference, and all because both riders were willing to make changes in themselves.

Making changes

Making an initial change can happen very rapidly, as with these riders. Getting changes 'into the muscle', so that they become your 'default setting', takes longer. But if you have the motivation of a happier horse, a better ride and a greater feeling of harmony – as well as the incentive of higher marks – you'll be prepared to put in the effort, because it really is its own reward, and because your horse will be telling you minute by minute how you're doing. Teach yourself to read a momentary hollowing as a possible sign that your elbows may have 'come adrift' or your middle back may have stiffened; train yourself to interpret a loss of energy or straightness as an indication that your legs are not stretched or draped close enough, or your heels have come up; remind yourself that a feeling of 'holding

Maxim | begin with yourself

hands' through the reins means that your hands are worth holding; learn that, when your horse steps forward into a downward transition and walks softly yet purposefully out of it into a lower gait, he's telling you that you have given him room to go forward both physically and emotionally. Read his signals, and they will tell you second by second not just how you are doing, but whether what you need to do next is something a bit different or perhaps – thank you – just more of the same.

What you are looking for

It can help to watch other riders and horses for some key signals, and to ask willing friends or family members to do the same for you. Swapping the observer role with other riders can benefit you both enormously.

- Is the horse stepping under his body with every stride, lowering his pelvis to do so, or is he pushing out behind with little energy passing through his back? Watch where his hocks are when they begin to bend: if they are roughly under the curve of his bottom, he's probably stepping under. If they are further back than this, he's probably not flexing his back and allowing his power to transmit through.

- Do his opposite pairs of legs make an open or a closed V-shape in trot? The closer the V, the more he's stepping under. An open V tells you he's not flexing his hind leg and back joints as much as he could.

- Can you see movement in the muscles behind the saddle? Is his neck soft enough to vibrate with each stride as his hooves hit the ground? Movements like these tell you that his energy is passing freely from his hind legs right through his top-line without any blockage.

Earning a more advanced outline

It's often said that 'you need to earn a longer stirrup leather'. What this tells you is that the length that once seemed right can, with time and practice, come to seem too short: as your hip ligaments stretch through correct riding, your legs will hang lower, and your back and buttock muscles will learn how to remain toned without the tightness that causes bouncing. You will be sitting deeper and your legs reaching down further. Good riding stretches your muscles and ligaments so that your old length seems too short: effectively, you have 'earned' the right to longer leathers. But if you go at it the other way, and start by altering your leathers to

The V-shape in trot. In the top picture, because Jay is not stepping under herself enough she is not transmitting energy through her top-line and is not actually working into the contact. She is dropping behind the bit – and is effectively behind her rider. Ali is offering her right hand forward to test – and hopefully correct – this drawing back. The lower picture shows the 'closed-V'; Jay is properly connected and working energetically through her body.

what you think is an appropriate 'dressage length', you will find yourself having to reach for your stirrups with dropped toes and raised heels. In the process, you will probably suffer a bouncy and unbalanced ride because you have taken away the support that allows your hip, knee and ankle joints to absorb your horse's movement efficiently. Take the time you need, and don't be fooled by seeing other riders' long, elegant legs. Check out by watching how they ride whether they have arrived at their long leathers the hard way – or whether they tried to take the short cut instead.

I want to add another piece of 'earning' to your agenda. It's my experience that you also need to 'earn' the higher head-carriage and arched neck that's a badge of more advanced horses. There are no short-cuts. If you fall into the trap of setting the kind of neck-frame you think your horse needs to have for his level of competition, and then trying to insist on him maintaining that shape, the chances are that you will be asking more than he's physically ready to give. He will find it tiring to arch his neck more than his muscles are ready for, and he will either hollow or drop behind the vertical – anything to escape the discomfort. If, on the other hand, you offer him a long enough rein to allow him to round through naturally – even if it's only a little curvature – and use your schooling exercises to help him build strength and gradually take more weight onto his hindquarters, you will find the triangular muscle at the base of his neck beginning to enlarge quite naturally. As it does, he'll round his neck more easily whilst carrying his head softly, as if it were just dangling. Then you'll begin to notice that your reins are a bit long, and it will be time to take in the slack. You will have *earned* your horse's higher outline and arched neck – and your reward will be that he offers you this with willing flexibility rather than a braced effort.

Trouble-shooting

Giving your horse a longer rein can feel unfamiliar and even scary at first. It highlights that almost automatic feeling that shorter reins give you more control. In fact, of course, they don't: a horse who is short in front is often long behind and if his quarters are out behind him you have less control, not more. Take an honest look at pictures of your horse – does there seem to be more of him behind the saddle than in front of it? Unless he is actually built with a long back and short legs, he should seem roughly square, with as much in front of you as behind you. How does the picture change if you give him two or three more inches of rein, while bending your elbows and taking them further back against your side?

As I explained earlier, in addition to helping you stabilize your hands, repositioning your elbows makes your seat more effective. Now think like your horse for a moment: imagine what it feels like to have unstable hands and arms waving about at the end of the reins whenever you move your head; then imagine what it feels like to have quiet hands that feel elastically connected to your rider's body as a whole, because even though her elbows and wrists are soft, her arms are close to her sides. No floppy dummy here! So her messages will be clearer and more consistent.

As a rider, how are you going to slow down if you have what feels to you like a long rein and you aren't supposed to pull back on it? Many riders I've worked with have been surprised to discover that they can now give slow-down messages by flexing their shoulder-blades, by deepening their weight down into their stirrups through more flexed ankles, or by slowing the speed of their rise in trot. Flexed shoulder-blades combined with closed, bent elbows offer a passive resistance that tells your horse clearly 'not so much, not so fast' (this is a key element in half-halting). Allowing your weight to sink down more into your ankles means that you feel heavier to your horse – again, a form of passive resistance to energetic forward movement. (This can also come in handy when your horse is taking off, or becoming unbalanced, out hacking.) In trot, rising more slowly takes you out of synch with his current tempo, and leads him to slow down to match you because it's actually more comfortable for him to do so. In an unwanted canter, posting as if to a trot has much the same mismatch-to-match effect. So who needs short reins or hauling hands? Put these subtle aids together with the way you use the shape of your school and your training patterns, and you have many effective and non-forceful ways of inviting your horse do what you'd like him to.

In this chapter I've tried to show how the lovely outline we aspire to is the result of offering invitations to our horses rather than issuing them with instructions. A classical outline is the result and badge of correct training, not an end in itself. Balance and self-carriage can both be improved, but not faked or short-circuited. My guess is that if you are still reading this book, you are after the real thing. For further clues, read on.

Maxim | begin with yourself

5 The training spiral

> The aim of basic training is to produce a pleasantly moving, obedient, willing, able and skilful riding horse.
>
> *The Official Instruction Handbook of the German National Equestrian Federation*[1]

Whatever kind of riding you want to do, you will enjoy it more if your horse can be described in words like these. It's highly likely that your horse will enjoy himself more, too. I think it's really important to remind ourselves that this is what dressage tests are actually seeking to benchmark. Stringing specific movements together is what you do in a test, but what the judge is really looking for is the way they are strung together, and what that shows about your ability to help reveal your horse's true athletic potential. Michelangelo said in one of his sonnets that the task of the sculptor is to reveal the statue hidden in the stone, little by little paring away whatever is surplus until only the essential statue remains. How would it be to think of your riding like this – as a means of revealing the best about your uniquely individual horse? How would it be to go into a dressage competition with the aim of helping him show himself as *'pleasantly moving, obedient, willing, able and skilful'*, whatever the level of training he has reached? How would it be to read your sheet in the belief that the judge's comments were intended to help you do this even more effectively?

When we begin to think like this, we are brought back at once to the question of training. What are we doing – both intentionally when we're teaching our horse or practising something with him, and unintentionally when we let our minds wander, put up with something we really know we shouldn't, get into battles with him or ourselves, or try to cut corners by insistence or the use of gadgets? Currently, many judges and trainers are agreed that their aim is for the horse to be a *'happy athlete'*. I'm sure this summarizes what most riders would also like to aim for. Athleticism comes from training and practising; happiness comes from less easily defined – and less reliably produced – experiences like state of mind, degree of rapport, confidence, mutual respect, stimulus, variety and absence of stress. The German Handbook goes on to remind us that the desired qualities in a horse are: *'...achieved by a systematic training programme which maintains and improves the natural abilities of the horse and allows the rider to use them in given situations.'*[2] It then continues by identifying six key elements in a horse's way of going and the order in which training should focus on developing them. Interestingly enough, the Handbook pays just as much attention to the less tangible mental/emotional components of training as to the physical ones. It implies very strongly that it's clear from a horse's way of going what his state of mind is, and also that training that respects him as an individual and tailors itself to his strengths and developmental needs will make him happier as well as more skilful. A contented, alert mind is reflected in a body that is *toned*, but free from unwanted tension. A mutually enjoying and confident partnership tends to show its best much more often than one that is anxious, or contains a dominant partner. That's what classical training is all about.

Often, disappointments in performance can be traced back to an insufficiency in one of the key elements, and that's why it helps us as committed riders to know about them and to work within the progressive training system they seek to develop. Judges are often reminded that it is more valuable to a rider if we indicate *why* something isn't good enough rather than simply pointing out the deficiency. *'Lacks bend'* may be a true snapshot of what we've seen – *but why does that matter?* *'Not enough impulsion'* tells you what's missing – but *what difference would more impulsion make, and what else would benefit from it?* Judges are sometimes told in training sessions that 'it is not their job to give a riding lesson' – and, of course, they are also under pressure of time both during and after the test. But, nonetheless, a good judge will try to point out to the rider where the specific faults in a test performance are coming from, and what might help in future.

The answers in each case take us back to the important elements, which are reflected in what the Handbook terms the Scales of Training. There are six of them: **Rhythm**, **Suppleness (Losgelassenheit)**, **Contact**, **Impulsion with elasticity (Schwung)**, **Straightness** and **Collection**. I have always found it easier to remember sequences like these with the aid of a mnemonic: maybe you do, too. So here is a suggestion:

Riders Sometimes Canter In Small Circles

or, of, course you could make up your own.

Maxim | begin with yourself

In this chapter I want to look briefly at each of the six Scales of Training identified by the German Federation, and show why it's valuable to bear them in mind in all your training and competing. The Scales of Training are set out in a sequence roughly corresponding to what should be asked step by step as a young horse develops, but this shouldn't be taken to imply that there is ever a time when we can say we've fully achieved any of them. So I prefer to think of training as a repeated visiting of the same issues but at progressively higher levels. It's a bit like going up a spiral – each circuit seems to revisit the points on the one below it, but if you keep following the circuits you gain height each time around. See the diagram below. This idea is well expressed by Paul Belasik, when he says: *'In my mind's eye I liken it to a map with a circular road on it. There is no point in rushing to the end, because it is only the beginning where you have already been.'*[3]

Advanced skills like collection depend on having laid more fundamental foundations such as rhythm, suppleness and straightness. So it is counter-productive to seek it before those foundations are in place. Yet a horse whose work is more advanced may still lose rhythm (the first of the Scales) temporarily when performing a difficult movement like a pirouette: the loss of rhythm tells the judge and rider that he has, for the moment, gone beyond his competence, however rhythmical he may have been in his collected canter or his medium trot. Loss of rhythm in the pirouette tells you that he is struggling – at his level – in essentially the same way as a Preliminary level pony who breaks rhythm in canter and runs faster and faster onto his forehand because he can't yet maintain his balance. Every horse and rider can make mistakes – that's about being a living creature, not a machine. But as they gain more knowledge and more experience, they will make mistakes less often, and recover from them more quickly. I think it can be comforting – as well as accurate! – to bear this in mind.

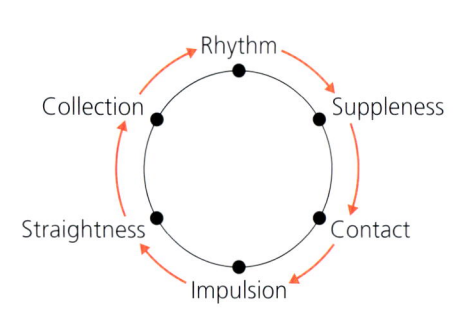

If you imagine this circle is the basis for a tubular shape, you can visualize how it is possible to progress up it in a spiral, revisiting each baseline issue at higher and higher levels.

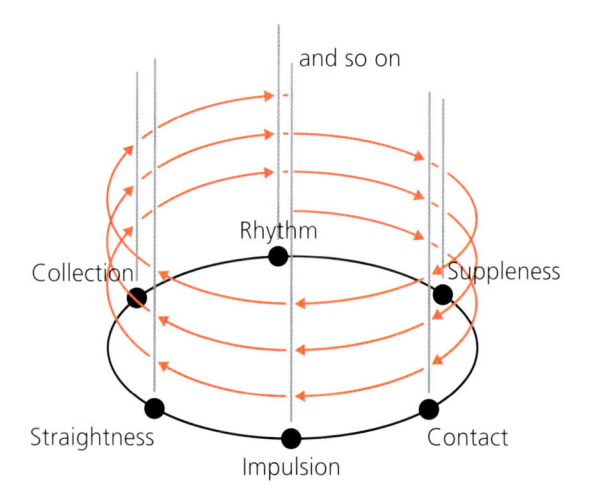

The training spiral.

Maxim | begin with yourself

It's usual for trainers and writers to look at what the Scales of Training mean for our horses. In this chapter I want to do more than this. I'm going to consider how they can help us to explore ourselves. What does your horse's rhythm, or straightness, or suppleness tell you about *you*? Only when you consider how well you – as well as your horse – are doing can you truly improve the partnership that the two of you make together. How is your particular centaur progressing around the training spiral?

Rhythm

Riders Sometimes Canter in Small Circles

'…establish rhythm by maintaining a certain tempo suited to the horse's own natural basic pace.'[4]

I hate shopping in London's Oxford Street. Why? Because crowds of shoppers make me go much more slowly than I find comfortable. Other people may be going more slowly than I am because they are enjoying ambling, or simply because any crowd as a whole ends up having its speed dictated by the slowest people in it. It's not anyone's fault – but I feel uncomfortable and become irritable when I'm forced out of my natural rhythm. On the other hand, I love striding along on a flattish road or track: I enjoy the feeling of stretching my muscles, and the rhythm soothes my mind into a free-floating state where I often come up with interesting reflections or creative ideas. Have you ever felt held back from your natural rhythm – or forced to go faster than you'd like to because you are late, or have too much to do? Alternatively, have you felt relaxed and released by walking or jogging at a tempo that suited you?

Have you ever recognized someone you hadn't expected to see by the way they walk? Or known that the person in a crowd looking so like someone you know couldn't actually be them, because their movement wasn't quite what you were familiar with? Have you ever been at a party and found yourself itching to get up and dance to a particular song? Or losing interest and energy when a track began that somehow didn't seem in the right rhythm for you?

There is rhythm in all of us – and each of us has our own *'signature rhythm'*. If you have ever done, or watched, dressage to music you'll know how important it can be to find a tempo that fits a horse's natural gaits. Tempo and rhythm are just as important when music is not involved. *Rhythm* means the *regularity* of the repeating beat (in this case, the horse's footfalls), and *tempo* refers to *timing* – the quickness or slowness of the rate at which they happen. When a rider has helped her horse find and maintain his natural rhythm in a gait, the tempo will hardly alter when his strides lengthen or shorten, because the lengthening or shortening

Maxim | begin with yourself

are produced not by changes in tempo but by variations in how his impulsion is used, how much ground he is asked to cover with each stride and what length of frame he is working in. When your dressage sheet tells your horse '*hurried in the lengthening*', it's telling you that he didn't keep his balance 'uphill' enough and so began running into a faster tempo.

You are the guardian of your horse's rhythm. It's your job to discover it by watching him when he's moving at liberty and by feeling what he offers you naturally when he's working well under you. Then you need to set that rhythm in your mind and your body so that it acts like an internal metronome. If you have it stored in yourself, it will help you preserve and enhance what he offers naturally.

Why does this matter? Because the very familiarity and regularity of a signature rhythm has a calming and soothing effect. Our first horse, Tristan, who was part Thoroughbred, could be very anxious and hot at times. Yet he was the best lunge horse our instructor had ever had. He never seemed to find lungeing boring. When a horse-walker was installed at the yard, Tris would get quite irritable if he was asked to go in the school while other horses were in the walker. It seemed that the regular rhythm of working in circles not only calmed him but actually made him happy. This may link with the research findings that children learn better when listening to baroque music, which is characterized by its rhythm as well as its sweetness. Regularity of rhythm appears to set off particularly calming brain-wave patterns. Perhaps we are helping our horses achieve more pleasant and more life-enhancing mental states when we help them discover and maintain these natural rhythms of theirs.

What might help you to do this?

- Notice your own natural rhythms, and what effect it has when they are disrupted or changed. Discover what helps you maintain them, and what distinguishes natural changes (momentary drifting-off in attention, or slowing down after lunch, for example) from externally-generated ones. Get inquisitive about the rhythms of other people, and other horses.

- Hum or sing songs that seem to match your horse in different gaits. You can do this out loud – which he will probably enjoy – or silently in your head. Either way, that regular beat will translate itself from your mind into the minute signals your body transmits to your horse. I have always enjoyed singing to our horses when I lunge them, and found that the same songs worked well for most of them. But when I was showing a client recently how to lunge, my familiar songs didn't fit her horse at all. He had his own, different, rhythms. Fortunately, his owner found other tunes that matched him better.

- Remind yourself that, when you are anxious or over-concentrating, you may become tense or begin to block your horse's natural forward flow. Concentration is an essential component for success in competition for both horse and rider, but, as I explore in Chapter 10 on the theme 'Paying the Right Kind of Attention', it can be a handicap if it is associated with mind-body tension. It's for this reason that I prefer to use the terms 'focus' or 'awareness', which indicate a state of mindfulness that can be relatively pressure-free.

- In competition, many riders mistake speed (faster tempo) for impulsion, and hurry their horses beyond their natural rhythm. This seems to happen particularly often in the trot. You may get the comment 'hurried' or 'rushing', or even 'losing rhythm'. It may be better to take off the pressure and let your horse flow along more naturally, even if sometimes you get the comment 'needs more impulsion'.

Suppleness (Losgelassenheit)

Riders **Sometimes** Canter In Small Circles

The German term 'Losgelassenheit' can be interpreted as suppleness combined with looseness and with a complete absence of any tension – i.e. the horse is unconstrained.

A correct rhythm can be achieved only if the horse's back is swinging. The muscles of the neck and back must not only be relaxed, but must work and swing with the movement of the horse's legs.

…Without the willingness of the horse there cannot be true Losgelassenheit.[5]

The important words here are 'unconstrained', 'swinging' and 'willingness'. They draw our attention to a state of 'flow' which is not inhibited either mentally or physically. But the relationship between mind and body, and between horse and rider, in this is quite complex. Think of each as a pair of interconnected circuits, where the elements are interlinked and can affect each other at any time.

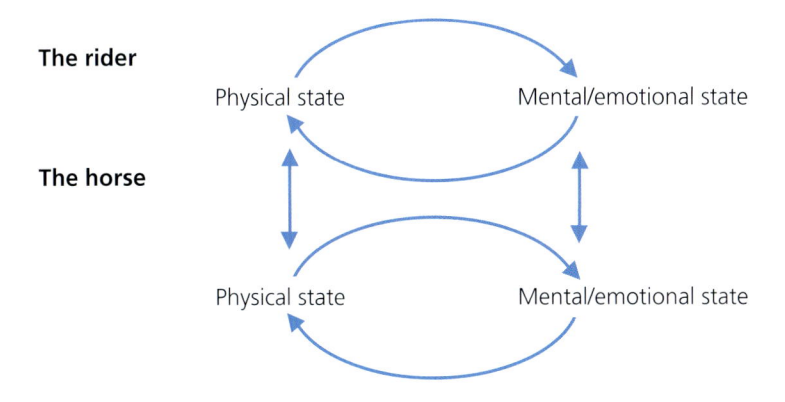

The rider
Physical state ⟷ Mental/emotional state

The horse
Physical state ⟷ Mental/emotional state

The mind-body relationship between rider and horse.

Maxim | begin with yourself

In order to influence your horse's state, the best place to begin is with your own.

- Anything you do to create an 'unconstrained', 'swinging' and 'willing' state in your mind and body will convey an invitation to your horse to do the same. If your mind is calm and focused, it will convey an invitation to him to become the same, because you will be transmitting subtle signals through your muscle tone, balance, rate of breathing and so on, which your horse will certainly notice and respond to differently from signals conveying, for example, agitation, anxiety or distraction.

- Anything you do to make yourself more supple and to follow your horse's movement with less constraint will invite him to respond in the same way. When I ask riders to soften their lower backs and tilt their pelvic bone upward 'as though you were trying to raise it to make room for your horse's back to lift beneath you at each stride', they become more able to flow with their horse's movement, keeping close to the saddle rather than bumping or coming adrift. Their flow helps the horse to flow. The swing in their back encourages a greater swing in his. When both backs are soft the horse becomes more willing to step under himself and allow his energy to be transmitted through without blocking. When the rider's hands are stabilized and her elbows bent and soft, the horse's energy can flow through his entire system – and through the rider as well. This is how the centaur develops.

Stiff backs and soft backs. In the picture above, Ali has braced herself and hollowed her back – and so has Wattie. In the picture on the right, though Ali is toned, she is soft, and so is Wattie!

Maxim | begin with yourself

- Greater physical harmony makes for greater mental harmony. Greater mental harmony makes for greater physical harmony. Willingness arrives because riding, and being ridden, is more pleasant. It's one of the proofs that you are on the right track.

The beauty of such an interconnecting system is that you can start to make changes anywhere. Change how you feel and think, and you will be changing how your body communicates. Change how your body behaves, and there will be corresponding changes in your mental and emotional state. Change yourself and you will be changing your horse.

Contact

*Riders Sometimes **Canter** In Small Circles*

Contact is a soft and steady connection between the rider's hand and the horse's mouth. While training progresses, the horse should be ridden more from behind into the elastically yielding hand. The contact will then be even on both reins when riding straight ahead, and a little stronger on the outside rein when riding on a circle.

To achieve a contact the reins may not be moved backwards. Contact has to be the result of well-developed propulsive power.

…To establish a contact the rider must bring the horse's hind legs further underneath his body. This stretches and elasticates the neck and back band muscles…[6]

Contact is not something you take but something that develops when you ride correctly. Charles de Kunffy often reminds riders that 'it is the rider's job to present the bit, and the horse's job to take it'. He adds that this should feel as if the horse is always moving towards the bit but never quite arriving at it, because it is always being presented just ahead of him as he carries the rider forward with him. So the idea of 'riding the horse from the inside leg into the outside hand', which is implied in the Definition, tells us that the 'framing' which these aids provide is still essentially elastic. The horse on the circle or turning the corner is *bending* without ever being *bent*.

Riding involves complex biomechanics, yet it is so much more than mechanical. That's why we find ourselves using metaphors to describe feelings (both physical and emotional) that are constantly evolving. If, even for a short while, you have felt your horse going forward with energy and willingness through his entire body, reaching towards the bit but not solidly on it, you will have a sense of what

'It is the rider's job to present the bit, and the horse's job to take it.' In a big, forward trot Jay is 'following the hand' by stretching into the longer frame in order to continue taking the contact.

'contact' is about. This is what test movements like 'free walk on a long rein', 'give and retake the reins', or 'stretch on the circle' are inviting you to demonstrate. When you lengthen the frame, does your horse actively follow the bit as he feels it moving away from him? Does he chew down onto it? If he thinks 'thank goodness' and sticks his head in the air, or jerks another few inches when he feels your hands opening, you haven't got contact in this cooperative sense.

Think of holding someone's hand while you are walking along. There's a physical contact, which is probably most comfortable and enjoyable when it feels secure and consistent rather than loose or clenched. There's also an emotional component – the sense of being held and holding, of being valued and valuing. Holding hands can tell you a lot. It's much the same with your horse. You are holding him through his mouth, a part which is both important and sensitive to him. It's one of his main sensory organs. Good hands respect this. Good mouths respect good hands. It's mutual.

The Handbook reminds us of another important aspect of contact: it's not just about body parts – mouth to hand through the rein: it's about generating energy and encouraging it to flow and be shaped without blocking it. You can block your horse's energy if your back is stiff and your seat comes adrift, and you can also block it with your hands if they are insensitive or pull backwards. Your horse is more likely to show willingness and offer you his energy if he trusts you to leave him a way forward. Learning to use various forms of passive resistance helps you become more effective and more confident in your ability to control that energy sympathetically.

Impulsion with elasticity (schwung)

*Riders Sometimes Canter **In** Small Circles*

'Schwung' is the transmission of the energetic impulse created by the hind legs, in to the forward movement of the entire horse. An elastically swinging back is the necessary pre-condition.

…'Schwung' is always the result of efficient training, which uses the natural pace but adds to it the horse's suppleness, looseness, elasticity and responsiveness to the aids.[7]

The proof of elastic impulsion is suspension, that moment in trot and canter when all four hooves are off the ground. Riders often hurry their horses forward, especially in trot, in the mistaken belief that this is demonstrating impulsion. In fact, rushing is the enemy of impulsion, because a hurried horse has no time to be elastic. He has to jump as fast as he can from one pair of legs onto the other in the trot, or to cycle as rapidly as he can through the phases of the canter. He will be relying on the muscles that propel him, not the ones that lift him. If you learn to use your legs and seat to ask your horse to step actively under himself, while at the same time your weight and your own swinging back help him stay balanced and convert some of that energy from a forward into an upward movement, you will be showing him how to become elastic. He will be learning how to carry himself, and you will be producing the suspension that is the real proof of impulsion.

Although a horse can certainly be going quite fast – even too fast – and have little impulsion (as in hurried trot) a horse working correctly in good balance can be going fast and have real impulsion, as in the case of a well-ridden eventer, for example. Also, of course, a top dressage horse doing extended canter has both impulsion and (in dressage terms) considerable speed.

Even a young horse can move with impulsion. You don't have to be in sitting trot, only to slow your rising and at the same time close your legs each time you sit. Most horses look relieved when this happens, and begin to use their whole bodies more elastically. It begins, though, with you.

Straightness

*Riders Sometimes Canter in **Small** Circles*

The horse's propulsive force, developed by the quarters, can only be fully utilized… if the horse moves 'straight'. A horse is 'straight' if the hind feet follow exactly the same line as the front feet. Only then can the rider transfer more weight evenly on to both hind legs increasing their carrying power.

…When a horse is straightened his spine is always shaped according to the line he is moving on, be this on a straight or on a circle line.[8]

Why is straightness important? When a horse's hind feet are stepping along the same line as his front ones, his weight is distributed evenly in a lateral sense and so he is using his body more efficiently and with less risk of uneven wear and consequent stress to muscles and tendons. He is also more easily directed, because his energy isn't escaping to one side or another. Some years ago a reader wrote to one of the equestrian magazines describing how dressage had saved her life. One day, when she was out hacking, a lorry had come fast and very close round a corner towards her. Instinctively, she put her leg on, and her well-trained horse stepped smartly – and safely – sideways onto the verge, just in the nick of time.

Straightness doesn't come naturally to animals any more than to humans. I have noticed our cats favouring one particular 'lead paw' when playing with balls or leaves; and if you watch dogs trotting along beside their owners it's amazing how many are going 'quarters in' – or out! Each horse tends to bend more easily to one side than the other, with his quarters in on the concave side. When a judge penalizes your horse for going *'quarters in'*, it's not just a cosmetic problem. It's a problem of uneven muscular use and development – and left unchecked long-term it could be a veterinary problem, too. (The dual nature of crookedness – the fact that it affects *both sides* of the horse, not just the 'stiff' side – is discussed by Paul Belasik on pages 67–71 of *Dressage for the 21st Century* – see Useful Reading.)

You cannot have a truly straight horse unless he is impulsive, which is why straightness comes after impulsion in the sequence. It's also true, of course, that lack of straightness impedes the throughput of impulsion. Straightness, like all the other items, is one to revisit again and again as you and your horse progress up the spiral.

Straightness is, of course, an issue for you just as much as it is for your horse – and you can work on your own straightness at any time, not just when you're on horseback. Straightness in you means that your shoulders and hips reflect the direction you're going in: like your horse, you should be straight on straight lines and turned on curved ones. But, like him, you will tend to have a 'lead side', a dominant shoulder, hip and foot. Notice when you're walking along which leg

Maxim | begin with yourself

'leads' each stride – I can almost guarantee that you will not be putting push and pressure into both your legs equally (certainly I didn't until I started to think about it). Also, you will probably carry your bag on one arm or shoulder most or all of the time. (Look at other people – many of them will have one shoulder more raised, perhaps even more-muscled, than the other from doing this over time.) You will have a favourite hand for lifting the kettle, turning taps, cleaning your teeth, brushing your hair and so on. Look at your forearms – one is likely to be more strongly muscled than the other. Bend sideways from each hip in turn whilst sliding your hand down the side of your thigh. Is there a difference between your hands in how far down they can slide? Turn from the waist – can you turn further in one direction than the other? When you sit in a chair, is one buttock taking more weight then the other? Almost certainly, the answer to all these questions will be 'yes'.

Now think about the implications this has for your horse. You may think you are sitting straight. You may think you are turning your upper body to mirror his shoulders through bends. You may believe your weight is central in the saddle. But are you giving him the clear signals you think you are – or are you unintentionally skewing your messaging because your body and its movements are not symmetrical?

Noticing your asymmetries is the first step. Experimenting with ways to even and straighten yourself is the next. Shortly before writing this, I broke three bones in my right hand. This meant that I had to use my left hand for everything for almost two months. I decided to take this as an opportunity to increase its skill. Even though my right hand is healing, I now have a choice as to which hand brushes my hair, cleans my teeth, does up buttons, spreads butter, cuts onions, holds a spoon or fork… And I intend to keep using those choices even when my hand is fully recovered. Work first to straighten and equalize yourself, and it will give you a start on helping your horse to do the same.

Not symmetrical. Annie is curling over to the left with inclined head and collapsed waist – so Red thinks he should (over)bend in the neck and lead with (fall out through) his right shoulder.

Maxim | begin with yourself

Collection

Riders Sometimes Canter In Small **Circles**

The aim of all gymnastic training is to create a useful horse which is willing to perform.

The deciding factor here is that the horse's and the rider's weight are distributed evenly over all four legs. To achieve this, the carrying power of the hind legs has to be increased. The front legs, whose original function was of a 'supporting and braking' nature, carried most of the weight. Their burden has to be reduced, whereas the hind legs, which by nature have a predominantly pushing role, must now take up some of the weight-carrying task of the front legs.[9]

As this implies, collection has its foundation in what has gone before. Rhythm and suppleness are the foundation that makes contact possible. With all three in place, impulsion can develop. Impulsion launches the energy that is essential if a straight horse is to become a collected horse. Only a (more or less) rhythmic, supple, impulsive, straight horse can develop true collection. As you work towards becoming more rhythmic, supple, energetically toned and symmetrical, you will also be developing the ability to collect your unique centaur being.

In a young horse, balance is a start. Whatever work you do that helps him to develop his ability to carry himself and you in balance is a good beginning. The Handbook describes how correct training both asks and helps the horse to do this:

> *When the horse is correctly trained, his neck shapes itself. The lowering of the quarters determines how high the neck is carried and arched: the horse carries itself. Whereas if head and neck position are caused by the reins mainly or solely, the rider has to carry the horse's head and neck with his hands.*
>
> *If the carrying capacity of the quarters is developed sufficiently, the horse is able to carry his own and his rider's weight in perfect balance.*[10]

Even at the earliest stages of the training spiral, your indicator of the degree of balance, then collection, that your horse has developed is the extent to which he can carry himself. When he hollows, he is pushing himself along, not carrying himself. When you feel him leaning on the bit, you are carrying him. When he is light, and his neck is arched *in relation to his age and level of training*, or when he can stretch down into a lengthened rein without becoming heavy in front, he is beginning to lay the foundations for collection in its more advanced forms. This is why some of the dressage test sheets say: 'When asked for collection, riders are only expected to show sufficient engagement to carry out the required movements'. Collection is relative.

There are many useful schooling exercises that can help you and your horse keep moving forward on your journey around the spiral, visiting and revisiting each of its key elements at higher levels. Charles de Kunffy's books *The Athletic Development of the Dressage Horse* and *Training Strategies for Dressage Riders* (see Useful Reading) are an invaluable source of understanding and practical help. It helps to remember, too, that the school movements are not ends in themselves but rather ways of progressing up our own particular training spirals. I would like us to be mindful that, every time we ride, something can be done, and something achieved, in relation to one or more of these six essentials in our training. And I am also sure that when we ask the same of ourselves as of our horses we provide them with a much clearer invitation to progress.

Finally, bear in mind that working on the spiral doesn't have to take place only, or even mainly, in a dressage arena. As the Handbook also says: *'Training should always be systematic but never uniform, as no two horses are the same. The training schedule should be varied and should be carried out at different locations if at all possible. Cross-country riding should form a large part of training.'* [11]

Maxim | begin with yourself

6 Working up the spiral and the competition levels

> The dressage test... serves as an opportunity for the rider to present his horse to the judge for comment as to his degree of success or otherwise in training his horse to the requisite level.... The rider should show that he understands the requirements of that level of training and that the horse is well prepared for the level of the test.
>
> **Wolfgang M. Niggli,** *Dressage: a Guideline for Riders and Judges*[1]

Every time you compete, you have an opportunity to benchmark how you and your horse are progressing up the training spiral. When you look at the ascending stages of the competition levels from this viewpoint, they can help you understand what your horse should be able to do, relatively easily, at each stage of his learning and physical development.

If more riders approached competition like this, judges would see fewer ungainly, unbalanced 'going-through-the-motions' tests. Being prepared to have a go at a higher level when you believe it would be a useful stretch is one thing; but asking your horse to do, for example, lateral movements if he hasn't yet learned to step under his body and carry himself sideways as well as forwards, produces an incorrect – often unsuccessful – imitation instead of the real thing. Much the same goes for lengthening or medium work. It's the genuine stuff you want. And so does the judge.

I'm sure that if you asked your horse he would prefer to do his new learning at home, without the pressures that busy surroundings, other horses – and you feeling anxious and perhaps distracted – put on him. It would be so much more relaxing – even enjoyable – for you both to use competition to show what you can already do comfortably rather than struggling to string it all together in public before it is naturally in your minds and in your muscles.

A good principle is to compete below the level at which you are currently working at home, and to test your readiness to go up a level only occasionally, perhaps at an unaffiliated competition. This is using the competition system to its best advantage, to rubber-stamp your existing progress. If you have a competitive nature, a fringe benefit is that this can also give you a better chance of doing well! And you will be able to use the judge's comments to refine, polish and improve – in other words, to do even better in future. If, on the other hand, you are daunted by competition, you are much more likely to be relaxed if you are doing work with which you and your horse are already comfortable.

In this chapter I want to look at what the different competition levels ask of you, and explore how working towards the next level can enhance your training by reminding you of your own progress up the training spiral. When I'm judging, I find it helpful to ask myself: *'What is required at this level?'* I also ask myself: *'What does this particular test focus on?'*, and I shall explore that question more fully in Section IV, the Strategic Skills section of the book, when I talk you through how to choose tests that best suit you and your horse.

For the time being, I'm going to: (1) describe what's required at each of the most commonly competed-at levels; (2) relate the specific movements to the training spiral and (3) suggest some exercises that will help you progress. If you are already some way up the levels, it will still be worth your while to revisit the lower ones you are no longer competing at, and to remind yourself of the basics that they require. So often the issues that cause problems at a higher level, and bring you disappointing marks there, relate to problems in more fundamental work. Going back to basics may feel disappointing, but it almost always helps you to secure your foundations, so that you can progress again more surely.

The competition levels

Preliminary level

What's required

Medium walk and walk on a long rein
Working trot and canter
Trot to halt
Brief transitions (2–5 steps) trot-walk-trot
Some transitions without the support of the wall (e.g. over centre line)
Some transitions between markers rather than at the marker

20-m circles in trot and canter
15-m circles in trot
10-m half-circles in walk
10-m and 15-m half-circles from track, returning to track on opposite rein
3-loop serpentines in trot
Give and retake of reins in trot

Maxim | begin with yourself

How this relates to the training spiral

What should be your aims at this level? Attentiveness, smoothness, flexibility, rhythm, balance and flow. With reference Chapter 5, be thinking of **Rhythm** and **Suppleness**. The most important aim for a young horse, or one just starting out at dressage, is that he should move forward freely. As we saw in Chapter 5, a horse will have his own natural tempo in each gait, and it's your job as a rider to allow him to show this while moving on the straight lines and large curves that are asked for at this level. You need to get that rhythm into your head and into your muscle memory, just like the beat of your favourite tune.

Often, if you lack rhythm, your horse loses rhythm too. The commonest causes are blocking with your hands or not moving rhythmically yourself. Count in time with his gait, if it helps you. *One, two, three, four; one, two, three, four* in walk. *One, two; one, two* in trot. *One, two, three; one, two, three* in canter. Or hum that matching tune under your breath. You can hum silently, or very quietly, to yourself even in a test!

If you feel the rhythm falter, slightly soften one hand forward, then the other. If you have been blocking your horse, this should help him to step freely forward again. If you find this happens often, but you can always correct it by releasing one or both reins, then it's probably a sign that you need to work on developing a softer, more elastic contact yourself.

If you lost rhythm on a turn, often it's because your horse wasn't moving with enough energy. Squeezing him with your inside leg as his inside leg lifts to step forward can encourage him to put more energy into that next step and help him keep both his balance and his rhythm. (If you can't yet feel which of his hind legs is lifting behind you, ask a friend to watch you and call out 'now' each time a particular leg lifts. Notice how your horse's rib-cage swings against your leg each time. Practise calling out yourself so that your friend can check you, until you can get it right automatically.)

Suppleness in a young or novice horse is going to show itself in two ways: the tail-to-head flow of energy through his back and neck (*longitudinal* suppleness), and his ability to curve his body (not just his neck!) when he's going round corners and circles (*lateral* suppleness). When they're moving at liberty, horses will often naturally look outwards on curves, especially in canter: in the wild they can balance quite effectively like this, but when they have to carry a rider as well it helps them to support the additional weight if they bend their whole body in the same direction as the curve and make more use of their inside hind leg. So, with you on board, if your horse curves his body inwards, he's more likely to stay in balance. Therefore, even at the beginning of his training, you will be helping your horse if you ask him to go straight on straight lines and curved appropriately at

Maxim | begin with yourself

other times. (I should add that a more advanced horse *can* curve outwards and yet remain in good balance – as, for example, in counter-canter – but this also requires some experience and skill in the rider, who has to help him keep an 'upright' posture and carry himself, rather than 'falling' through his shoulder or disengaging behind and pushing instead of carrying himself.)

Rhythm and suppleness are truly the foundation of all that follows. Focus on monitoring and enhancing them from moment to moment, whatever you are doing with your horse, and you will keep yourself alert and interested. And if you are alert and interested, he's much more likely to be so, too.

Useful training exercises

- All the Preliminary movements – with rhythm and suppleness in mind! Ask for changes of direction – with appropriate changes of bend. Try figures of eight.

- Can you keep your horse straight if you ask him to go along the quarter-line rather than staying on the track? Can you keep him straight out hacking? Are you straight yourself? Check that your shoulders and hips are horizontal and facing forward if you are on a straight line, or in alignment with your horse's shoulders if on a curve.

- When you make a downward transition, make sure that you soften your hands immediately the horse responds to your aid, so that you don't block his first steps in the lower gait. He should step forward positively from trot into walk with free, purposeful strides, not shuffle with little ones or almost stop before lurching forward again. When you want him to drop from canter into trot, first warn him by rebalancing your own weight and flexing your inside shoulder back in rhythm for a couple of strides before you actually ask. If you have your elbows flexed and close to your sides, this shoulder movement will signal to him through increasing pressure from your inside seat-bone, and without any pulling back on the reins, that you want him to step under and rebalance himself. Thus he will be encouraged to shift his own weight back and carry himself through the transition. Then he's less likely either to tip onto his forehand, or stop abruptly – two common problems with downward transitions.

- Get the horse used to making transitions between the gaits, making sure he also steps under himself like this into halts. Do lots of transitions. Ask for them when you're out hacking, as well. Make sure that you don't get sloppy about them; otherwise he will get confused about what's wanted. Always warn him, always rebalance yourself first and always use your legs to ask him to step under himself rather than just taking your legs off his sides and only stopping him

Maxim | begin with yourself

with your hands. The former Chief Rider of the Spanish Riding School, Arthur Kottas, uses the maxim: 'Seat, leg, rein' to remind his pupils that every change a rider wants should use *all three* means of aiding and be signalled to the horse *in that order*. Warning him by rebalancing your seat and asking him with your leg means that your reins only need to *verify* what you have already told him and what he is already well on the way to doing. If you make this your maxim, too, you and your horse will build good habits and they will become automatic.

Novice level

What's required

As for Preliminary, plus:

Halt, rein-back and proceed in walk
Halt for a specified number of seconds
Some medium trot strides
10-m circles in trot
Ability to make transitions from trot to walk and vice versa with only 2–4 steps in between (i.e. half-halts)
Allowing the horse to stretch in the trot
10-m loop in from the track and return to the track
4-loop serpentines in trot
Collected trot
A few strides of counter-canter
Give and retake the reins in canter
Change of canter lead through trot
Some medium canter strides
15-m half-circle in canter and return to track with a change of direction
5-m loops from and returning to the track in canter
Walk to canter between two markers

How this relates to the training spiral

Be thinking of rhythm, suppleness and contact.

If you have been building your horse's ability to carry himself, and building your own ability to preserve his natural rhythm in a supple, forward flow, you will have laid the foundation for the tighter turns and more precise transitions needed at this level. If the horse has already begun to learn to carry his own weight, with-

Maxim | begin with yourself

out depending on your hands to support his forehand, and if his circle work has begun to teach him to step under his own body when you sit up and use your legs gently, he will find it easier to lengthen. But if he rushes forward onto his forehand when you ask him, you'll know that you need to do more, more, more transitions!

If you have been teaching yourself and your horse that the reins are there for guidance rather than for balance or stopping, you will find that you have built a trusting relationship that allows energy produced by his hind legs to flow freely through his back and neck, so that your hands can receive and direct it with increasing subtlety. The proof of this trusting connection through to the rein will be what happens when you lengthen the reins. What you – and judges – are looking for here is for your horse to stretch his neck in order to keep the contact. As the rein gets longer, for example in the free walk or some 'lengthen the rein' exercises, he should stretch forward and down to keep in touch with you. For you, it can almost feel as though his hind legs are stepping right under him to reach towards your hands. If he sticks his neck forward and out on the same level, he isn't 'through' his back: he's just relieved that there's less pressure on his mouth. The same goes for snatching and jerking, in which cases the focus must go back to your hands again.

However, if he can make a soft, rounded stretch when you lengthen the rein in trot (or canter), this shows not only that he is trusting you, but that he is able to balance himself without your support.

As though his hind legs are stepping right under him to reach your hands… Ambrose is well balanced while clearly 'seeking the bit'.

Maxim | begin with yourself

Giving and retaking the reins in the higher gaits tests balance and the genuineness of the contact at the same time. Your horse should keep the same outline he had before you released the contact, or stretch out and down just a little; and he should neither hollow nor come behind the bit when you take the reins back again. If he hollows on release, he's telling you that you didn't have him balanced or genuinely into the contact, and if he hollows when you retake he's telling you that you need to practise your rein-shortening technique to make it smoother and more subtle!

The greater precision required at this level (transitions at specified places, tighter movements, quicker succession of transitions) help to benchmark the extent to which you and your horse understand each other. How precise – and how effective – is your aiding? How willing, and immediate, are his responses?

Useful training exercises

- Transitions within as well as between the gaits. Begin to teach yourself and your horse that there can be many kinds of trots, not just the working trot you've got used to. For example, ask him to trot just as energetically, with more bounce rather than more forward movement. Think of bouncing a large, soft, rubber ball underneath you. When you do this, you are helping him stay in balance while giving him the incentive and the time to use his hocks actively underneath himself, rather than just to propel himself faster and more onto his forehand. This kind of trot work now will be the foundation of collection further up the spiral. When he is able to use his hocks well in energetic balance, ask him to use this as the platform for launching himself forward-upward for a few steps (think controlled lift-off). By doing this you are beginning to build towards medium and eventually extended work. Be content with a few longer upward steps at a time, and then ask for shorter steps again before he has had a chance to lose his balance. Only increase gradually the number of steps you ask for at a time. Build your vocabulary of trots now – you'll both enjoy using it later! Play with the 'language' and find out what you can do with it. Play a bit with the same process in canter, too, when he begins to be reasonably well balanced. Try to stretch your skills by working briefly at the leading edge of what you can do in every session, but try also to avoid asking so much that you 'fail'.

- Teach your horse to move away from the pressure of your leg. (Teach yourself to use one leg for aiding rather than always using both at once. Think how you use your legs alternately to ask for an active walk: now you want to achieve the same independence in other gaits and in more taxing movements.) Do turns on the forehand – opening and closing gates provides a good opportunity for this. Or pick an imaginary point somewhere near the centre of the school and spiral in towards it then out again, keeping him slightly bent to the inside of the circle, using your outside leg to bring him in and your inside one to take him out again. (There is a picture of Shane and Ted doing this on page 259) Use your other leg to help him stay balanced and to control how far and how fast he moves in or out with each step.

- Come off the short side of the arena just after the centre line and use your inside leg on the girth each time you feel the horse's inside hind leg lift, so that instead of stepping straight forward with it he places it further underneath his body and creates a sideways shift. Try it on a loose rein sometimes – you will be pleased to discover that you don't need to use your reins to contort your horse into sideways work! This is the beginning of leg-yielding. Ride forward again if he begins to walk diagonally towards the fence, or if you, or he, start to 'kink' in the middle. Don't try to shape the movement with your reins until you and he both know that his quarters are what motivate and carry him sideways. When he goes sideways reliably whilst staying more or less parallel, begin to ask for a little bend around your inside leg, away from the direction of the movement. Once you've got lateral movement, you can ask your horse to increase the degree of his bend or his angle. The important thing is that he first understands the principle of what you are after. You can fine-tune it later.

- Play with weight aids – what happens if you put more weight into one stirrup? Your horse will probably move towards the weighted leg to rebalance himself. Be careful that you don't tip to the side you are weighting – your body should remain straight and upright with no collapsing in your waist, shoulder or hip. Turn down the centre line – can you 'invite' him to make a zigzag with alternate weight-aiding?

- Can you use your weight to help your horse make downward transitions in balance and without either of you relying on your hands? A couple of strides before you want the transition, allow your weight to travel down more through your ankles. Let them become very soft and flexible, so that gravity helps your weight into a gentle downward aid ; down, down, DOWN with your third and final stride. Be amazed at the smooth, flowing, forward transitions you can get!

Maxim | begin with yourself

Elementary level

> **What's required**
>
> As for Preliminary and Novice, plus:
>
> Halt – rein-back – canter depart
> Extended walk
> Large half-pirouettes
> Medium trot between designated markers (instead of 'a few strides')
> 8-m circles in trot
> Leg-yielding
> Canter from walk
> Medium canter to trot via few steps of collection
> Canter between designated markers
> 15-m canter circles
> 4-loop canter serpentine with a simple change of leg each loop on the centre line
> Canter half-circle to centre line, simple change, canter half-circle in opposite direction
> Working canter on a long rein
> Longer periods of counter-canter
> 5-m canter loops away from and returning to the track
> Simple changes of leg
> Shoulder-in
> Quarter pirouettes
> Rein-back to trot

How this relates to the training spiral

Be thinking of rhythm, suppleness, contact, impulsion, and straightness.

Elementary tests ask you to make changes: in direction, in ground coverage, speed, and between one movement and another. They put an increasing premium on balance and self-carriage, as well as on the speed, precision and effectiveness of the 'aiding conversations' between you and your horse. For these, you need impulsion: energy from the hind legs freely transmitted through the whole of the horse's body and received by the rider's hands via the bit. This is what will help the horse engage and carry himself in those circles, loops, and transitions.

As a judge, I can easily spot the difference between a horse who *steers* around a small circle and one who *carries* himself and his rider, or between one who makes a simple change look like a single, flowing process and one who jerks his way through a series of barely-connecting bits and pieces. What do your circles, or your simple changes, feel like? Without impulsion there can be no real self-carriage, and certainly no straightness. Without impulsion the horse will neither be using his hind leg muscles properly nor, almost certainly, lifting his back to cushion your weight. Without straightness he will be loading different parts of his body unequally, with the risk of strain and even damage. When a judge tells you that your centre line was *'quarters right/left'*, or that he was *'quarters in'* on the circle, this is the implication.

Having begun lateral work with leg-yielding earlier in your training, you are now going to be asked to show another movement where your horse has to step under his body and lift himself laterally. The test of a good shoulder-in is just this: that it is a movement where your horse lifts and carries himself at an angle to his direction of travel rather than pushing, drifting, or falling. If he can balance himself and uses his hind legs actively; if you and he both know how to activate a specific leg more than its partner; and if you know how to use your outside elbow to stabilize your hand and rein to help prevent him falling out through the shoulder, you will already have what it takes.

Everything depends on what has gone before. So, what are your most basic stops and starts like? So many riders lose marks when their horse moves, or swings his quarters, in halt. Think broadly – does your horse stand still when you mount? Will he 'park' on a loose rein? You are aiming beyond competition marks here – aiming, in fact, for a calm and handy horse. Will he readily back up in the box when you say the word, or raise your hand, or put a tiny bit of backward pressure on his chest? Properly taught and properly practised, halt and rein-back should be easy, everyday activities, not special competition manoeuvres.

Useful training exercises

- Watch other horses and riders. Are they steering or carrying?
- How do you feel the difference between when your horse is steering and when he is carrying himself? Find out what it is that tells you.
- Practise detecting which hind leg is lifting by riding with your eyes shut. Get a friend to lead or lunge you, and call out what you are feeling. Whilst on the lunge, do the same in canter to get used to recognizing which foreleg is leading.
- Straightness starts with you, so begin by checking yourself. Are you looking straight ahead on straight lines? Are you looking over your horse's inside ear on curves? Are you sitting in the middle of the saddle, equally weighted on both sides of his back?

Maxim | **begin with yourself**

- It can be helpful to work on taxing movements, such as tight circles, a bit at a time, as I suggested about lengthening strides. Try a 12-m circle… Try a 10-m half-circle…Work down gradually to what you want. Compound movements such as simple changes can be approached in the same way. Try getting your canter-walk transitions really smooth – then walking forward again….And when that comes easily just add an upward transition on the other end. Then reduce the number of walk steps.

- Continue building your vocabulary. Eventually, you will need to produce four walks: free walk, collected, medium and extended. Can an observer tell which kind of walk you are doing? Can you? Can you change from one to another cleanly and crisply? Is each of them energetic, with active hind leg steps? The walk can easily be interfered with if you don't really know what you are doing: ask your trainer or a knowledgeable friend to help you with this.

- Practise lateral work out hacking as well as in the school. The section 'A hack with Roy and Cori' in Chapter 8 explores how this and other 'school' work can be done equally well on tracks, along hedgerows and in open fields. Use natural markers such as trees and bushes to work towards. This can also be a brilliant way to hold the attention of 'looky', spooky horses.

- Use every daily opportunity to help halt and rein-back become easy and natural for yourself and your horse. If he is well-balanced in halt, with his hind legs well under him, he will not find it hard to move off in trot, or even canter. Once he can rein-back rhythmically without either hollowing or dragging back with his nose on his chest, he will be able to pause at any moment when you cease giving the backward aid, and move forward in walk, trot or canter. Play with the component elements, then begin putting them together in different combinations.

Medium

What's required

As for Preliminary, Novice and Elementary, plus:

Collected walk	Give and retake the reins in medium canter
Half-passes in trot and canter	
Extended trot	20-m half-circle in counter-canter
Canter-halt on entry	Halt-rein-back-canter
Extended canter	Travers

Maxim | begin with yourself

How this relates to the training spiral

Instructions on the test sheets remind you that 'collection' means the ability to perform the movements required at this level – in other words, it is relative. It's not so much the movements that are new, apart from half-pass and travers, but the way they are put together and what it takes for you and your horse to perform them more or less fluently. You are moving up the spiral, though the elements are still the same. You are now revisiting them at a higher level, as you and your horse will continue to do throughout your work together.

Useful training exercises

If you know from experience that your four limbs give you control over your horse's four legs, and have developed your ability to use your limbs independently and effectively, then you have what it takes to motivate his hind legs, create a bending of his body around your inside leg, and at the same time control his neck and shoulders. These are the conversational building blocks that allow you to tell him 'half-pass' or 'travers' – just as earlier on they allowed you to say 'leg-yield' or 'shoulder-in', or 'turn on the forehand'. Problems with lateral movements should refer you back to yourself and your aiding: ask yourself, first, 'Can I give clear, unilateral aids?' And, second, 'Does his response tell me that he has understood?' If not, which part of the instruction has he not understood? Remember, his behaviour gives you all the information you need. Any difficulties will give you the exact recipe you need to improve!

While I have stopped my detailed account of training for competition at Medium level, the training spiral itself never ends. Every time you go around it you revisit the six key items at a different level. Rhythm, suppleness, contact, impulsion, straightness and collection are the basics of training because, together, they add up to producing a healthy horse who is a pleasure to ride – and who is more likely to enjoy being ridden. Time spent revisiting earlier levels and recapitulating the work you did there is never wasted. Time spent exploring the boundaries of your current abilities is time that helps you take the next steps upwards and onwards. Whether you have a Grand Prix Warmblood or a native pony, a Thoroughbred or heavy cross, there is something here that can give you practical help towards making your riding more enjoyable and your competition results more successful. You have a framework which is both clearly structured and, in practice, almost infinitely flexible. It will guide you without constraining you – the ideal training instrument!

Tips for trainers

If you are involved in training riders, the training spiral is a wonderful aid for you, too, especially when you take the horse's behaviour as a mirror that reflects the rider's ability and learning issues. Here are some tips to help you make the most of your time with your clients.

- Each time you see a rider, ask her what she has been up to since you saw her last. Does she know how that relates to the training spiral? Explore this with her.

- Find out if she knows what she is doing to bring about the behaviour she is getting from her horse.

- Get her to experiment, playfully and inquisitively, with different versions of what she is doing and to notice the different results she gets.

- Don't just tell her she is 'right' or 'wrong': encourage her to find out for herself what works – and why.

- Always encourage her to discover more techniques, more strategies, more approaches. Her search and her discoveries will keep her motivated and allow her to own her learning rather than becoming dependent on you.

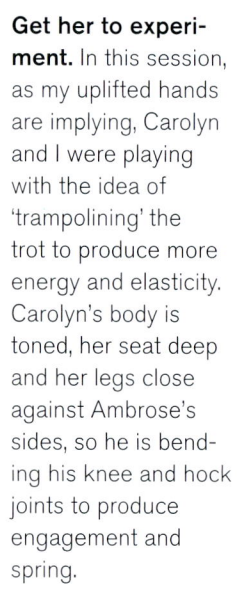

Get her to experiment. In this session, as my uplifted hands are implying, Carolyn and I were playing with the idea of 'trampolining' the trot to produce more energy and elasticity. Carolyn's body is toned, her seat deep and her legs close against Ambrose's sides, so he is bending his knee and hock joints to produce engagement and spring.

Maxim | begin with yourself

- Every time you see her, aim to have the bulk of her session within her comfort zone, but with some work inviting her and her horse into their stretch zone. *Always avoid their panic zone.*

- Make sure that she knows how to replicate any new learning for herself when she's not with you. Get her to tell you (and of course herself!) just how she did that.

- At the end of your session, get her to recap what she has learnt and will be taking away. Don't do it for her – and don't correct her if what she remembers is not what you thought she learnt. What she remembers *is* what she learnt! If it's not what you intended, give some more thought to how you communicated with her, and pick the point up another time, in another way! Remind yourself, every time you teach, that your rider reflects your teaching in the same way as her horse reflects her!

- Help her to relate what she and her horse are doing now to the foundation work they did at lower levels, and to recognize how they are building towards more effective and subtle communication with each other – and, through this, leading to more advanced skills and (by the way) higher levels of competition.

Maxim | begin with yourself

7 Decoding your test sheets

> A really competent judge does not only observe and mark inaccuracies and irregularities; at precisely the same moment he positively recognises their underlying causes…[1]
>
> Exactness is not all that matters; the influence of a judge has to be constructive and therefore he must not fail to commend what is good as much as condemn what is wrong.[2]
>
> **Kurt Albrecht,** *A Dressage Judge's Handbook*

You are looking at the judge's comments on your test sheet, and asking yourself: '*What did she mean by that?*' In this chapter I'm going to offer you two route-maps for finding your way from your test sheet comments back into more effective training. The first (Reading Your Sheets Right) has to do with getting yourself into the right frame of mind to use the comments – and of course the tests themselves – most productively; and the second (Decoding Specific Comments) helps you extract practically usable information from the specific comments themselves.

Reading your sheets right

Most judges make use of relatively standard phraseology in their comments. As part of their training they will regularly have attended judges' training courses, where a shared set of values and criteria for judging are learnt and practised – and tend to be expressed in 'judgespeak'. And they will also have 'sat in' with more experienced judges during actual competitions and noted not just what those mentors have picked out for comment, but also the kind of wording they use. Time is pressured when you're judging, so we all tend to seize on phrases that sum up common issues neatly and clearly. I suspect, however, that even though we know what we mean when we dictate our comments, it may not always be so clear to the competitor! By the time a judge has reduced an opinion like 'not stretching downwards as well as forwards into the rein and therefore not lifting the back as he should' (for a free walk) to the words *'not through top-line'* or *'not taking the contact'*, she may be in danger of forgetting to ask herself whether the competitor even shares her understanding about what's correct. The technical knowledge that a judge may have accumulated over a number of years may not be shared by someone attempting a Riding Club Preliminary test for the first time. Even if the rider does have theoretical and technical expertise, do our words convey our meaning to her clearly? Do we share the same understanding as to what is meant by words like *'through'* and *'contact'*, for example? Is the rider even in the right frame of mind to hear what we have to say?

If you understand the principles of classical riding and the key features of the spiral of training, it all becomes both simpler and clearer. First, however, it's important to check that you receive the comments – any comments – in the frame of mind that helps you make best use of them.

Reading in the right frame of mind

Often, when we read sheets, we do something like this. First, we look at the percentage. *'Only 58%?' 'Only 52%?' 'Only 64%?'* ('Only' of course is relative!) Next, we scan for the 'good' marks and 'good' comments (saying *'yes!'* mentally to ourselves). Perhaps pat ourselves on the back. Maybe we mentally pat the judge for having spotted and rewarded that transition that felt so light; that circle that seemed so balanced… Then we spot the 'mean' marks and have a grumble about them. *'That leg-yield was better than a 5. What does she mean "not enough bend?" Felt like plenty to me. This one was no worse than the one he did in that test last week, and he got a 7 then. Must be a mean judge… Oh well, better luck next time.'*

Does this sound familiar? I have taken this approach to reading sheets myself in the past. It's very natural – but when we read with this good/bad mind-set we often miss the opportunity of getting any real benefit from our sheets. The words 'judge' and 'judgement' are unfortunate, because they feed straight into this way of thinking, and the feelings about being good or bad, that so often go with it. Feeling judged – whether the judgement itself is pleasing or displeasing, often means you don't really reflect on the content of the judgement or its deeper implications. Discovering that your horse didn't come up to scratch – even if deep down you know he didn't – can make you feel very defensive.

I believe that you will get the most out of what judges say if you consider their comments in relation to the themes I've been exploring so far in this book. I'm

Maxim | begin with yourself

inviting you to step aside from your immediate feelings and responses and read your test sheet as something that really can give you helpful guidance for your journey around the training spiral. What value can you get out of it if you try?

What happens if you assume that *the judge is there to serve you?* For those five or so minutes that you're in the arena, her knowledge and experience are at your disposal. She is doing the best she can, just as you are. She owes it to you to tell you what she sees and how it measures up to the standards she has painstakingly learnt (yes, this is where judgement does come in); you owe it to her – and to yourself and your horse – to try to understand what she has said, and why. Then you can feed it back into your continuing journey around the training spiral and up the levels of competition. You can pay yourself – and the judge – the compliment of mining those brief comments for the training nuggets they contain.

In doing this, you will have made some really important changes in the way you think and feel. You will have:

- **Got yourself looking to the future,** where you can take action, because you will be asking yourself the question: *'How can I use this information?'* rather than looking backwards passively to the past (how you did on that day), which you can't change.

- **Put yourself in a positive mindset** by deliberately setting out to ask yourself: *'What value does this comment have for my training?'* rather than just seeing whether the judge does or doesn't agree with how you felt about your performance.

- **Connected the test sheet** (and the performance it relates to) **back to your everyday work with your horse.** That is something you are in charge of and can get expert help with if you need to.

- **Got yourself some items for your current work-in-progress check-list.** Some comments will confirm what you know already. *'Yes, that did feel like one of the best shoulder-ins we've ever done.'* Or, perhaps: *'Mm. I know he isn't really going forward enough yet in those downward transitions'.*

Sometimes there will be pleasant surprises, sometimes an idea you hadn't thought of.

> Each time you read a sheet, try asking yourself: *'What can I take away from that to help me next time I ride?... And in the future?'*

Maxim | begin with yourself

Understanding judges' shorthand

One way to approach the judge's comments is to ask yourself: *'Which item(s) on the training spiral can they help me with?'* We are considering two things here: the level of training your horse demonstrates through the Scales of Training, and the way his level of training is displayed in specific movements. Judges will have been taught to compare what you do with the FEI definitions – you can find those in your national organization's Handbook. Often, comments can seem to focus just on performance details; but that is only half the story! Think how much more you can get from them if you keep pegging them back into ideals of classical riding and the aims and concerns of the training spiral!

When we think of revisiting the same issues time and again as we progress higher up the levels, it makes it easier to take on board a further notion: though the essence of a gait is always the baseline for judgement, what is acceptable at a lower level in terms of balance or engagement will not usually be judged good enough at a higher level. For example, a true four-beat walk remains just that, but as you progress you'll have to demonstrate that you and your horse can maintain its rhythm and purpose *while at the same time* lengthening or shortening and elevating the stride itself.

Decoding specific comments

I've already emphasized how important it is to be thinking *forward* as you read your sheets. So don't just glance over the sheet as soon as you pick it up at the end of the class: give yourself time to read it on your own in a quiet environment and in the right frame of mind.

Pointers for your work on the training spiral

Ask yourself first of all how the comments highlight your horse's individual progress and needs on the training spiral. Look over the sheet quickly to get the overall impression: what themes are emerging? Are you hearing the same old story as you've heard from other judges? It can be uncomfortable to recognize that your horse still doesn't seem forward enough, or settled enough in his mouth, or whatever your particular bugbear may be. This time, though, you can see which bit of the 'ideal training recipe' it relates to. When I was a teenager I had a cookery book that contained a section on 'Why Cakes Fail'. Common causes of failure were all listed – cracked top, sunken middle, doughy texture and so on – and against each was given the cause. So you knew what to do to improve the next time. If you can

Maxim | begin with yourself

read your test sheets like this, you'll find even the most critical ones have something really useful and positive to offer you.

Rhythm

A judge's first concern is with the essential rhythm of the gaits: is the walk made up of four even beats – or is it verging towards two (becoming lateral)? Is the canter energetic enough, does it have enough jump, to keep it three-beat – or is it becoming sluggish and tending towards four beats? Is the trot like a metronome in its one-two, one-two rhythm – or are there slight hiccups? A horse may temporarily lose rhythm or change tempo (the speed at which the recurrent beats in the rhythm follow each other) – as, for example, when making a small circle or tight turn without enough impulsion, when he will tend to slow down or become irregular. He may lose rhythm because he is becoming unbalanced or hurried. As we judge, we ask ourselves: 'Is this a brief variation in rhythm with a discernible, immediate, cause – or does this horse's rhythm lack consistency much – even most – of the time?' Whichever answer seems to be correct, a comment about interruptions in rhythm should take you back to basics in your schooling before you can progress again up the spiral.

Phrases relating to rhythm
Rhythmical
Losing rhythm
Lost rhythm
Uneven steps
Unlevel
Lateral steps
Almost two-beat [in walk]
Four-beat [in canter]

Suppleness

Horses can appear stiff for many reasons: age, arthritis, lack of fitness, training that hasn't helped them learn to bend in the body, training that hasn't taught them how to engage both hind legs equally (essential for both longitudinal and lateral suppleness) or, conversely, how to deliver – when asked – more thrust from one hind leg than the other (as for example on tight turns or in lateral work). All horses by nature tend to be less flexible on one side of their body than the other: it should be one of your continuing aims in training to exercise your horse in such a way as to help him acquire greater evenness in strength and flexibility on *both* sides.

Maxim | begin with yourself

A horse who is stiff through the back may be being blocked in the rein by unyielding or over-dominant hands; or you may be flattening the surf-wave of his movement by stiffness in your own back, or by leaning behind the vertical so that you effectively drive his back down and his hind legs out behind you. It's easy to see this happening at Preliminary and Novice levels when a rider asks for lengthened or medium strides and, instead of the horse stepping under himself, lifting his back and shoulders in a powerful, undulating fashion, he produces only a flattened scurrying. All too often, a rider driving in mistaken fashion, or one whose own back isn't flexible enough to 'surf the wave' and ends up bouncing, will be causing the very plank-like flatness she'd most like to avoid.

Phrases relating to suppleness
Stiff
Lacks bend/needs more bend
Falling in
Falling out
Supple
Elastic
Needing/showing suspension
Not over the back/through the back

Roy and Cori in medium trot. We had been working on softening Roy's lower back and 'unpinning' his knees and thighs to help him absorb Cori's movement better.

Maxim | begin with yourself

Contact

While younger or less highly trained horses may be relatively reliant on the support of their rider's hands, the contact through the reins and bit should never be harsh, 'dead' or backward in its feel. Neither horse nor rider should 'set themselves' inflexibly, as this blocks the complex flow of energy that involves the horse's hind legs, his back and neck, his mouth and the rider's hands and body. People often describe this as some kind of a circuit, but though this is a nice concept the reality is much more complex! A blockage in any part of this complex system of inter-relationships will have far-reaching (and sometimes long-lasting) effects. Conversely, a horse and rider duo who are able to carry themselves in balance and with appropriate muscle tone may well feel that they are sharing a flow of energy – and look like that to those who watch them. Judges are reluctant to seem critical of riders, and their comments are more likely to imply that your horse is at fault than that you are. But is this in fact the case? Be honest with yourself – a horse who doesn't take the contact isn't being difficult for the sake of it: he's resorting to avoidance tactics either because he hasn't been trained properly or because he is uncomfortable. A comment about contact should be a signal to you that you need to explore what you can do to make it comfortable for him to work from behind into your hands.

Phrases relating to contact
Above the bit
Behind the bit
Behind the vertical
Contact varying/inconsistent
Not through the neck
Overbent
Too deep
Too much neck bend [in lateral work] – not taking the contact
Resisting
Against the hand
Working well into the contact
Good connection through the reins
Not seeking/stepping into the contact
Elastic contact [or, contact needs to be more elastic]

Impulsion

Why does engagement figure under this heading on the test sheet? Because the source of both impulsion and engagement is in the hind legs. A horse without impulsion cannot be engaged in either its physical sense (stepping forward with energy and intent) or in its emotional sense (willingly committed to what he's being asked to do). If he has no impulsion you have nothing to work with. Neither has he – so he will not be able to carry himself in balance through turns, transitions or school figures. He will only be able to potter along, perhaps even pulling himself along with his forelegs rather than driving or carrying himself with his hind ones.

Cori can easily over-bend and disengage behind rather than lifting and carrying himself, as this canter picture shows.

Cori and Roy usually produce soft, rhythmical lateral work, but this can result in a lack of purpose and thrust. This shot shows Roy attempting a half-pass in medium trot – with an explicit permission to go for energy rather than striving to achieve perfect bend and positioning. Though Cori needs more bend, he is moving very freely both forwards and sideways and taking the contact positively.

Maxim | begin with yourself

Critical comments or low marks that relate to impulsion should get you exploring your horse's commitment in both its physical and emotional senses. Does he like his work? Is he free and comfortable in the back, neck and mouth? Is he balanced enough to carry himself onward and upward or is he falling onto his forehand and ploughing 'downhill' into the sand?

Phrases relating to impulsion
Not forward enough
Lacks impulsion
Well engaged
Lacks engagement
Quarters swinging
Forward-thinking
Active
Fast
Running

Straightness

The further up the training spiral you progress, and the higher the level of your horse's schooling, the more important is straightness as a benchmark of correct training and working. It's also intimately related to balance. Once a horse is producing enough forward energy (impulsion), that energy has to be directed. If your horse isn't straight in relation to his line of travel, the force (energy) produced by his hind legs will not travel properly along that line but will escape to one side or the other – as, for example, in falling in or out. He will not be able to carry himself in balance along the line of a circle, loop or change of direction, but will be 'spilling out'. The more taxing the movement, the more this shows up – and the better a test of straightness that movement becomes!

Phrases relating to straightness
Quarters right/left
Quarters in
Quarters swinging
Falling out
Falling in
Losing the outside shoulder
Well engaged/not engaged enough /lacks or needs more engagement

Collection

I find it fascinating that, in writing each of these sections, I have found my finishing thoughts about one item in the training spiral leading straight on into the next. Just as impulsion led into straightness, so straightness leads into collection. Without impulsion and straightness, there can be no true collection. (I could of course go further and include all of the Training Scales by saying without *rhythm, suppleness, contact, impulsion, and straightness, there can be no true collection.*) A horse who demonstrates collection in relation to his level of training is one who *carries* rather than just *propels* himself. Physiologically, this means that he has developed and is using his whole musculature. The muscles involved in the correct posture are developed by training and, as you progress around the spiral, your horse will be showing the results by taking more weight onto his quarters and becoming lighter and more mobile in the forehand. To someone watching, he will seem to be 'sitting' more and going more 'uphill'. As he moves, he will be bending (articulating) his joints more whilst stepping well under his body. He will be able to convert some of his forward energy into upward thrust, generating elasticity and suspension from the shorter, yet just as active, strides that result. He will *give the impression* of being shorter from head to tail than he used to, and compact rather than strung out. (This is a quite different type of 'shortness' from the winched-in head and rammed-under hindquarters that riders sometimes produce when they don't understand what collection really involves.)

A horse who demonstrates collection in relation to his level of training is one who *carries* rather than just *propels* himself: Ali and Jay.

Maxim | begin with yourself

Phrases relating to collection
Unbalanced/well balanced
Running on
Not in self-carriage
Steps too free/large
Not collected enough
Strung-out

> Compare some recent photos of your horse at work with ones taken earlier in his training. Has he changed in any or many of these ways?

Comments on the gaits and specific movements

Individual dressage movements, and their combinations and sequences, help you and the judge benchmark how your horse is progressing up the training spiral, because they require the horse to demonstrate that he has progressed further through the Scales of Training. Let's consider the basic gaits before moving on to some of the specific movements you'll be encountering in the most competed-at levels – Preliminary to Medium. I have given a selection in each case of commonly-used negative comments: good judges will also try to highlight what they find good in your tests, and are likely to be using much the same phraseology, but in a positive form.

Walk

What is the essence of the walk?

The walk must consist of four equally-spaced footfalls. It should be free and purposeful, with good ground coverage in free, medium and extended versions. If the rein is released (free walk), the horse should seek to maintain contact with his rider by stretching his head downwards and forwards, lengthening his top-line until his neck is below the level of his withers. He should not jerk the reins, or resist when they are shortened again. He should track up, and overtrack (if his back isn't too long, in which case he may find it difficult or impossible) except in collected walk, where his steps should be shorter and higher.

Phrases relating to the walk
Not covering enough ground
Not tracking up
Not overtracking
Lateral steps
Not taking the contact
Losing rhythm
Tight/short steps
Not stretching down over the top-line
Lacking purpose

Trot

What is the essence of the trot?

The trot is a two-time gait with diagonal footfalls. A good trot will show active hind legs stepping under the horse's body. If the hocks seem to rise behind a line dropped vertically from the horse's tail, rather than within that line, it's likely that the horse is not engaging and that he is not working through, or over, his back. Where a horse is well engaged, his diagonal pairs of legs will give the impression of a V-shape as he shifts his weight from one pair to the other. A well-engaged trot will show very little gap on the ground at the point of the V, which tells you that the horse is stepping under with his hind legs. You can see a good example of this contrast with Ali and Jay in the photos on page 57.

Phrases relating to the trot
Not tracking up
Lacking impulsion
Needs more engagement
Lacking activity behind

Canter

What is the essence of the canter?

The canter is a three-beat movement with a moment of suspension after the third beat. The outside hind leg starts the sequence, then the same side foreleg and its opposite hind leg together, followed by the inside foreleg (the leading leg) on its own. A young or novice horse in good balance will seem to progress in parallel with the ground; an advanced horse will lower his quarters and seem to 'go uphill'; and an unbalanced horse will have a 'downhill' appearance and may use his head and neck in an exaggerated movement to help himself balance as he moves through the sequence.

You should be able to see a clear distance (separation) between the hind legs. Where they are close together ('bunny-hopping' at worst) the canter energy will not be travelling freely through the back and the rhythm will be compromised. Where there isn't enough energy/impulsion from the hind legs, the diagonal pair may not hit the ground at the same time, and the canter may become 'four-beat' as the hind leg of the pair gets left behind.

Ted bunny-hopping in left canter.

Phrases relating to the canter
Losing rhythm
Becoming four-time
Lacking suspension
Flat
Needs more swing
Not through the back
Together behind
Disunited
Cantering in front, trotting behind

Halt

What is the essence of a halt?

The most important feature of a halt is its stillness. In order to achieve this, your horse needs to be in balance, which means that he must step positively into the halt with his hind legs as well as his forelegs. He needs to finish his stride, so that he stands square with his weight comfortably distributed. He should be thinking forward into the halt, which means that he should not come above (or against) the

Trot to halt, sequence one. *top left* In the approach, Wattie is not quite 'through' and his head is tilted. *top right* Ali's weight is tipping forward and her elbows are disconnecting from her sides, weakening her seat: Wattie is leaning into the rein and running onto his forehand. *bottom left* Ali has had to rely on the reins to stop Wattie pitching as far forward as he would otherwise have done. Though he is well-trained enough to step under into the halt, his weight is on his shoulders. *bottom right* Wattie is not square in front or behind and the halt looks as though it could destabilize and shift at any moment.

bit, nor drop his poll. This is the image judges will have in their minds. Inexperienced horses often fail to engage properly (thereby leaving their quarters out behind, not squaring up, or moving), and more experienced ones may move or fidget if they have begun working on more advanced movements such as piaffe.

Trot to halt, sequence two.
top left As he approaches, Wattie is in an active, well-balanced trot and Ali is also well-balanced and toned. *top right* A half-halt from Ali (there's a slight but visible increase in muscle tone in her back) warns Wattie to take his weight back in preparation for halting. *bottom, left and right* Wattie is shortening his steps behind as Ali 'rides his hind legs under him' so as to help him not to drop onto his forehand. The last picture in the sequence is shown on the opposite page.

Maxim | begin with yourself

Wattie is square in front and about to plant his remaining hind leg to complete a correct and well-balanced halt.

Phrases relating to the halt
Not engaged enough
Losing immobility
Not really established
Not square behind/in front
Thinking backwards
Not straight

Rein-back

What is the essence of a rein-back?

It should be straight, with a clear two-time movement of paired diagonal steps. It's often said that the horse should be 'thinking forward' in both halt and rein-back – meaning that he should be accepting – even actively 'taking' – the bit willingly rather than resisting or dropping behind it. He should seem to carry himself positively as though motivated by his own intent, not his rider's compulsion.

Phrases relating to the rein-back
Dragging
Resisting
Steps not diagonal
Not straight

Shoulder-in/travers

What is the essence of these movements?

The essence of a correct shoulder-in or travers is that the horse can carry himself at an angle to his line of forward travel, without losing balance, impulsion or straightness. He will only be able to do this if he has learnt to carry weight with his inside hind leg to support the movement, if he is free enough in the shoulder and stifle to stretch sideways as well as forwards, and if he can create and maintain a bend through his body rather than just in his neck.

Phrases relating to lateral movements
Not enough bend
Losing shoulder/quarters
Not enough angle/too much angle
Falling out
Inside hind needs to carry more
Needs to be more seated
Too much bend in the neck

Transitions

What is the essence of a transition?

The essence of correct transitions is that they feel and look freely forward, without hesitation, jerking, stiffening or resistance in the mouth. Time spent in getting your transitions soft, forward, 'through' and on the aids is time spent progressing up the training spiral. A clear and harmonious transition feels great and is a delight to behold! (I recently judged – with great pleasure – an Elementary level horse and rider whose transitions were exemplary in their soft connection and forward flow. Not surprisingly, the rider's elbows were bent, close and flexibly absorbing the movement, with no blocking at all.) As you progress up the spiral, you should be helping your horse make transitions within each gait as well as between them. I heard an Olympic judge tell one of his pupils: '*Upward transitions within the gait should take one stride; downward ones should take three strides.*' If you make that your aim you will know how well you are doing! And you will not end up getting the comment, '*Lacked a trans. back again*' because you let your lengthened/medium strides just peter out rather than asking your horse to sit and carry himself, with each stride now taking him over a shorter space of ground.

Phrases relating to transitions
Not forward enough/nicely forward
Against the hand
Hollowing
Transitions within the gait need to be clearer/crisper
No transition back [after lengthening or medium strides]

Walk pirouette

What is the essence of a pirouette?

The horse must be centred and seated enough to walk a relatively small circle with his hind legs (centred more or less on a particular spot) while his forelegs walk a slightly larger one around them. The walk rhythm should be maintained as an even marching. To an observer, the pirouette should look centred, whether it is the larger quarter- or half-circle required at lower levels or the full-circle demanded higher up. For a well-centred and well-balanced pirouette, see the photo of Roy and Cori on page 267.

Phrases related to pirouettes
Not centred enough
Stepping wide
Sticking
Pivoting
Crossing over
Needs to be more seated

Collective comments

In their training, judges are encouraged to highlight the overall picture that you and your horse made, and to emphasize the underlying causes of problems you experienced in the test rather than just pointing out the details of what went wrong. Good judges whom I know also try to give hints on what you can do in future – for example: '*To progress, needs now to…*' Often, judges don't give a separate comment for each of the four headings: *Paces, Impulsion, Submission and Rider,* but instead try to summarize what they have seen and what they think you need to address in order to improve.

When I came to write this summary in judging you I often realize just how little I know about you. I don't know your horse's history, and whether this is his first test or his fifty-fifth. I don't know about any problems he may have had. I don't know how he – or you – feel about being in a competition, and whether that makes you perform better or worse than you do at home. But I can tell you what I have seen; I have some idea of the common causes of the problems and limitations your test may have displayed; and I can give you an idea of where I think you could focus in order to improve. In other words, I can and should be using my knowledge of the principles of classical riding and the training spiral to assess what I see in front of me and to frame my comments in a way that can help take you forward. That's what I hope to do, and what I hope you'll give me credit for aiming at.

It's usually fairly straightforward to make comments on the horse but, as I mentioned earlier, many judges shy away from making comments about the rider, because they fear hurting your feelings or putting you off. I can think of one set of comments I received in the past that kept me out of competition for nearly two years. I'm sure the judge didn't intend this to happen – but she certainly didn't have my feelings much in mind as she wrote! I always prefer to assume that every rider is fond of her horse and wants to do her best: she didn't set out that morning to ride badly or make her horse uncomfortable, even if I happen to think those were the results. Judges are advised 'not to give riding lessons' in their comments. Sometimes this is hard; if you are somehow getting in your own way and limiting your horse despite your good intentions, I think I owe it to you both to point out where your riding may be implicated, and what you might do about it.

Let's take an example. I have often seen Elementary and Medium level horses, for example, going flat and fast when asked for medium work – in part because their rider is leaning behind the vertical in an attempt to produce a 'driving seat', which actually prevents the horse from swinging and connecting over his back. In such cases, I might offer one of the following comments: *'Try to soften your back more, to help him soften his'*; *'Try asking for a little less speed'*; *'Rising to the trot might help him lift his back more'*; *'Try to keep more upright so you don't flatten his back.'* It's also common for me to write: *'Rider's legs too busy'* when a never-ending thump, thump, thump with heels or spurs is actually causing the horse to switch off. It takes humility and openness to learning for a rider to accept personal criticism as the help it's intended to give but, in my experience, if you can take feedback as a guide to improvement you are helping yourself to feel empowered.

Meeting a young rider after a competition, I was asked: 'Were my legs better today?' She continued, 'I've really tried to keep them quieter since I read your comments on my last sheet. It's very difficult, because I'm getting too tall for my pony now, but I know it doesn't look good and it doesn't really help us in the long run.' This led us into a very interesting discussion about using her calves rather than her heels for leg-aiding. I reminded her of the tradition of men riding Iberian horses or Lipizzaners: often the riders' heels hang well below the horse's belly, yet their leg aids are subtle and effective! When I began working with Roy and his

15.2 hh horse Cori, Roy often had his heels up in an attempt to reach Cori's sides, yet with thought and practice he was able to teach himself a more classical position and way of aiding (see the photos on page 269).

In summary, if you can read your test sheets in a positive frame of mind and with an eye to the future, you are much more likely to find them clues to buried treasure, instead of the punitive sentences they can sometimes feel like. Everyone is human: the judge intends to do you justice just as much as you intend to do your best. Sometimes we both fail to live up to those high intentions – but if we are willing to take feedback as helpful suggestions for the future we can always improve!

8 No arena, no problem

> I no longer just hack, I work on transitions, leg-yielding, shoulder-in, half-pass, flying changes, lots of changes within the gaits, because I realize it's not fair to climb on your horse once a fortnight and say, 'Just for this 5½ minutes I want you to go correctly, but for the rest of the time just slop around and go however you want.'
>
> **Roy Brown,** *Notes on Working Together.*

You don't need amazing facilities to ride according to classical principles. You don't even need an arena to do dressage. You just need the right attitude and a spot of ingenuity. When I was about 19, I had the chance of riding a sweet-natured, just-backed Thoroughbred/Shire cross who belonged to the farmer up the road from my parents' house. I had barely heard of dressage then, and certainly knew nothing about it. But I did feel honoured to be allowed to ride Silver Queen, and excited at the prospect of helping her learn. Two things I did with her then have always stuck in my mind. I taught her to respond to leg aids by tapping her off one leg then the other and so zigzagging her from hedge to hedge across a 'green lane' between fields, saying firmly, 'Right, right, right' and 'left, left, left' as I did so. (I wonder now why I thought she needed to know about right and left, and whether she remembered and responded to those words later on in her life!) And I followed the farmer's daughters' instructions and spent a bit of time during each hack riding round a tiny oblong field with high hedges (had it once been the garden to a defunct cottage?). I didn't know what 'schooling' was, but we trotted around this natural 'school' anyway.

Looking back, I think I probably learnt more than Silver Queen did – in particular, that hacking can be more than pottering about and that you can train a horse anywhere. That's what this chapter is about. Many successful dressage trainers do, in fact, use open-country work to encourage their horses to go forward, as well as cavalletti and jumps to help them work through their backs freely and correctly – and I'd urge you to take the same wide-angle view of what training can involve.

Schooling without an arena: the guiding principle

Remember that your horse learns something from everything you do

You may make a distinction in your mind between 'work' and 'play': your horse doesn't. If you allow something at one time or in one place and not in another, he just gets confused – or switches off. In this sense, there is truly no 'time off' with a horse. Time off for him is when he's in the field or the stable: time off for you is when you're not with him. To put it another way, you can enjoy the freedom of the wide-open spaces of fields and bridleways together and at the same time know that you are not undoing or contradicting anything valuable about your mutual understanding. If you are always consistent in what you tell your horse and what you expect from him, hacking out will be a genuine and valuable part of the way you train and develop him, whether or not you have a school. And if there are no mixed messages between you, you will be able to enjoy your time together, *and* feel a sense of freedom, even while remaining attentive to each other and to the learning implications of what you are doing.

Use the landscape

Train yourself to spot the possibilities of slopes, angles, corners and landmarks. What opportunities will they help 'set up' for you and your horse? Look for ways in which natural and man-made landscape features may make something easier, so that it comes naturally: ask for canter, for example, where the corner of a field or the bend in a track will encourage your horse to strike off on a specific lead and help him associate that lead with the appropriate aiding. It is also very helpful for young horses starting canter work to first be asked for short canters in a straight line on a flat or slightly uphill stretch in the open – they can learn to manage their balance in this way more easily than if they have to keep going round corners in the arena. On the other hand, look also for ways in which land formation may add a useful level of difficulty: trot uphill, for example, to encourage your horse to develop his hindquarters, or diagonally across a slope to encourage him to manage his balance for himself.

Keep the training spiral in mind

Ask yourself how the training spiral can guide you today – every day is different and it's important to assess yourself and your horse afresh rather than just repeating what you did yesterday. Therefore, use the first few minutes of a hack to 'tune in' to your horse and assess what he is offering, and what he is in need of. Perhaps he is sluggish or tired today – would a brisk trot or canter wake him up and establish a good rhythm, or would it be more respectful of his state to work on stretching, or on exercises that can be done in walk? Is he stiff – does he need to have a chance to stretch his muscles and really swing through? How does the contact between you feel? Dead or alive? Friendly or irritable? Is he carrying himself – or are you?

Be opportunistic

'Pretend you wanted it', Charles de Kunffy often says when a horse does something his rider wasn't asking for. You wanted some lengthened strides along that flat bit and he gave you canter instead. He gave you what he thought you wanted (he's your mirror, remember), so don't just return to trot straight away – use the canter first! Otherwise you will just confuse or annoy him. What can you do with that extra forwardness? Or perhaps he is a bit inclined to hesitate and have a good look at something – this might be just the moment for a shoulder-in, looking the other way, until you have safely passed the danger. What can you do usefully with what you get? The benefit will be that you avoid conflict while at the same time re-establishing your role as leader, reasserting a positive yet quite playful emphasis on training as an incidental by-product of having fun while you are out together.

Give your horse the experience of a new movement now; polish it later

If you are highly motivated and something of a perfectionist, you may be inclined to think that 'real' dressage can't be done unless you're in a dressage arena. Even in an arena, perfectionist thinking can easily make you and your horse lose delight in being and moving together. Think like your horse for a moment: before he can come to understand what he has to do to produce a 'good' leg-yield, transition, rein-back or whatever, he has to do something approximately like the movement and receive praise that tells him he's heading in the right direction. He has not only to learn what the movement feels like but also to associate it with a particular combination of rider aids. If, like Silver Queen, he's willing to move off your leg from one side of a track to the other and back again without too much heaving and shoving, you can praise him. Later, you can look out for a reasonably well-defined field corner and leg-yield across it as if you were stepping purposefully yet softly from D to E or B in an arena. When that comes easily, think about finessing the bend and the angle.

Look for analogies to test movements

Dressage movements are based on everyday manoeuvres. Gates can offer you brilliant opportunities for halt, rein-back, and response to unilateral leg-aids, in a variety of combinations that lay the foundation for many sequences required in tests. If you are doing an out-and-back hack, make your turn-about to come home through a walk pirouette that starts facing a gate or hedge. This barrier will act as a natural brake that will help you collect your horse's steps. Don't just let him swivel – keep him walking but make the steps small and active and 'draw' the shape with intent by sitting upright yourself and activating each hind leg in turn. You will have started yourselves on the road to those walk pirouettes!

Break test movements and sequences down into their component parts

Ask yourself what is involved or presupposed in a simple change, for example, and take the opportunity of practising that. Can your horse collect and carry himself sufficiently to stay soft and 'through' in a canter-trot transition – and then in a canter-walk one – and immediately go forward freely and positively in the lower gait? Once he can do canter-trot in balance and thinking forward, then practise canter-walk. When he can do that, you will finally be able to add the upward transition to canter again, and you'll have built yourself balanced, forward and flowing simple changes.

Always be thinking ahead to more advanced possibilities

Be content with what you are getting – and yet have an eye to where you and your horse are going next. All your work is part of the training spiral, and should be flowing out of what has gone before and at the same time leading on to what comes next, as you revisit each of the Scales of Training at higher levels. Each time you remember to deepen your seat and collect your horse for a stride or two before asking him for a downward transition (whether between or within the gaits) you are securing the foundation upon which you build his self-carriage and collection. Without this, you would never get to piaffe. Even if you have no intention of aiming at piaffe, or know your horse isn't built that way, knowing that piaffe is one of the ultimate expressions of collection adds purpose and lustre to less ambitious everyday acts of engaging and rebalancing.

Schooling 'outside the box'

I want you to think 'outside the box' – literally – and begin to appreciate how your everyday riding in the fields, tracks and roads can support your horse's progress around the training spiral and, ultimately, improve his performance in dressage tests. If you ride him attentively and with an eye to the spiral, you will find this comes quite naturally. If you don't have a school, or only use one when you actually have a lesson, you will be able to continue your training naturally and easily. Even if you do have one, you won't have to make that choice between 'working at dressage' and that tempting, 'time off' hack. By changing the way you think, and making the most of the opportunities that the wider world offers you, you can benefit from the great open spaces even while enjoying them. As a start to your own new way of thinking, I'm going to list some of the ways you can do that.

Riders	Sometimes	Canter	In	Small	Circles
Rhythm	Suppleness	Contact	Impulsion	Straightness	Collection

Rhythm

- Monitor rhythm (regularity) and tempo (length of interval between footfalls) on longish stretches of walk, trot and canter.

- Work towards lengthening or collection by counting the number of strides you take between two natural markers (e.g. trees) – then come round again and cover the same distance with fewer, longer, strides, or more, shorter ones.

- Sing songs that match and reinforce the rhythm of particular gaits or variations in a gait.

Suppleness

1. Longitudinal

- Get your horse swinging through his back by riding him with a light or 'event' seat on longish stretches of canter. Encouraging a horse to stretch the top-line muscles and supraspinous ligament in a free canter or gallop like this can have enormous benefits for his general 'throughness'.

- Make yourself light on his back by standing to the trot, allowing your hips, knees and ankles to absorb the movement.

2. Lateral

- Ride into the corners of fields rather than automatically flattening off the curve.

Maxim | begin with yourself

- Don't always ride in straight lines – build in circles and loops, or even serpentines.

- If you are on a green lane or bridleway, ask your horse to leg-yield or half-pass across it. Do shoulder-in one way, then the other.

- If you spot something ahead that you horse may not like – something flapping, for example – put him into shoulder-in facing away from it before he has had a chance to notice and react to it.

Contact

- Always have your horse on an elastic contact, even with a long rein. Contact isn't just about short reins or a rounded shape: contact is communication, and even the lightest, but consistent, feel between you means that your lines of communication remain open the whole time. Hacking out can also be a good time to practise free walk on a long rein. The kind of free walk you are after is the one he offers you on the way home when he's thinking about his dinner!

- Keep a conversation going through your hands – the contact should remain a living means of connection between you so that neither of you switch off from it.

- Ask your horse to use his hind legs actively rather than just slopping along. Engagement from behind is what really creates the contact, so ride every stride from your seat and leg – don't just sit there!

Impulsion

- Notice how your horse walks on the way home – then ask for the same walk on the way out!

- When you slow down for any reason, don't just let your horse peter out by stopping your forward aiding. Ask for the slower tempo or the lower gait with a half-halt, a rebalancing of your own position and a reminder from your seat and legs that energy is still required!

Straightness

- Get into the habit of monitoring yourself. Are your shoulders facing straight ahead – or is one more forward than the other? Are they level in height? Are you sitting upright, or is your back rounded and your waist collapsed? Are you

Maxim | begin with yourself

stretching down equally into your stirrups, or is one hip creeping up more than the other?

- Monitor your horse, making use of relatively straight edges such as curbs, tracks or hedges. Is he straight behind you, or is he carrying his quarters to one side? Bear in mind that, as a horse's hips are wider than his shoulders, you will have to place his shoulders in a little from the edge to make sure that he is straight behind you: if you find your horse tends to trip on roadside curbs, check your straightness.

- When riding across open spaces such as fields pick a marker, such as a tree or gate, on the far side and aim for it with your eyes until you reach it. Your body – and therefore your horse – will mirror the intensity of your gaze. This is a very useful skill for eventers to cultivate – it can help you keep the correct line between fences, thus helping to set up approaches and save time.

Collection

- Remember that collection is about balance and self-carriage, not just relative shortness of stride.

- If you are out with other people, don't just stop and wait for them if they get left behind – take the opportunity to ask your horse to shorten his stride whilst continuing to walk actively.

- If you are the one who gets left behind, ask your horse for more energy or a longer stride to catch up. Don't just jog or trot every time!

- Use corners of fields and tracks – ask your horse to maintain positive energy and maintain his tempo whilst travelling through the corner. If he tends to slow down, use more inside leg to help him engage and keep his balance.

Making the most of what you've got

When I judge and take clinics, I meet a lot of riders who don't have dressage arenas to work in, yet with determination and ingenuity they get their schooling done all the same. For a while, our first horse was kept at a yard where the 'school' was actually a field – complete with a central clump of trees and bushes – entirely topped with sand. During the autumn, this space also had to be shared with the flock of turkeys that the yard's owner was rearing for Christmas dinners! A designated dressage arena is a bit like central heating: once you have it, you tend to take it for granted and to forget that there are other ways of achieving the same things. And even if you do have a school (or central heating) it is a pity if it makes your life easier at the expense of narrowing your life experience. Whatever the context, schooling really starts in your mind, and when you have its aims at heart they will be readily transmitted from you to your horse. Schooling can be free and fun as well as thoughtful and disciplined. It can happen when you are not sitting on him as well as when you are on board, and it doesn't have to be done in a designated arena.

To set you thinking, here are three real-life examples of schooling that doesn't have to be done in a school.

Loose-schooling with Nikki and Ollie

I once heard Arthur Kottas, the former Chief Rider of the Spanish Riding School, telling an audience of professional instructors that the School's Lipizzaners were not just worked in high school movements – they were also regularly loose-schooled and loose-jumped – for elasticity, for variety and for sheer fun. Of course, if you have a school, it's easy to set this up. But loose-schooling with or without jumps can also be done in a small field or a sectioned-off part of one. Loose work invigorates horses mentally as well as physically and, as my friend Nikki finds, it can also be a great way of bonding and refining communication with them. Nikki has always enjoyed loose-schooling her dressage horses. She believes that it encourages them to go forward, to take responsibility for their own balance and to use their backs without constraint. We photographed a session with Nikki and her Medium level Warmblood, Ollie. See pages 116–17.

Field work with Annie and Red

Annie doesn't have a school: she has a field. The field isn't level, and the 'track' she has made within it is on a slope: one 'long side' is higher than the other, and the 'short sides' that connect them are either uphill or downhill depending which rein she is on. As Red is an eventer, rebalancing like this is good for cross-country work; and in our sessions we have also tried to make use of the short sides to encourage him to step under and engage more. Red has a longish back so this is not as easy for him as it would be for a more compact horse – but of course, by the same token, it's good remedial training!

The sequences of photos show the 'land use' we have made of Annie's field – plus some of the other natural hazards she and Red contend with, like the family sheep and George the pony! See pages 118–19.

Maxim | begin with yourself

Loose-schooling with Nikki and Ollie. Below and opposite page.
Lungeing and loose-schooling can be great ways to loosen your horse and to strengthen the bond between you.

1 Ollie is still wearing his 'lungeing kit' but the lunge-line is no longer attached – it is all in Nikki's hand. She is trotting as actively as Ollie!

2 Despite the physical gap, the mental connection between Nikki and Ollie is quite evident.

Maxim | begin with yourself

NO ARENA, NO PROBLEM • 117

3 Back on the lunge, Ollie is really rounding in his back – just as a dressage or jumping horse should.

4 Note how giving Nikki's contact is. The lunge-line is only there to prevent Ollie cantering off to the far end of the school after he lands.

5 With his saddle cloth removed, you can clearly see the freedom and movement through Ollie's back and neck.

Maxim | begin with yourself

Field work with Annie and Red. Above and opposite page. These pictures were all taken in the same session – one in which we used the slopes of the field to help Red learn to engage more and carry himself in better balance.

1. A canter in which Annie and Red are balancing each other through the reins.
2. Down the slope and onto his forehand... again, Annie is holding Red up, with something of a chair seat. Red's mouth is open and there is a sense of pressure in the contact.
3. Same place, a little later. Red is now stepping under, and is 'through' in his back and neck. He's in a much better balance, and Annie is more toned and upright.
4. A rather hollow, though forward, canter uphill. Annie is behind the movement though her hands are still quite soft.

Maxim | **begin with yourself**

5 Later, Red is stepping under more and Annie is in better balance with him.

6 The downward slope. This time Red is carrying himself (Annie is giving the reins forward to check), but his weight is a little on his shoulder.

7 Later, Annie is more toned and upright, and Red is carrying himself in much better balance.

8 A lovely, balanced, well-connected trot (note the closed V-shape Red's legs are making). Because of Annie's soft hands, Red's mouth is comfortably closed and his ears are listening.

Maxim | begin with yourself

A hack with Roy and Cori

It was Roy who unintentionally prompted me to write this chapter, because he phoned one winter's morning to say we couldn't do the session we had planned because his school was frozen. 'I shall go for a hack instead,' Roy said, 'I can always do half-passes down the lane.' An hour or so later Leo and I both realized that we really should have gone with Roy and taken photos of that hack instead! So we arranged to do it another day.

Roy has often said that our work together in the school has led him to think differently about how he rides *all the time*, and how he has made use of anything that happened on hacks to improve his own riding and Cori's way of going. The sequence of photos follows them round their hack, just as it happened on the day. There was no pre-planning – Roy made the most of his opportunities and we enjoyed them with him.

I hope you will find that this chapter and these riders together give you not only food for thought but also the inspiration to spread your own wings, and in so doing gain even more benefit from every bit of the riding you do.

A hack with Roy and Cori. Above and opposite page.
Photos **1**, **2** and **3**. Dressage helps with gates and there is a really nice rein-back to close the gate. Note Cori's rounded top-line, lack of resistance to the bit, and clear diagonal steps. It would be good to see this in the competition arena!

Maxim | begin with yourself

NO ARENA, NO PROBLEM • 121

4 Riding forward past an imaginary dragon.
5 Travers (quarters in) to the right.
6 Half-pass right.
7 Collected canter.

section three

Pathways to performance: the mental skills

Is your mind on the job?	**124**
Paying the right kind of attention	**136**
Where do your assumptions get you?	**148**
Self-belief, self-talk and rehersal	**163**

9 Is your mind on the job?

> It is the thesis of this book that neither mastery nor satisfaction can be found in the playing of any game without giving some attention to the relatively neglected skills of the inner game. This is the game that takes place in the mind of the player, and it is played against such obstacles as lapses in concentration, nervousness, self-doubt and self-condemnation. In short, it is played to overcome all habits of mind which inhibit excellence in performance.
>
> **Timothy Gallwey,** *The Inner Game of Tennis*[1]

Riding well is as much a matter of your mind as of your body. In this section I'm going to explore some of the differences that you can make when you know how to have, and keep, your mind on the job. As you read, you'll learn how to recognize, create and change your own mind-body states; how to create shared 'bubbles' of focus that help you and your horse produce your best; and how to spot and change the ones that don't. You'll pinpoint what concentration means for you, how you make it happen, and how to work with its natural changes and flows. You'll discover more about the way you and your horse learn, as the unique individuals you are; how to create and keep a shared zone of mutual attention and respect when you're together; and how you can begin to turn patterns that don't work into ones that do. And you'll find your own personal mental pathways to improving your positioning, reactions and strategies for schooling and performance. All through what your own mind does naturally and effortlessly every day. For the key to all this is the miraculous mind-body connection.

Maxim | how you think shapes what you do

The mind-body connection

When you were little, did you ever walk along garden walls? Walks with our daughter Charlotte when she was a small child often got routed to take in as much wall-walking as possible. Even older people can find it a fun thing to do – only recently we turned into our road and found a couple of teenagers strolling along our garden wall! Even when you're little, walking along a narrow surface is usually more thrilling than terrifying; but if that walkway was a parapet twenty or thirty feet up, would you feel the same? What about if it were six or ten feet above ground level? For most people, there will be an invisible threshold height above which wall-walking seems risky, or even dangerous. As they approach the 'risky' level, they will tense up and probably balance less well; nearing the 'dangerous' level, they may panic, wobble, or simply freeze.

The difference has nothing to do with your physical ability to walk a straight and narrow pathway, and everything to do with what you think and feel about it. It's your mind that makes you relaxed, even playful, on a low garden wall, and that makes you tense and awkward – even to the point of being unsafe – on higher ones. What you think affects how you feel, and it also translates directly into your body. Think of talking with someone: they say something you agree with and you nod; they say something amusing and you smile or laugh; they say something you disagree with and you frown or purse your lips. These reactions aren't conscious or deliberate – they are just your thoughts expressed in immediate 'body language'. We all learn to observe and read this language when we're tiny, and it is an essential part of the way human beings communicate with each other.

This automatic mind-body connection, with its corresponding expression of thoughts or feelings in body language, is always an ingredient in the conversations we have with our horses – sometimes, as we all know, with unfortunate effects! It can, on the other hand, be a key means by which we can actually *think* ourselves into developing better relationships with them and enhancing the subtlety of our aiding. How does this come about? Horses read our body language because, over millions of years, they needed to read each others' if they were to survive. But because they are horses, not people, they interpret us and react to us not in our terms, but in theirs: tension means danger; anger means fear or flight; your confusion sends confusing messages to your horse and may, itself, make him feel unsafe because, for him, it means that you are not offering him clear leadership. He makes his own sense of everything you do – in *his* terms. Your horse doesn't imagine himself into your shoes: he interprets everything as it relates to *him*, and he responds in relation to what has just happened or is happening *now*.

In this chapter I want to explore the pitfalls and possibilities of your mind-body connection as a way of laying the foundation for this whole section on

Maxim | how you think shapes what you do

mental skills. We don't have to be at the mercy of our wayward or unwanted thoughts and feelings provided we learn to recognize them, modify them when they're not helpful, and – better still – develop the skill of *intending*, rather than allowing our actions to send *unintended* or accidental messages.

How the mind-body connection works

When you pick up your coffee mug for a drink, or reach for the hoof-pick, you don't need to give your body detailed instructions as to how to do it. Probably, you are focusing solely on the end-result – mouthful of coffee, pick out hooves. Your conscious mind doesn't need to be involved in working out and masterminding the full sequence of actions, because you already know a lot about stretching out, taking hold, adjusting the amount of pressure in relation to anticipated size and heaviness of the object to be lifted, etc. (Like me, you may remember times when you picked up what you thought was a full mug but was, in fact, an almost empty one, so that you 'threw' the contents upwards because you were using too much force for the weight the mug actually carried!) Babies and toddlers, on the other hand, do have to think about basic movement, because it is new to them.

Deliberate learning always follows the same sequence:

1. **Unconscious incompetence:** don't know something, can't do something – don't even know you don't know it.

Then

2. **Conscious incompetence:** know you don't know something.

Then

3. **Conscious competence:** you can do it, but need to monitor consciously how you're doing it.

And finally

4. **Unconscious competence:** you can do it without even thinking about it.

Every time we learn a new skill, however old or experienced we are, we go through the same sequence, more or less rapidly. Speed and ease of learning will depend on many things, including natural aptitude and also whether the learning is entirely new or a modification of something already known. Riding offers lots of examples, from the early struggles novice riders have to master the rising trot, to more subtle adjustments of position and aiding that help transform the rough-and-ready rider into a sophisticated performer, concerned with finessing the

Maxim | how you think shapes what you do

communication that enables rider and horse to look as though what they're doing flows naturally and without effort. As a dressage judge, I'd say that horses go through a version of the same sequence, even though their consciousness is different from ours. Watching a less and a more experienced horse doing the same test, I can often spot which is which by the contrasting expressions on their faces: the more established horse is likely to have the calm and confident look of one working with unconscious competence, whereas the less experienced horse may seem anxious, tense or even unhappy as he tries to perform movements which, for him, are more taxing because he is only just 'consciously competent' at them.

You can make use of this learning sequence to develop both your mental and physical skills. While you are unaware of how you think or feel about something, or how your body behaves, (stage 1, unconscious incompetence), you can't do anything to change it. So your first step forward is always to switch on your self-awareness, for the time being putting yourself into a state of conscious incompetence (stage 2). For example, you might feel fine riding at home but become nervous and 'freeze' when you compete. You know that you do this, but to change it you need to know *how* you do it. (Competition strategies and nerves have their own place in Section IV of the book.) Or you might be surprised by a judge's comment that you lost your horse's quarters, or his shoulder, on circles because you hadn't noticed it happening. Once you train yourself to become aware of what's going on, you can find out what you need to do to catch and correct, or even prevent, it. As you find out the details of your personal 'recipe' for nervousness, or your recipe for allowing your horse to swing out rather than helping him carry himself, you can begin to design and practise the mental or physical strategies you need to put things right. You are moving into conscious competence, stage 3 of the learning sequence. The more often you practise your new strategies, the more habitual they become and the less you have to think about them. You are now becoming unconsciously competent (stage 4) at getting yourself into an effective state for competing, or at engaging your horse so that he carries himself in good balance through tight turns as well as on straight lines.

From intention to action

Earlier on in the book I said that horses offer us the ultimate feedback about ourselves because they react to what – in their view – we *actually* told them rather than to what we *think* we told them. We can take this even further when we take the mind-body connection into account. Apart from the times when something makes him revert to his ingrained 'wild' reactions – mostly factors of alarm or discomfort – *your horse responds to what he takes to be your intentions.* So, if you're not getting what you thought you intended, it's worth asking yourself two questions. One: 'Did I succeed in making my intention clear?' And, two: 'Was what I got really, deep down, my intention after all?'

By 'intention' I mean more than just a vague 'what you'd like to happen'. I'm talking about something which is more like 'commitment' – something you want in your heart of hearts. When your heart is divided, when your mind goes one way and your true feelings go another, the message you give your horse will be just as divided, and he will almost certainly pick up and act upon what you *feel* rather than what you *think*, or what you believe you 'ought' to want.

For example, sometimes you may need or want to lunge your horse instead of riding him. Suppose he doesn't make a transition when you give the command. What assumptions do you make about this 'failure to obey' you? Do you think it's because he is enjoying having a wild canter when he has been in his box all day? Do you get cross because you think he is deliberately ignoring you? Or do you remind yourself that it's not the content of the words that conveys your intent to him but the tone – and make sure that next time around you suit your tone to the meaning, with a heavier, lower pitch for transitions down and a brighter, more upbeat tone for transitions up? Are you really intending him to work out there, or are you subtly giving him the message through your own casual body language, tone of voice and sluggish responses that it really doesn't matter what he does so long as he keeps moving for twenty minutes?

A while ago, I attended a course for business leaders that used work with horses to help reflect back to people how their personal leadership style came across – when there were no words to disguise or confuse the issue of how they communicated their intention. The horses were all used to lungeing, but the business people weren't. Some of them succeeded in getting 'their' horse to move out, away and forward with relatively little trouble. One man, however, found that 'his' horse just kept coming in to him and stopping for a cuddle. After this had happened several times, the course leader asked: 'How do you feel about this happening?' After a little thought, the man replied: 'Actually, I rather like it!' The horse had unerringly picked up that, at heart, what this man wanted was the feel of closeness and connection that came when the horse approached him voluntarily. The man hadn't seen that he had anything to do with it! Having acknowledged that he did, he then set out to discover what would happen if he really wanted the horse to move out and forward. Only by committing mentally and emotionally to that aim – because he did, truly, want to find out more about the power of his own intentions – was he able, after a couple of attempts, to get the horse lungeing in a 'normal' way.

Of course, intention is only part of the equation: as a real-life rider you need the knowledge and the skills too. But, however much knowledge you may have, however much technical skill you may have, it won't get through clearly to your horse without a committed intention on your part.

Maxim | how you think shapes what you do

So, if your schooling is lackadaisical because you feel you *ought to* rather than because you truly *want* to, or because your trainer told you that you should practise that shoulder-in a bit more, or if you are riding a dressage test worrying all the time about the comparisons people will be making between your little daisy-cutter Thoroughbred and those socking great Warmbloods with their flowing, elevated, flashy gaits – is it really a surprise if your horse is half-hearted or does less well than you know he can do?

This brings us back to the question of what you want. One of the great challenges and delights of riding is that, because horses respond so straightforwardly, they continually confront us with ourselves – yet, at the same time, they don't judge us. I suspect that, while this can be very difficult at times, is it also one of the reasons why people get so involved, and why they keep going even when things are difficult. I recall working on a clinic with two horses who had both been rescued – one from the meat lorry and one from being put down because various owners had found her behaviour so impossible. By the time I saw them, their rescuers had helped both the little, round pony and the big, leggy mare to settle and start to realize some of their athletic potential. The riders had been truly committed: their initial sympathy and belief that each horse had something to offer had carried them through the daily problems of schooling as well as, in the case of the big mare, some major problems of handling and trust-building.

So, a first step for each of us is to ask ourselves what it is that we truly want. Taking on a horse who is nervous, or irritable, or simply young and green, is not for everyone. Honesty begins with you: if you are tempted by a horse like this, ask yourself if you can commit the time and energy that will be needed, if you have the technical skills and support, and if you have what it takes emotionally. If the answer to any of these is 'no', don't go ahead: that doesn't reflect badly on you. The same applies if you like dressage (or jumping) but don't like competition; if you prefer working with youngsters rather than established horses (or vice versa); if you want riding to be a relaxing enjoyment of different activities rather than a semi-professional commitment to a single discipline. And, of course, the same honesty applies in assessing whether you have the right horse for the riding you really want to do. Where you are clear and consistent, you will be clear and consistent with your horse. And where you take the trouble to find the right kind of partner – and maybe make the hard decision to change partners if the match isn't right, or decide to modify your riding aims because your commitment to your unique horse is more important to you – then everything will come together and flow more than if you struggle on in conflict or indecision. Your mind and your body will be congruent with each other, and the messages you give your horse will be clear and consistent so that, together, you turn your intentions into action.

Maxim | how you think shapes what you do

Using your mind bank

It's become clear through research and through different kinds of therapeutic work that our minds store virtually everything that our senses have registered during our lifetimes. This doesn't mean that it's all consciously available, neatly filed in some kind of accessible and clearly-labelled mental filing-cabinet. But it does mean that you have potential access to more than you think you know, and more than you are aware of in consciousness. Within the rich deposits of your mind is stored a wealth of information that can help you become more effective in your riding (and, of course, in much else!), if only you pause and tap into it. Just as Roy was able to connect with his memories of the way his teacher Marion rode his horse and, without even realizing how he was doing it, use her as a kind of template that transformed the way he rode, so you potentially have access to models of effectiveness that you have watched or seen in photographs, and to your own best moments and peaks of skill as well.

> Take a moment to stare off into space, or close your eyes, and watch again in your mind's eye an outstanding piece of riding that you have witnessed. Maybe it was one of the freestyle performances at the Olympics, seen on television or video. Maybe it was something you saw in person, at a competition or a demonstration. Notice how you are seeing it: how much detail, natural speed; whether slowed down or speeded up. Is it in colour? Is it close up, or far away? Can you step into the picture and feel something of how it must have felt to the rider? And as you went through the experience, did you find yourself making any changes in your posture here and now? When outstanding trainers work with riders, I have often seen them echoing the rider's position and even their movements: as Charles de Kunffy says, 'I ride with them.'
>
> Now take the same memory, but substitute yourself and your horse. Feel how it feels to produce that long-striding extended canter; that balanced collected trot; that flowing half-pass.

Next time you are about to ride, take a moment to run through a memory like this that can inspire you and quite literally shape your own riding for the better. If you have trouble visualizing, don't worry. Many riders find it easier to remember the past or imagine the future in terms of recalling and even recreating physical sensations in their minds. Work with what comes naturally to you – and aim at training yourself gradually to enrich your imagining with a greater range of information. If

Maxim | how you think shapes what you do

you can easily create how something feels (that is, experiencing movement, pressure and texture quite readily in your mind), try asking yourself what you would be seeing, and hearing, at the same time. If you find pictures easy, ask yourself what sensations you might be experiencing at the same time. As I'll go on to show you in Chapter 13, it's really worthwhile getting fluent in this kind of imagining. Not only does it enable you to draw on your mentally stored skills of people you admire, it can also help you to shape better performances in the future through using the practice of mental rehearsal to go alongside your actual practice in the school. As you rehearse, so you shape your intentions; as you intend, so you give clear messages to your horse; as you clarify the messages to your horse, you make it easier for him to do his best; as your partnership becomes more harmonious and more effective, so you achieve more together.

Aiming your mind for your chosen destination

Riding happens in the here-and-now, but it is always on the way somewhere. This is because your horse always learns something from every interaction he has with you. He draws some kind of meaning from the way you behave and the way you respond to him. If you are consistent, and if you ensure that even relaxing or playful times together carry the same 'messages' as your serious schooling sessions, then he will get clear and consistent information about what you want; what's acceptable and what isn't. If you vary your standards *you* may understand why or when you are doing so, but you will be making it harder for your horse to know what you want: it shouldn't surprise you to find that when you want a purposeful walk in the arena, or a balanced, responsive canter on a small circle, you may have to re-establish the ground rules each time and perhaps find it rather an effort.

Consistency starts in your mind, and needn't be an effort if you are clear and, if necessary, firm. Of course what you actually ask your horse to do *will* differ between hacking and schoolwork, but asking for the same rapidity and quality of response in both contexts will help your horse build good habits and make them secure at the level of unconscious competence. This means that you will both be free to apply your conscious effort to what's new, or difficult, or unexpected. Consistency and high standards actually increase the amount of freedom and head-space you both have.

Having a clear idea of where you're aiming doesn't mean that you should be satisfied only if you achieve exactly what you have in mind. In fact, the opposite is true. Having a clear longer-term goal means you are free to recognize and reward even quite small steps in the right direction. If you are aiming to teach your horse lateral work, for example, break it down into simple chunks that can be achieved relatively easily, and praise both him and yourself for every small advance. Does he respond to the leg, moving willingly in and out on a spiral, or sideways in a leg-yield when you ask? If you are starting to teach him something entirely new, be prepared to praise his attempts, even if he is unbalanced or hollow at first: he has to have the experience (of going sideways in response to your aiding, for example) before you can start to help him refine *how* he does it. Usually it's best to ask for brief episodes of the new work – just a few steps sideways, just a few lengthened strides, for example – so that you maximize his chances of understanding what's wanted. If you allow him to keep the new movement going long enough to lose his balance, fall through the shoulder, race onto his forehand or flatten out, he will be learning these faults alongside what you really want him to learn. The art is to ask for a minimum and give him the best chance of producing something acceptable, even if unpolished.

Think of zooming in and out as you might with a camera lens. Focus close-up on the here-and-now, then zoom out to check how here-and-now relates to where you're aiming for. If you're on track, you can be pleased and show it. You can take the same attitude towards bigger issues and achievements. Is your horse working well at Novice now (close-up)? Then it's time to zoom out and have a look at how his current work is preparing him for Elementary. What needs to be in place before he can carry himself in a more advanced balance, do lateral movements and manage to demonstrate clear differences within the gaits? Zoom in again, and begin to introduce these new elements into some of your schooling sessions. Only if you work at developing this mental flexibility yourself will you be in the best position to help your horse take his training and athletic development forward.

Pre-flight cockpit checks

With clear intention and the ability to use regular zooming in and out to help you relate what you're doing this minute to your longer-term aims, your mind is at its best to make the most of your riding. Like a pilot preparing for take-off, you still need to run through some cockpit checks each time you ride. Some apply to you, and some to your horse.

- *What's your internal weather?* In other words, what state of mind are you in? If you are hot and bothered, distracted, rushed or worried, your intention will be harder to maintain and will come through less clearly to your horse. Try to develop the habit of putting aside any mental clutter as you approach the yard. You might do this by metaphorically 'parking' non-horsy thoughts as if on a mental shelf or in a mental cupboard marked 'refer to later' (use your visual or kinesthetic imagination to help you do this); by using your physical journey to the yard as a metaphorical shift between one set of thinking and another; or perhaps just by thinking forward to what it is you enjoy most about being with your horse. If you really can't put your mental clutter aside, don't ride: loose-school or lunge your horse instead. It is not worth compromising what you can do now, and letting an unsatisfactory session interfere with your longer-term work and pleasure with your horse, by pressing on through a sense of duty. If you bring extreme tiredness to the yard with you, or strong and absorbing emotions such as anger or frustration, your messages to your horse will lack clarity and consistency and your riding will suffer. If the mental baggage from your day is not as debilitating as this, use the everyday routines of grooming, tacking up and so on to help you clear your mind and get focused. Paying attention to things you can so easily take for granted (in other words, changing deliberately from unconscious to conscious competence for a while) is a great way to do this. If you would normally flick a brush over him quickly, take time instead to give him a thorough grooming. Talk to him about anything or nothing. Tune in to how he is in himself today. Locate yourself *here* and *now* instead of *there* and *then*.

- *Take your internal weather into account when thinking about what to do.* Your horse, and your dressage, can benefit from many kinds of working together. If you are tired, or stiff, or tense, think of loose, forward, free work. Play with poles or small jumps. Enjoy. Your horse will not go back to his box thinking, '*What happened to those simple changes we were going to practise?*' In itself, taking the pressure off like this at the beginning can often get you into the right mood mentally and physically to do more ambitious things later in the session. But if not, so be it. Another day will give you other opportunities. Today you are both looser, freer, more forward. You could even spend a whole session usefully in walk if you haven't the energy to do more – so long as it's a purposeful walk and you use it as a vehicle for confirming aiding and response (off the leg, longer and shorter frame, etc.).

Taking the pressure off. Here, Roy and Cori are experimenting. By asking Cori to try a half-pass in medium rather than collected trot, Roy is hoping to encourage Cori to produce more engagement, impulsion and connection. Roy's light-heartedness encourages a rather puzzled Cori to 'have a go'.

Maxim | how you think shapes what you do

- *If you run into unexpected turbulence or static, be prepared to change or even jettison your plans.* Spooking, external distractions, horse feeling fizzy? Can't seem to concentrate, other people milling about, other horses being difficult? A day is just a day. Cut your session short, get off and lunge instead, loose-school over a jump, or perhaps stop schooling and go for a brief hack (or start with one). Successful leaders in all spheres are people who keep their long-term aims clearly in mind *and at the same time are prepared and able to be flexible about the means of achieving them.* There are so many ways to work towards improving the partnership you have together, so many routes to greater suppleness, balance, lightness and responsiveness...

- *What's your horse's weather today?* Is the spring grass getting to him? Is the wind bothering him? Is he a bit stiff from that fooling around in the field yesterday with his friends – or from that journey back from the show? He has been living his own life while you have been away from him leading yours, so connecting with him is an essential part of preparing for your work together. Tune in to him as you bring him in from the field, or in the box as you get him ready. What mood is he in? How energetic does he seem to be? How ready is he

Tune in to him. Roy and Cori in the yard.

Maxim | how you think shapes what you do

to pay attention to you, as opposed to his friends or incidental distractions in the environment? Fine-tune in the first few minutes of your working session. How is he going today? What is he offering you? Have your own aims in mind, but remember that you will get the most from him and from your partnership if you start from *where he is*. Accept his state and work with it before you ask for more or different.

- *Plan your route for today*. I suggest that you build every ridden session around the following sequence: *match him; loosen him; stretch him (physically and mentally); relax him*. Think of a bell-shaped curve (see drawing). Start low and slow; recap and remind; increase intensity and energy; consolidate, wind down again. New or demanding work need only take five or ten minutes from your session. Remind yourself that time spent in loosening, recapping, and unwinding is *essential* – without the first two elements your new or more taxing work will lack a proper foundation and may not be adequately integrated into what you and your horse already know, and not winding down properly could induce stress or even injury.

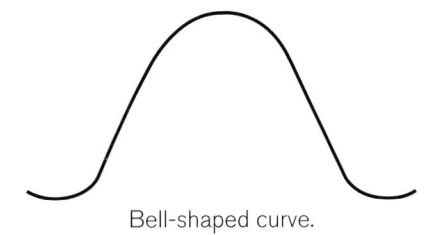

Bell-shaped curve.

Finally, remember that recapping builds confidence and encourages both of you to try a little more. Consolidating new learning through repetition helps you both to store and remember it.

Now – are you ready to fly?

Maxim | how you think shapes what you do

10 Paying the right kind of attention

> In a pitch-black cave, a hurricane lamp shedding a broad, dim light, which enables you to see the overall size and shape of your surroundings, is what you need first. If all you have is a torch with a fine beam, you will not be able to get your bearings so well. But once you have orientated yourself, it is useful to be able to home in on details, and now the spotlight comes into its own. The diffuse illumination gives you a holistic impression; the focused beam enables you to dissect and analyse. Both are needed.
>
> **Guy Claxton,** *Hare Brain, Tortoise Mind*[1]

How best can you pay attention in your riding? In this chapter I want to explore some important themes. First, just *how* do different people go about paying attention? Second, how concentrating can put you into a 'bubble state' that can sometimes be helpful, and at other times may hinder you in your riding. And, third, how you can benefit from cultivating your ability to use, and to move between, the fine-beam and the broad light types of awareness. As always, flexibility enables you to make the most of yourself – and of your horse.

Just how are you paying attention?

When you are really paying attention, which of your senses (sight, hearing, etc.) is most involved? Everyone uses their physical senses to receive incoming information about the world – but also as an *internal* means of remembering, recreating, reflecting and rehearsing it. Many people naturally use visual information for doing this – talking, for example, about something being 'clear as daylight' or, by contrast, feeling that they are 'working in the dark'. This indicates that, for them, thinking or imagining probably means they are seeing images inside their head – 'in their mind's eye'.

Many riders, though, tend to rely more on physical (kinesthetic) sensations, both as their main channel for receiving incoming information from the outside world and as their major mental mechanism. If you are not primarily visual, and are reading, or hearing your trainer use, ideas that are expressed mainly in visual language, you will of course know the words being used, but to understand their message fully you will be having to 'translate' them. What you understand will not feel so immediate or be so effective for you because it's not expressed in your 'first language' of physical sensation. The word *'focus'* is visual: if you are kinesthetic, finding something *'heavy work'* or having a *'light-hearted hack'* might more accurately describe what you do. For you, paying attention might feel like *'switching on'* with its opposite (if you are bored) being *'switching off'*. 'Kinesthetic' is not just about feeling something specific ('I'm putting more weight into my right seatbone now') but also the more subtle, unconscious 'feel' of being at one with your horse's rhythm, being aware of how he is breathing, etc.

If you are one of the (rather smaller) number of people who process primarily through hearing, your natural metaphors might involve things like *'wavelength'*, *'receiving loud and clear'* – and at the extremes *'tuning-in'* and *'tuning out'*.

None of these sets of metaphors is inherently 'right' or 'wrong' in themselves, but they can make all the difference to whether you 'get' an idea easily so that you can manage yourself more rapidly and effectively, or have to struggle and take longer. (And, as we know, time is of the essence in riding!) With this in mind I shall try to use all three frames of reference as I go through this chapter: please feel free to read what you need when I use the metaphors that don't work so naturally for you!

> Take a moment to think about what you are doing in your head when you concentrate, and check which of your senses you are relying on most. Think of a time (or an activity) when you concentrate effortlessly. How would you describe that?

Bubbles of concentration – helpful or unhelpful?

People often assume that concentration is always helpful – but is it? Concentration is a specialization of attention, which means that it rules some kinds of information in and others, out. I think of it as a bubble which can either protect horse and rider from unwanted features of the outside world or cut them off from some of

Maxim | how you think shapes what you do

its potentially useful 'realities'. If your bubble is such that outside distractions don't get to you and you are thus free to do your best, that's one thing. If it is such that you are caught up in fear or anxiety about what *might* happen rather than what *is* happening, or even what *might be likely to* happen, your bubble will be insulating you from the reality of the outside world, and may even insulate you from your horse. Terrified self-absorption is something that many riders have experienced (myself among them), and it can start a rapid downward spiral in which things get even worse. (See Chapter 13 for some helpful 'Strategies for Managing Competition Nerves'.) For the time being, let's look at these contrasting possibilities in a bit more detail.

Good bubbles

A 'good bubble' can be really helpful if it means that you and your horse are attending fully to each other and to what you're doing. The easiest way to get this going is to set the example yourself: if you are truly focused on him, your responses will be quicker and more subtle, and this will effectively be telling him, 'I'm with you: you matter.' This is a great confidence-giver, and invites your horse to give you his concentration in return. I remember Arthur Kottas teaching a friend on her spooky mare, and telling her: 'Watch her ears. Watch her ears all the time. If they go forward, you have lost her. When they start to go forward, at once do something to catch her attention again.' Ears are usually a good indicator of where your horse's attention is going, but individual horses may also have their own additional ways of showing this. Mild grinding of teeth, or lip-smacking, may tell you either that your horse is really thinking about what he's doing, or that he's worried or distracted. You know him – what signals is he giving you? And what are you doing about it? You can create this bubble by having an open, curious awareness about your horse's every feeling, every movement, every response. It's about Noticing... Wondering... Comparing... Experimenting... Allow yourself to zoom in and out from time to time – compare how he is now with yesterday, with five minutes ago, with how you'd like him to be in twenty minutes, in six months...

A bubble of concentration is also helpful when it enables you to filter out distractions. As part of our case-study sessions for this book, I was working one day with Shane on her sister's horse. As she started to warm up I noticed a column of smoke rising somewhere near her neighbour's house, and wondered if it was a bonfire – or something accidental. We decided that it looked alarming, and Shane's sister went off to phone the fire brigade. During the forty minutes of so of our session, the fire got worse, rapidly devouring the whole of the neighbours' barn, with flames crackling and roaring, timbers shifting and collapsing. Pretty

PAYING THE RIGHT KIND OF ATTENTION • 139

soon, three fire-engines came down the narrow lane with their sirens going... And for pretty much all of this time Shane kept the 7-year-old with her in a bubble of attentive work.

If you are visual, you could make use of the focusing metaphor to help you create and maintain your helpful bubble: imagine that what you want to concentrate on (the test movements, or your horse's way of going, for example) is crystal

A test for any horse and rider! Shane's neighbours' barn is well alight – and very noisy!

Stringer is not too happy as he turns towards the fire…

…but Shane rides him forward, transmitting her own confidence and creating a shared 'bubble' of concentration, which results in correct and expressive work.

Maxim | how you think shapes what you do

clear in your mind's eye, and potential distractions are fuzzy. Yes, you know there's a person with an umbrella just by the fence, or two bored children playing with a dog while their mum calls out the test for a friend in the next arena, but you can keep them out of focus – or perhaps allow their colours to become dim and muddy in your mind, rather than bright.

If you are auditory, think of having an important conversation on a crackly line – you need to filter out the irrelevant noise and concentrate on what you really want to hear.

If you are kinesthetic, think of distractions in terms of mild physical discomfort, which it's pretty easy to ignore when you are doing something important or fun. Everyday examples might be something like disregarding a small piece of grit in your shoe on a cold day when you really don't want to take your gloves and shoe off to deal with it, or blanking out a mild itch when your hands are full and you're in too much of a hurry to put everything down and free a hand to scratch it.

Bad bubbles

Bad bubbles occur when you lock down on incoming information and concentrate only on what alarms or bothers you. *'I'm going to forget the test. I just know it. My mind will go blank like it did last time. Then, even when the judge tells me what I need to do next, I'm bound to forget again. And then my horse will get fed up stopping and starting and that's just when he switches off, or finds something he can spook at...'* And, surprise surprise, it's pretty likely that with this mind-set you will forget, and maybe some of your other predictions will start to come true too. We all have our own natural mind-set: what none of us benefits from is a 'set mind'!

Allowing information to keep flowing in means that you continue to have the possibility of choice about what you pay attention to. *'Turned left instead of right... Stop, start again... Let's get this entry really straight and rhythmical ... Eyes on C all the way, trampoline that trot; boing, boing, boing, lovely; lost his shoulder a bit on the turn, get that elbow in so we get him back in balance, there we go, now we need inside leg to activate the hind leg for that shoulder-in... What's that going on over there – some kind of rumpus in the collecting ring – let's have a little shoulder-fore so he doesn't see it so clearly and a bit of a gee-up to distract him...'* Some riders may actually 'talk themselves through' in words – my husband Leo does. Others will be feeling this same sequence without words, or seeing themselves as if they were watching a video. Whatever sense tends to frame your thinking, the point is that ongoing information provides an ongoing reality check for your worried fantasies – and offers you potential ways to avoid fulfilling them!

Another simple yet helpful strategy is to keep breathing – yes, that simple! I am sure that most riders have been reminded of this by their teachers more than once. Breathing can be controlled either voluntarily (you think about it) or involuntarily (it happens without your awareness or deliberate control) as it is most of the time. When we're anxious, or frightened, or even concentrating hard, this automatic process tends to be interrupted, and we hold our breath. This momentary holding of your chest muscles has immediate knock-on effects on many other muscle groups that are involved in riding, and it also reduces the amount of oxygen your muscles have available. That's why you may start to feel exhausted! Your tension is rapidly picked up by your horse. He may echo your tension physically, mentally or both, which you in turn perceive, increasing your anxiety and tension... Now you have a reinforcing loop, which can lead to a downward spiral... The bubble is beginning to close you off.

It's not always easy to remember the importance of breathing when the bubble has closed it – you're more likely to start getting puffed and red-faced as your automatic control kicks in to keep you going. But you can train yourself to hum or sing quietly as a regular part of your riding. Your horse will get used to the tunes and recognize even a quiet hum when you are competing and are not allowed to use your voice. Matching the gaits with tunes helps reinforce rhythm and can have a calming effect on both you and your horse. And when you're humming or singing, you can't help but go on breathing!

Broad beam or narrow focus – your choice

When you are concentrating, you are in a mind-body state that potentially gives you access to a rich range of information. If your concentration is broad beam, you will be monitoring information at a mostly unconscious level, and are likely to be in a quite passively receptive state. It's a bit like daydreaming: there are things going on in your mind, and you are quite able to monitor yourself and your surroundings, but you do it on automatic. This kind of state can help you in riding because it usually calms your mind and body. Calmness of this sort allows you to be both alert and receptive: able to take information from the outside world and from the inner world of your own sensations and emotions. Much of your mental processing is 'off-screen', until your mind signals the need for you to become aware of it by raising it 'on-screen' into your conscious awareness. In broad-beam attentiveness you are less likely to have your feelings strongly aroused by others (including your horse!). Instead, the quality of your attention is shaped and enhanced by interest and curiosity. The pioneering coach Tim Gallwey, who formulated the Inner Game approach to sports and business, found when he coached people that they learnt and progressed most when they were alert and

Maxim | how you think shapes what you do

curious: they *noticed more* and they *noticed relevantly*. Other writers on coaching have described this state as one of 'wondering': wondering (being curious) *why* something is happening, and often wondering (marvelling) *at the very fact that* it's happening.

> Think of a time when you have been in a curious and wondering state like this. How did it come about? What were you doing at the time? Do you ever feel like this when you are riding? If so, what triggers it? If not, can you learn from how you do it at other times and copy your own 'recipe' across when you are riding?

By contrast, narrow-beam attention can allow you to spotlight (or tune in to, or really get a feel for) exactly what is happening, so that you can really work on it and manage it to the best of your ability. Narrow-beam awareness is primarily a function of the conscious part of the mind. The objects of your attention are 'on-screen'. You can make use of this effectively to create a flow between the movements of a dressage test instead of simply stringing them together. You will need that homing in, too, when something unexpected happens, when something goes wrong, when you have to cope or to improvise. However, pinpointing can sometimes be a hindrance. One example would be those times when you find yourself flitting about from one idea to another, one sensation to another, rather than having an overall map of the situation into which all the different bits can fit. In such situations you are so busy seeing the individual trees (narrow beam) that you can't see the wood they are part of. Or you could be tuned-in – but to the wrong things! Riders often report 'freezing' with anxiety in competitions: strong emotions such as worry, fear or anger can occupy all your sensory channels and seriously interfere with your ability to have a broad-beam awareness or overall 'feel' in riding. It's as though they drown out other information – particularly the subtle signals you need to refine your responses and clarify your intentions.

If you are consciously distracted or overloaded by too much information, whether it comes from outside or inside you, you may not even be able to maintain your focus on the most basic things, never mind having enough attention available for new ones. I remember trying to work in at my first dressage test. We were in a huge field, with lots of horses and riders milling about in various states of excitement. I tried to ride a 20-m circle – but without the familiar boundaries of the school I had nothing to guide me, and whenever I lost the shape and thought I'd better start again someone would cut across my vision (or even the pathway I

Maxim | how you think shapes what you do

had planned) so that I lost my direction as well as my attention. Small wonder that my horse got more confused and wound up!

Having a flow between narrow focus and broad beam

For truly effective riding, we need to cultivate the ability to use both narrow focus and broad beam, and to switch between them at will. That way, both can enrich what we're doing. Guy Claxton explains it like this: *You cannot spend all day focused and concentrated. You have, gradually, to develop the quality of attention of a cat: relaxed and watchful at the same time.*[2]

There is so much information coming at you when you ride. Your conscious mind can't possibly deal with everything. How can you manage, at the same time, to monitor your position, deepen your seat, think about using your hands independently and subtly, check whether your horse is forward enough, and 'through' enough, and soft enough – and in addition learn how to ask him to go sideways, or do a proper walk pirouette rather than a smallish circle? You can't, of course. While you are struggling to assimilate new information (conscious incompetence) you will be having to rely on habit (patterns you have stored in unconscious competence) to help you use what you learnt previously. And when you are in narrow-focus mode, it's also difficult to be playful or experimental – two states which require broad focus and often set up good learning, problem-solving, or new discoveries. Broad-beam awareness also has its disadvantages: it can be de-energizing and fail to give you the detail you need to make rapid decisions and actions.

In other words, you need both parts of your brain to be working for you, each in the way it knows best.

How can you help this to happen? The key is to learn how to move at will from broad to pinpoint awareness. In *The Ethics and Passions of Dressage*, Charles de Kunffy describes an ideal state for riding, in which both are potentially available: *'The rider's attention span will lengthen... Their powers of concentration will deepen to a meditative state, oblivious of anything outside the harmonious absorption of the communication with the horse. Their focus will sharpen to cut the irrelevant details away, making them steadfast in body, mind and spirit.'*[3]

Let's go back to the way cats do this: they monitor what's going on around them, even if their eyes are closed. Our cat may be sleeping peacefully, yet when she hears our car turning into the road she gets up, goes out through the cat-flap and is there to greet us in the driveway. We have had cats for over thirty years and, whenever we have got a new car, it has taken them at most a couple of days (sometimes less) to recognize the sound of the new car and know that 'their people' are coming home. The cat's senses monitor her surroundings even when she is asleep:

she is unconsciously aware of her surroundings. When something changes she begins to pay conscious attention.

I believe that this offers a helpful model for our riding. The 'meditative state' described by a number of outstanding riders and writers, including Charles de Kunffy and Paul Belasik, is a good place to begin every ride, and to return to at regular intervals. By first putting ourselves into a state of broad-beam receptivity, we make it possible for the unconscious part of our mind to tell us what we need to pay specific attention to with our conscious narrow-beam attention. If you watch an expert rider, their riding will often seem to be effortless. This is because their level of skill allows them to rely on unconscious awareness to monitor a very substantial amount of what is happening, and thus take appropriate action at the level of unconscious competence. This leaves perhaps quite a small amount of information for them to process in consciousness – which is why they can set something up or prevent something else happening with such apparent ease. With so much taken care of at an unconscious level, their conscious awareness can notice and help them respond to subtle or minimal signals from the horse, from their own body, or from their surroundings. They can correct a potential loss of balance or straightness, almost before it happens. This is why they seem to have so much more time than the rest of us to prepare and to react.

Of course, sheer hours in the saddle make this easier by creating good habits and providing varied experiences and strategies for dealing with them; but, even if you ride just a few times a week, you can learn how to create a receptive awareness so that you can make the most of the talents you have and pay attention where it's going to be most useful.

Learning to switch your forms of awareness

Cultivating states of unconscious receptivity helps you to switch off your conscious processing until something calls for you to apply your narrow-beam attention. The sorts of things that call for narrow beam are things that change, things that are interesting, things that are puzzling, and things that you sense may turn out to be in some way relevant for you. Broad-beam receptivity allows you to notice these kinds of things sooner. When you notice a difference at this unconscious level, you will become alert to it, so bringing your conscious attention to bear on it.

There are some simple things you can do to help yourself get into a receptive scanning state.

1. Clear your mental and emotional clutter before going to the yard, as I explained earlier (see pages 132–3).

2. As you do your warm-up, make sure your eyes are defocused by staring into space, looking into the distance beyond your horse's head rather than down at his neck. Having 'soft eyes' like this opens up a physiological link to your unconscious ways of processing: having a crisp focus connects to conscious processing and tends to close down that link with the unconscious. You will find yourself switching the type of focus you use quite often as you ride, matching the way your mind switches from receiving mode into attending mode. As a useful side-effect, you will find it easier to sit upright with a tall neck if you are defocused, and to learn to 'feel your horse through the back of your neck', as Charles de Kunffy puts it. What this means is that you will be creating a 'seat' that includes not just your bottom but the whole of your spine and head. Think how much more available that makes you for conversing with your horse! One advanced rider I know said that, even though she was experienced and successful before learning how to defocus, it proved to be a key step in helping her finally achieve her now exemplary upright 'dressage position'.

3. Begin every ridden session with at least ten minutes of purposeful walking, on a contact but with a long rein, so that you and your horse can tune into each other and you both begin to get a feel of how each other is today. This is the foundation for attentive conversation, and helps you make the right decisions – both deliberate (conscious) and intuitive (unconscious) – about what it might be best to work on.

4. Warm up your trot with suppling and stretching work. Begin with rising trot. Set a rhythm that is not too fast, but full of energy. Feel it like a heart-beat, if you are kinesthetic. Hear it like a metronome, if you are auditory. Or, if you are visual, imagine yourself tracing the line of your rise and fall in the air in front of your surroundings like the regular peaks and troughs on a monitor screen. Best of all, expand your awareness from what comes most naturally to include the other ways of sensing: that way, you are beginning to train yourself to develop a multi-sensory awareness which will become more automatic – and so more useful – over time.

When something switches on your narrow-beam attention, or when you deliberately want to use it, make sure that your eyes are working in focus. This is the simplest and most effective way of changing from one state of awareness to the other. For broad-beam focus, look at something, then up and away beyond it into the distance… It's a good idea to practise this in many different situations – waiting at traffic lights or in the supermarket queue, standing by the sink as you wash up, walking along the road… Get familiar with making the change so you know you

Maxim | how you think shapes what you do

can do it easily and instantly. Do it riding round the school: broad, narrow, broad, narrow... Notice what feels different as well as what looks different when you do it. It's likely that your breathing will become slower when you're in the broad-beam state. In fact, you can deliberately make your breathing slower in order to help you switch to broad-beam state. The two factors will reinforce each other and create an even more powerful switch. Through practice, you can learn to get broad beam (defocused eyes, slow breathing) and narrow beam (focused eyes, 'normal' breathing) rapidly and easily whenever you want. As with all new habits, frequent practice is what helps.

What's in it for your horse?

However well you manage your own awareness, and however versatile you train yourself to be at tapping into both conscious and unconscious ways of operating, for effective riding you need your partner to attend with you! Why would he want to bother? Think of having a good conversation with a friend: it might be serious or playful, it could be about something trivial or something important – but when both parties feel a conversation is 'good', it's likely that you are both sharing the same kind of state and enjoying the quality of your mutual attentiveness just as much as the quality or content of what you're discussing. It's the same for your horse: if you ensure that you are in your best frame of mind for riding, with the right kind of conscious-unconscious flow to give him both clear guidance and understanding responses, you'll be more able to make the most of whatever happens – and you will be making it worth his while to give you his attention in turn. Your state will be influencing his through your body language. He will hear the changes in your breathing, feel the differences in your muscle tone, and begin to match them himself. You will be influencing him in very subtle ways – and you will be increasing the chance of having a good conversation together. And good conversations tend to lead to good outcomes.

Tips for trainers

1. Train yourself to notice what kind of sensory metaphors your clients are using. Do these suggest that they are primarily visual, kinesthetic or auditory? Try to monitor the language you use yourself to match each client. Many outstanding teachers often unconsciously cover a 'spread' of sensory language – with the effect that they reach more people in their 'first language'. But you can do better than this if you identify the primary processing sense of each client individu-

ally. Then you will really be sure of 'speaking the same language' and making it as easy as possible for her to benefit from what you have to teach her.

2. Encourage each client to use both kinds of awareness – unconscious and conscious. You may have to explain the benefits that each can give her, and show her how easily she can access them by changing the kind of eye-focus and breathing pattern she is using. In particular, make use of the exercises I've suggested in this chapter to help her get into a broad-beam state when she begins each lesson.

11 Where do your assumptions get you?

> Our beliefs are a very powerful force on our behavior. It is common wisdom that if someone really believes he can do something he will do it, and if he believes something is impossible no amount of effort will convince him that it can be accomplished... Our beliefs about ourselves and what is possible in the world around us greatly impact our day-to-day effectiveness. All of us have beliefs that serve as resources as well as beliefs that limit us.
>
> **Robert Dilts,** *Changing Belief Systems with NLP*[1]

Assumptions are beliefs that have sunk below the threshold of awareness – unconscious mental short-cuts based on our past learning and experience. We can't get by in life without making them, but simply because they operate 'under cover' they can sometimes be even more powerful than the beliefs we consciously know we hold. Assumptions are either generalizations based on events that remain more or less constant (e.g. the sun will come up today because it comes up every day) or on powerful past experiences (I touched the top of the stove and got burnt – better not touch stoves in future). Once an assumption has become a part of our mental furniture, it saves us time by acting as a filter for organizing and making sense out of incoming information so that we can react quickly and make any decisions that are necessary. Much of the time, of course, assumptions are useful. They help us to predict the likely effect of our actions, so that we can manage ourselves effectively in relation to the world around us. But simply because an assumption functions as a mental short-cut or template, we rarely check whether it is actually supported by evidence, so we can't be sure how good a guide it is really going to be.

This means that, in addition to useful assumptions, we each carry round some that may need updating (the information they were based on is no longer valid – things have changed, or we have changed, or other people have changed) and many that are not based on 'hard', factual information at all. Assumptions that involve beliefs, for example, can be less reliable than ones about the natural world. I remember as a child learning that chestnut horses are 'hot'. No doubt some are – but we have owned two and known others and none of them were 'hot' in the way I'd been led to believe. An additional cause of error is that the learning and experience on which our assumptions are based isn't just our own – it often rests on what we have been told by influential people in our lives – parents and teachers, for example. This means that when we take their assumptions on board as our own, we may be accepting as correct information that is actually inappropriate to our circumstances. I remember standing with my mother watching my daughter having a jumping lesson. 'Aren't you frightened she'll have a fall?', Ma asked. I wasn't – my personal experience hadn't led me to assume that this was likely – or dangerous if it did happen. Ma's experience of horses, though, went back to the much more dangerous situation of being bolted with whilst travelling in a friend's dog-cart: horses in general were always potentially dangerous so far as she was concerned, even though she learnt to love, and to an extent even trust, the ones we owned.

We make all kinds of assumptions about horses: *'A horse kicks at one end and bites at the other'* leaves out a great deal, but it's worth bearing in mind because every horse has the capacity to react defensively or aggressively in certain circumstances. If you approach a horse with the assumption that such behaviour is likely, though, you'll almost certainly be sending a message via your body language that makes him uneasy – and perhaps increases the probability he'll behave in the very way you'd rather avoid. One of the reasons why riders often have less trouble communicating with other people's horses than with their own may be that they come to a relatively strange horse with fewer assumptions – and so their minds are more receptive to what actually goes on between them as they ride. There are fewer filters in the riders' minds to colour (and distort) what happens. Some years ago, my editor, Martin, attended a trainee judges' course at which two fairly competent club riders acted as guinea pigs. Both rode a prescribed test on their own horses and, later, both rode the same tests on each others' horses. He tells me that it was universally agreed that each rider performed their better test on the other's horse!

In this chapter I want to examine some of the assumptions riders often make about why horses do the things they do, how they think and how they regard their work. Taking an honest look at the assumptions you are making about your horse is an important step towards understanding how you are actively shaping the relationship you have with each other. Your assumptions will be affecting what you think, how you act – and how you feel – in many subtle, as well as obvious, ways. And much of this will be crystal clear to your horse. Bringing this hidden information to the surface, asking yourself what assumptions are useful and why,

Maxim | how you think shapes what you do

and what aren't and how you can change them, is a great way to clean up communication and take your partnership forward.

What happens if you don't run this 'audit' on yourself? Each time you make an assumption without checking the evidence you may, in fact, have taken a first step away from reality. And it can get worse: because assumptions act as filters for incoming evidence you will tend to interpret subsequent events in the light of what you've assumed. Before long, you can be way off track.

With horses, this progressive drift away from reality can happen very easily, because you can't ask the horse, and even if you could he wouldn't be able to tell you. Or can you, and would he? In this chapter I want to explain how you can get fuller and more reliable information about your riding if you learn to recognize and work with your own assumptions – and also take on board your horse's behavioural 'comments' about them! And I want to propose that you adopt some assumptions which, by contrast, have the benefit of leading almost invariably to outcomes that are both valid and helpful.

Assumptions about physical problems

Let's start with a physical issue that affects Shane's horse, Ted. Shane has had Ted since he was a youngster, when he had a habit of hollowing and then kicking out when asked for left-lead canter. Although he doesn't do this as much nowadays, it's still enough of a pattern for Shane to be concerned that he will do it and lose marks when they are competing.

Shane is just asking Ted for a left-lead canter, and even though she is being careful not to pull back on the reins he is hollowing and tightening at the very idea. What is causing this response?

Maxim | how you think shapes what you do

When we don't get what we're asking for, we naturally start to look for reasons. And it's a short step from seeking explanations to making an assumption about what the most likely ones might be. If human beings are involved, we can at least ask them why – though actually it's surprising how often people don't do a reality check like this. What kind of assumptions might a rider be likely to make about Ted's behaviour – and where could they lead her?

- *'He's against the leg.'* It's a form of disobedience. He's over-reacting to a normal aid. Keep it up till he gets used to it (the 'inoculation' formula!).

- *'He's more sensitive on the left side.'* Maybe he has a physical problem that needs investigating.

- *'He resists bending to the left.'* That could be his more difficult side – more suppling work is needed to help him become more equally flexible.

- *'He's naughty'* – this is his way of saying, 'Don't put your leg on – I don't want to work harder.'

- *'Maybe the rider's aid for canter left isn't as subtle as the one for canter right'* – rider needs to become more equal in her aiding.

Any of these could prove a useful explanation, so the rider needs to do her best to check them out by seeking more evidence, experimenting to see what happens if she changes something, and so on. But there's something else going on here, because these explanations are of very different kinds. They are based on different kinds of assumption:

1. *The horse is responding to a physical discomfort or limitation of his own.*

2. *The rider is being 'told off' by the horse about a discomfort she is creating through her aiding.*

3. *Horses would prefer not to work and become resistant when they are asked to do so.*

If you make the first assumption, your next step is to check the horse out physically. You may find yourself taking pressure off him because you don't want to cause him discomfort or pain. If you make the second assumption, you may think that your riding isn't good enough, probably feel bad about your inadequacy, and seek further lessons. If you make the third assumption, you may do none of these things, but instead get irritable and blame the horse each time for being difficult and lowering your competition scores.

What might be a more effective way of taking things forward? The answer lies in making a *different kind* of assumption – and then following up and checking out the information it gives you. Here's a step-by-step process than can help you.

Maxim | how you think shapes what you do

1. **Assume that what the horse is doing makes sense to him.** Like people, horses usually show resistance when they find things uncomfortable, painful or difficult. If you make this assumption, you avoid getting into areas of blame and feelings of irritation or anger. You have chosen instead to be an inquirer, an investigator, in a realm (the horse's experience and understanding of his world) that is different from your own. So, when Ted kicked out in one of my sessions with Shane, I encouraged her to assume that Ted had a good reason – in his terms. How does he behave generally? Does this habit seem to fit in with the rest of his behaviour, or does it somehow stand out as different? Though spooky as a youngster (less so nowadays), Ted was never mean or ungenerous: kicking out doesn't 'fit' with the rest of who he is.

2. **Gather more evidence.** Does he do this every time – or only some times? When does it *not* occur – and can you find any pattern in common between all the times when it *doesn't* happen. When I asked Shane these questions, she told me that Ted doesn't kick out every time. He *doesn't* kick out on the right rein. He *doesn't* kick out when worked with a light seat or when he's 'through' in his back. With this information we could begin to build up a possible explanation. Since he is usually obedient, it makes sense to assume that he's showing us in the only way he can that being asked for left-lead canter when he's not 'through' and/or when his rider's full seat is on him (as in dressage, as opposed to cross-country or jumping) is, in some way, objectionable to him. Further evidence came from some of the photographs, which showed that in left-lead canter Ted sometimes made almost no separation between his hind legs – he was almost 'hopping together behind'. One possible explanation we thought of was that it's the *right* hind which has the problem: in left-lead canter it's the right hind that performs the strike-off and has to carry the horse's entire weight for the first phase of the stride. If Ted finds this difficult or uncomfortable he might be kicking out as a protest when the strike-off signal is given.

In an early session Ted is hopping together behind in left canter.

Maxim | how you think shapes what you do

3. **Check for any physical problems.** If you think a minor strain or injury may be involved, check if it's better when rested, or if your vet offers some anti-inflammatories. As a eventer, Ted is regularly seen by a physiotherapist. She had seen him recently and found nothing amiss, so there were no answers there.

4. **Experiment to discover whether you can make a difference to the pattern.** Only make one change at a time, so you know what's causing what. For example, when we had our discussion Ted was about to go away for two weeks schooling while Shane was on holiday. We hoped this would give her the chance of finding out whether the problem also occurred when her trainer was riding him, which would suggest it was a learnt response to discomfort (either in the past or currently), or whether it only happened with Shane, in which case we might have to consider whether Shane's riding (like that of many riders) differs depending which rein she is on. However, although during his 'working break' Ted never kicked out against the leg, the change of rider as such didn't answer our question. As mentioned in point 2, Ted was known not to kick out when ridden with a light seat and Shane's trainer – a showjumper – always rides that way.

5. **If you think a problem may be caused by ill-fitting tack, check that out without changing anything else.** In fact, getting the saddler in to check Ted's saddles gave Shane the information she needed: because Ted had put on so much muscle on his shoulders that his dressage saddle was now too narrow, and the points of the tree were digging in. Shane was able to borrow a different

In a later session, with Shane sitting deeper and with more tone, there is more separation between Ted's hind legs and he is in a much better balance.

Maxim | how you think shapes what you do

dressage saddle for our next lesson, and even though it wasn't perfect for him Ted stayed much softer and more 'through' – and we had no hopping behind and only one kick-out (on the right, not the left, rein!) even though Shane spent some time working on trot-canter transitions.

6. **Sometimes you may have to test out a number of possibilities** before you begin to clarify what's causing the problem. For example, mineral deficiencies can cause behavioural as well as physical problems, and I have known of a previously charming and well-schooled horse who became positively dangerous when moved to a different yard – only to revert to his former easy-going self when moved back again.

7. **Take a hard look at what happens in response to each and every change you make.** If things improve, you are probably on the right track. If not, try something different.

Assumptions about what horses think and feel

In my experience, assuming that a horse's behaviour makes sense to him opens up a range of possibilities, as it did in Ted's case. If you make assumptions based on the idea that horses think and behave like human beings, you are lumbering them with baggage that doesn't belong to them – and lumbering yourself with difficulties that can feel much harder to overcome. Assuming that horses are 'naturally lazy', that they want to 'evade work', or that not doing what you want means they are 'resisting' or trying to manipulate you, only gets you into unpleasant places – and ones I believe you can relatively easily avoid. I'd like to suggest some assumptions that it's useful to make about your horse – not out of some woolly idealism, but because they take into account the fact that horses are not like us, and help you keep your mind open to noticing, evaluating and acting on *evidence*, not unquestioning belief.

Some assumptions it *is* useful to make about your horse

Horses don't think like people

They don't have agendas that lead them into manipulative, controlling or strategic behaviour. They are not devious or deceitful. They are motivated by straightforward things like the need for food, exercise, warmth, shelter and companionship. They prefer comfort to discomfort, ease to pain. Even though they have long-term memories for some things, and can learn and build on their learning, they don't work towards long-term goals – and they have no understanding of ours! They don't think and plan ahead. If you try to think like your horse you are likely to find him easier to understand – and to work with.

If I make it worth his while he will want to join in and play with me

If he has fun he will like schooling more

These two can be taken together. Why ride a bored, reluctant horse when you can have an enthusiastic one? If your horse is a different character in the school from the one you know when you're hacking, change something in the school! Variety works both mentally and physically – it supples the body and refreshes the mind. As we saw in the section 'Loose-schooling with Nikki and Ollie' in Chapter 8, even a 'serious dressage horse' benefits from working over cavalletti, loose-schooling over jumps and hacking out: they help him use his hind legs actively and swing through his back, and the enjoyment he feels when he's using his body energetically helps build the forwardness and elasticity the judges are looking for in competitions. This kind of forward thinking is something I notice when I judge eventing dressage – no cramped, over-rehearsed, cautious, behind-the-leg movement there!

Horses live life in the moment, but with long memories! Events, places, objects and people all carry associations of pleasure, discomfort, sometimes even distress, based on past experience around them. (Sometimes the connections are obvious, but sometimes the thing that triggers fear, resistance or pleasure may have been quite irrelevant – in this instance, there are parallels with the motivation that may lead a competitor may wear a 'lucky hat' into a state of total shabbiness because she once won a class whilst wearing it! Through a similar 'illogical logic', your horse's anxiety might be triggered by a 'background' feature of a stressful situation – even if the situation itself isn't repeating.)

If your horse is reluctant or lethargic when you head for the school, though, it's usually a comment on what he associates with being in there. Like the rest of his behaviour, this is free, valuable information – feedback you can use. Why not break down that dour expectation by having fun in the school and, like Roy, schooling outside it?

Riding is a conversation – if it isn't two-way, it's a lecture

If you listen to riders describing their schooling, you'll often hear words like 'tell' and 'ask'. *'He didn't do what I told him.' 'He found it hard to do what I asked him.'* But you don't often hear, *'He let me know that...' 'He wanted me to...'* You might

Maxim | how you think shapes what you do

hear someone saying: '*We had an argument about that*', but rarely: '*We negotiated our way out of that*'. It isn't always easy – or comfortable – to take your horse's behaviour as his way of 'telling' or 'asking' you something – but if you can be that honest with yourself it will really pay dividends. I'm not suggesting that you try to please your horse all the time: he's naturally programmed to prefer spending all day moving about gently grazing with his mates, and work of any kind isn't part of that in-built agenda! But since we have chosen to use horses for our purposes rather than theirs we have a responsibility to make it worth their while in emotional as well as physical terms.

This is something the great riders know and strive to do. As I mentioned in Chapter 8, under Arthur Kottas' direction the Spanish Riding School's Lipizzaners were regularly loose-schooled and loose-jumped – for elasticity, variety and sheer fun.

If I start where my horse is, I stand a better chance of taking him with me

This is a maxim that you can put into practice every time you are with your horse and every time you ride. 'Starting where your horse is' means trying to understand how his world is to him – especially today. What impact has the departure of his next-door neighbour to a new yard made on him? Is he grumpy or off-colour? Maybe he's missing his friend. Some years ago we loaned out our first horse, Tristan, and he went away for some months. The arrangement didn't work; nor did the next one. It was over a year later that he returned to our yard. It was summer, and we put him out in the field with our other horse, Lolly, for company. They hadn't been great friends as far as we knew, though they had hacked and schooled together many times. So we were surprised, and moved, to see the obvious delight they took in being with each other again. Had Lolly mourned when Tris went away? I don't know – but I certainly noticed the general depression among the horses in the barn when Lolly died last year.

Another example is the way your horse reacts to any changes in routine (for example, when you go on holiday, or when new people come to work at the yard). Routines help horses feel secure. Again, it's best not to make automatic assumptions, but to ensure that you monitor their responses and take them into account when you assess how your horse is going. If he's wound up next time you school him, it may be because he's uneasy with the new helper on the yard, rather than reacting to the weather, or the horses in the next field. Some horses seem more or less unaffected by things like this but, for others, they can have a significant impact.

Take ongoing patterns into account, too: just because they're a feature of life in the yard doesn't necessarily mean they work for all its inhabitants. For example, many yards leave a radio playing on the assumption that background sound is reassuring. But have you checked the horses' expressions and behaviour to make sure that they all actively like this? Some may dislike but tolerate this (for them) quite unnatural 'noise pollution' and learn to 'switch off'. Others may be irritated, but of course unable to do anything about it. A good look at their body language will let you know which are which – then you may have some decisions to make. Personally, I think it's better to give horses the opportunity of making their own decisions about whether to doze or do something when they're in their box: perhaps by providing footballs or pony-nut containers that they can roll about if and when they wish, giving them a stimulus *they* each can control.

And when you get on and ride, do you begin by wandering off round the school or down the lane doing your obligatory warm-up with your mind in neutral, or chatting with your friends? Or do you take these minutes as a really valuable opportunity to tune in with how your horse is *today*? Think of meeting a really good friend: even if you saw her yesterday, it's likely that part of those first moments of reconnecting will involve information-gathering, not just about what you've each been up to since then, but how you're both feeling. Much of this information comes, not through what is actually said, but through body language, expression, and tone of voice.

As a coach, I've learnt to use the first minutes of any working session for this kind of information-gathering: I'm asking myself, '*Where is my client starting from today?*' I know from experience that if I can start where she is, I can begin to sense what potential and direction our work could have today – and take her with me. You are your horse's coach, and you can do just the same. Ask yourself how he is, and what that rules in and out for today's riding conversation together. Is he stiff? Does he seem tired? Is he fizzy? Is he dying to get his muscles moving? Is he listening – or is he in flight mode, spooky and twitchy, attention everywhere and elsewhere? Assuming that you did your personal 'baggage-dump' before you got on him, see pages 132–3, this is your chance to dovetail with him. And when you dovetail and the fit is right, you can suggest appropriate things to do together, and you can make the most of today's conversation.

Thinking differently

You will solve most problems more easily by thinking 'outside the box'. In other words, think and do something *different!*

Usually, the very way you frame a problem in your thinking sets limits to how you go about trying to solve it. Have you come across the nine-dots puzzle?

Maxim | how you think shapes what you do

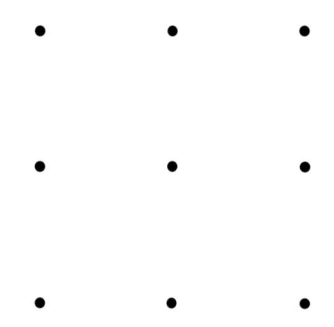

Join all the dots using just four straight lines

Most people get stuck because they *assume* that they have to stay within the (imaginary) boundary created by the square outer shape of the puzzle. They make an assumption – and literally box themselves in! This is where the phrase 'thinking outside the box' actually came from – because the solution is to go *outside the box*. Here it is:

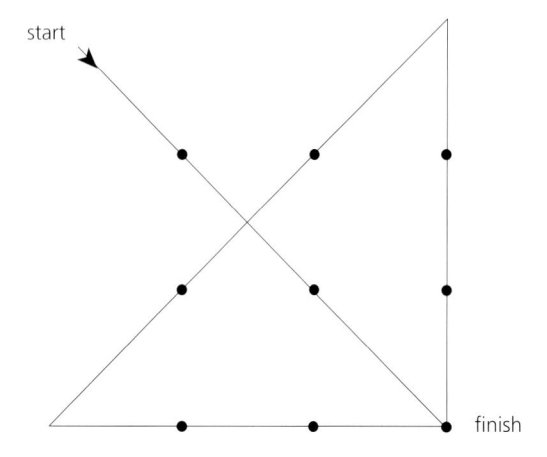

A good way of telling when it's time to think 'outside the box' is when you find yourself trying to solve a problem by repeating an attempted solution. If it didn't work the first time, the chances are you need to think again – and think *differently!* Let's suppose your horse isn't going forward enough. Your first thought may be to use your legs more strongly. Still no response – use your whip. Still no response – put on your spurs. This is thinking '*inside* the box', because the attempted solutions are all of the same kind. You are amplifying the signal strength – but it's still the same signal. And the assumption behind it is something like: 'He isn't listening. *So I'll shout louder.*'

Once you recognize this and go 'outside the box', other causes, and other solutions, may suggest themselves. Maybe he tired himself out in the field yesterday?

Maxim | how you think shapes what you do

Maybe it's time his saddle was checked? Maybe he needs more feed, or different feed, or a supplement?

Sometimes the horse himself has to be shown that he can venture outside his own 'box'. At a clinic given by an international judge/trainer I saw two examples of this. One was a green but nice-natured Spanish horse who just wouldn't go forward. The trainer realized, after a few minutes, that the horse was holding himself back, probably because of the strange venue and the presence of an audience. Rather than asking the (professional) rider to attempt any 'dressage', he got her to ride with a light seat, gently waving her whip near the horse, but without touching him. For this horse, the whole lesson consisted of learning that he was permitted to go forward and that in these circumstances that was enough to earn him praise. He was being asked to come out of the 'box' of physical tightness self-created by his emotional caution.

The other example was my friend Nikki's horse, Ollie, who is much more widely experienced but who also tends to 'hold' himself when he's on show. Nikki and the trainer both felt that he was doing this during the lesson. Given that Ollie is working at Medium level, trainers thinking 'inside the box' might have chosen to focus the lesson on bending work at that level (for example, lateral movements). This trainer, however, thought outside the 'box' of the level Ollie was working at, and instead went back to basics. He asked Nikki to come to halt and ask Ollie gently for a big bend first to one side and then to the other, just as if she were asking him to do carrot stretches in his box. After some minutes of this Ollie gave a great big sigh and relaxed into the bend, willingly yielding his whole neck and body. For Ollie, the trainer's decision to use a very simple exercise that Ollie could do easily, instead of one he and his rider associate with 'work', 'performance' and 'trying hard', had taken the pressure off. So Ollie came outside whatever mental and physical 'boxes' were involved in being schooled away from home with a different trainer and a gallery full of spectators. When they went back to 'proper dressage' after this, Ollie took his softness, suppleness and ability to relax with him. He had come out of his 'box' – because the trainer had first come out of *his* and shown him the way.

Chunking down

When you see dressage performed well, at whatever level, it seems effortless. Arthur Kottas says, 'If it looks easy, it's well done.' But the ease is achieved through many small steps and many repetitions, and most new learning is easier if it's broken down into small chunks. To illustrate this, let's analyse something as apparently simple as a circle in trot. A good one, even at Novice level, is distinguished by balance and self-carriage, bending along the line of the circle, a clear

V-shape as each diagonal pair of legs meets the ground, and an unfaltering, almost mesmerizing rhythm.

To get to this point, however, is a different matter! Let's list briefly what's involved in achieving each of these ingredients. I've put them in a different order below because, though the effortless balance is probably what catches your eye when you're observing it, it's actually the result of having the others in place. Remember the Scales of Training...

- **Rhythm** – this is inherent in the horse, but needs to be cultivated, guarded and regulated by the rider. You have first to recognize your horse's signature rhythm, then ensure that you ask for it, match it with your own movements, respect it and work with it always, whatever you're doing and wherever you're doing it.

- **Clear V-shape** – the V-shape comes from engagement; it happens when the horse is bending his hind legs and using them actively to step under himself. It happens when he's 'in front of the leg'. If there's a gap between the diagonal hind and forefeet then he isn't engaged enough. Engagement comes from thinking, and going, forward – without losing balance and running onto the forehand.

- **Balance and self-carriage** – all of our training should be aimed at helping the horse carry himself in better balance as he progressively builds his muscles and learns to take more weight on his quarters. Balance at Novice level doesn't look the same as balance at Advanced. It's easier, too, for a horse to carry himself in balance on a large circle than a small one – which is why the size of the circle required in tests gets smaller as you go up the levels. Balance means that the horse's quarters don't spin out behind, nor do his shoulders pop out in front. It means that he doesn't fall in and lean like a motor bike, using the rider's legs to hold him up. To achieve it, we need to get him used to rebalancing through frequent transitions and changes of direction. Every transition you make, every corner you turn, can be a small step on the way. Or, of course, it can also be an opportunity missed. Or, worse, letting it slip by just one time can confuse your horse and erode what you've been working hard to achieve at other times.

- **Bending** along the line of the circle – bending is about carriage and engagement as well as about flexibility. They all help each other out. Sometimes you have to prioritize one above another in your training. For example, Bertie seemed unwilling to bend through his body and tended to fall in, especially on the right rein. But this problem disguises a deeper one – he is built a little 'downhill' and finds it hard to engage and carry himself. Our friend Nikki showed us some useful exercises for supporting and controlling Bertie's shoulders and getting him to engage more: once these have helped him engage and he can carry himself regularly more 'uphill' like this, he will be able to bend more easily through the body rather than just in the neck. It's a question of bit by bit…

Assumptions are an essential tool for living. Like any other tool, though, they can help us most when we know their capabilities and can use them in the right places, because every assumption has its history, and its consequences.

Good balance on a novice horse.

Ambrose is stepping well under his body. His face is a little behind the vertical but he is carrying his head on well-defined top-line muscles rather than 'propping it up' from underneath.

At the start of this leg-yield, Carolyn's well-stretched right leg is encouraging Ambrose to step across and under his body. Her upper body posture, deep seat and softly 'framing' elbows are helping him carry himself in balance.

Maxim | how you think shapes what you do

- What assumptions are you making in your riding?

- Where did they come from?

- What's the evidence you have for making them?

- Where are they getting you?

- Are they serving you well – or are there any changes you need to make?

Tips for trainers

- What assumptions are you making about horses and, especially, about the way they learn? How do these help you and your clients? Might there be any ways in which your assumptions limit you, or them?

- What assumptions are you making about your clients? Do you assume that they need – and expect – your detailed comments and guidance throughout the lesson, or to be 'pushed' or 'stretched' to try harder, achieve more, or enter competitions? What are the positive consequences of such assumptions – and what might be the disadvantages?

- What assumptions are you making about your role as a trainer? What do you think being a trainer requires of you? For example, do you assume that you should be able to ride your clients' horses better than they can? Do you believe you should help them through difficulties by sorting the horses out for them when they hit a problem? Does this ever result in you getting irritated because clients become dependent on you? Or when they can't seem to 'get it'? Or if they get it this week – but lose it again before the next lesson…?

- What messages do you think your assumptions are implicitly conveying to your clients, and what effects do you think this is having on them and their horses?

Maxim | how you think shapes what you do

12 Self-belief, self-talk and rehearsal

> Events are lived the way we interpret them. Life, essentially, is lived in our minds.
>
> **Charles de Kunffy,** *Dressage Principles Illuminated*[1]

In the previous chapter I invited you to identify the assumptions you bring to your riding, and to consider the effects these may have on your thoughts and actions. Now, I want to move on to the related but deeper question of what you believe about yourself. It is because riding engages us at a level that is both deep and comprehensive that it can bring out both the best and the worst in each of us! From a positive viewpoint, this is why Paul Belasik can say: *'In the right concentration your whole being is listening.'*[2] Equally, though, we need to bear in mind something else he says: *'...the biggest challenges are always self-made. The escape, therefore, must not be from the trap but from the dangerous process of building the trap for yourself.'*[3]

In this chapter I'm going to start with the traps that you can make for yourself, and show you how you can escape from them. These traps are the traps of negative self-belief. The escapes are offered by recognizing, changing and liberating self-belief. Then I'm going to look at two powerful processes that often play a part in both: self-talk and mental rehearsal. Like most mental processes, these are neither good nor bad in themselves, but their effects can be limiting, damaging and depressing or liberating, healing and uplifting. The trick is in recognizing the nature of the process and learning how to use it as a tool that can help you.

Maxim | how you think shapes what you do

Self-belief

What kind of a rider are you?

amateur	professional	experienced
newcomer	all-rounder	specialist
owner	sharer	have lessons
pretty skilled	happy hacker	competent
trainer	anxious	confident
prefer experimenting	prefer being taught	still learning
got as far as I can go	at my best	plateauing out
better than many people	not as good as my trainer	good match for my horse
my horse deserves better	happy how I am	

You can probably add other categories, and I'm sure you will have ticked several – mentally if not with an actual pen – as you read through the list. The point I want to make about this is that whatever experience we have, and whatever level of skill we have achieved, every one of us will hold beliefs about what that involves; what it makes easy, possible, difficult or impossible; whether we can progress further or have reached our ceiling... and so on. And as I've explained before, what we believe is a powerful shaper not only of what we actually do but also of what we *may be able to do*. Belief, in other words, often becomes self-fulfilling.

It's important to recognize that believing in something doesn't necessarily mean it is true – you could actually say that belief often involves going beyond what's provable. There are some things you *know*, and you will use different ways of expressing yourself when you talk about them. 'I know they're shut on Mondays' is not the same as 'I believe they're shut on Mondays.' It's unlikely you'd hear anyone say, 'I believe it's Christmas tomorrow' or 'I believe my name is Susie.' But when you say, 'I'm not good enough' (to compete at a higher level, for example), you are expressing what is actually a belief as if it were a fact. And when you treat something – especially something negative – as a fact it tends to become one!

What you believe will lead on to what you assume. And, as we know, assumptions are often powerful but unrecognized shapers of experience. Self-limiting beliefs have self-limiting results. If you believe, for example, that being a pupil means you are less competent than your teacher (a common, but not always accurate, belief), then you may approach your horse and your work together as *someone who is less than competent*. As Roy found when I asked him to 'ride like Marion' (his trainer), his level of skill shot up and Cori responded accordingly. (See Chapter 16 for the full story.) This has to mean that, for some of the time at least, Roy is underperforming! If you are a trainer yourself, and you believe you have to demonstrate greater skill than your pupils, what kind of pressures does this put you under? It could help you produce your best – but it could also lead you to over-ride and over-teach.

The teacher-knows-better mind-set that many pupils and teachers share can easily result in pupils becoming dependent and much less resourceful than they need be. Carolyn put it admirably clearly in her reflection on our case-study sessions together: '*I'd become stuck in a way of riding that I didn't feel able to get out of: trainer tells me exactly how to ride, leg here, hands here, weight there, I do it and hey presto it works!* **Wait until next week's training session to be able to get it again**.' [My emphasis]

What had been happening here was that the rider and trainer were unwittingly colluding in building a rider dependency on the trainer that effectively disempowered the rider when she was on her own. This is a very common occurrence! We could put it another way by saying that their assumptions dovetailed with one another: the trainer assumed that she was (and perhaps also has to be) better than the rider and so needed to show her what to do; the rider assumed that she needed the trainer to tell her what's good and bad and what she should change – and probably because of this didn't learn to feel how her horse was going and make these judgements for herself. Even more importantly, though, the rider became confirmed in believing that she was not fully capable or independent. This goes against one of the fundamental aims of good teaching, which is to make the pupil *less* dependent on the teacher.

When Roy found how much better he could ride when he 'rode like Marion', it had profound effects on his self-belief. He had shown himself, in front of witnesses (Marion herself, my husband Leo and me) that he had the ability to ride with a level of effectiveness and style that matched his hopes and aspirations. Shortly afterwards, he went to watch international dressage at Wembley. 'I saw those riders and I thought "*I can do all those things!*"', he said. Roy's basic issue in riding and competing changed dramatically after that. It was no longer a matter of whether he could ride better and get Cori to work in a more advanced way: instead, it was about whether they were living up to what we all knew they were capable of *already*. When they had slightly disappointing scores in a competition just after Christmas, Roy explained that as Christmas is always one of the busiest times of year in his business he should have known he would be tired: 'I'll avoid competing at that time next year', he said. Where such a disappointment would have given many riders (including Roy himself in the past) a knock in confidence, this time he wasn't left doubting his ability – only feeling realistic about how tiredness could prevent him from living up to it.

Many people under-perform quite substantially in competition. I suspect that

Maxim | how you think shapes what you do

one cause is what they believe about judges' levels of knowledge and skill. Unless the judge is a competitor herself, her level of ability is usually *assumed* rather than actually *witnessed* by competitors but, for many riders, being judged is, in itself, enough to trigger a mind-set that leads to under-performance. For other riders, of course, the reverse can be true: being visible is, for them, an opportunity to show off their lovely horse and produce their best work. I remember being asked by my trainer to 'demonstrate' a movement to another of her pupils who couldn't do it. Even though I was quite novicy myself at the time, the word 'demonstrate' was enough to help me produce my best performance!

Let's take another topic that involves belief. Many riders believe they *ought* to compete. Some *want* to compete. Others actually *like* competing. What differences do you think these beliefs might make to their ability to compete effectively and to achieve the level of work of which they are technically capable? Many riders stick to Preliminary or Novice – for years! They think of themselves as 'a Novice/Preliminary/Elementary rider' and label their horses likewise. Even those who are confident enough to have a crack at higher levels may remain unaffiliated: they somehow believe that affiliating is some kind of boasting, which then has to be lived up to. For them, it feels like making a statement about *themselves*. However, the Finnish Olympic rider and trainer, Kyra Kyrklund, makes use of predictive thinking in the opposite way – to get the most from her horses. At a judges' demonstration, she explained that, even with the youngest and least experienced horses in training, she thinks about what they need to be able to do at Grand Prix – even if she knows they will never reach this level. Thinking *as if that's where they're going* helps her to train them in the right way, and it also ensures that they develop as far as they are capable of.

> How are you 'pegging' your horse in terms of his current, and future, levels of work? Is it easy, or difficult, to think of yourselves performing comfortably at a higher level? What sets a limit to your thinking and your aspirations? Are limiting assumptions, unfortunate experiences, or remembered criticisms playing a part?

Another factor that can affect your self-belief is whether you truly 'own' a goal for yourself. If you do something because you want to, your heart will be in what you do: action and belief ('I really want to do it, I like it') go together and will help you do your best. If you do something without really wanting to but because you believe you *ought* to – or because *someone else* important to you believes you ought to – then there's a dislocation within yourself: your beliefs, emotions and actions are not congruent (all of a piece) with each other. This can lay you open to self-doubt or anxiety and lead to a tentative performance.

What are your beliefs about yourself as a rider, and about what you can achieve?

> Thinking about my riding, I believe....
>
> The effect this has is...

> Thinking about competing, I believe...
>
> The effect this has is...

Self-belief can affect how you deal with successes and set-backs. In competition, the 'window for winning' is small! I hope that by now you will be more equipped to know how to evaluate for yourself how your horse is going, how he is progressing up the training spiral, and whether, in any competition, you and he were going as well as you could – whatever mark you actually attained. If you can approach competitions in the belief that you and your horse both start with the best of intentions and will do as well as you can *in the circumstances*, then even if you don't do as well as you know you can, you will be cushioned against possible knocks to your self-esteem. A less-than-ideal performance may disappoint you, but it won't make you feel less worthwhile *as a person or as a partnership*.

One of the easiest ways to undermine your self-belief is by dwelling on a failure or mistake and generalizing from it. For example, *'I never can get him straight on that centre line'; 'He's always falling in on the right rein'; 'I make such an effort to learn the test but somehow I don't remember it once I'm in the arena'*. Even if it is true that your centre lines often wobble, that he is stiff to the right and that you tend to forget the test because you're anxious, generalizing these events into statements like those above will make you feel bad, tend to get built in to how you think of yourself and your horse, and so become predictive. While you're in the arena, the art is to accept, deal with and put aside mistakes that arise (see Chapter 13) and, afterwards, use them as potential feedback to help you review and, if necessary, redirect your schooling and preparation. In other words, do the opposite of generalizing: view each event as a one-off that needs one-off treatment.

A good way to destabilize the effect of generalizations on self-belief is to 'reality test' them by having a conversation with yourself.

Maxim | how you think shapes what you do

It might go something like this:

'I'm not as good a rider as my friend at the yard.'

'Never?'

'Well, perhaps there are some times... Or maybe the way I do xxx is better than the way she does it.'

'Really? So can you honestly say you're not as good a rider as she is?'

'Sometimes I'm as good – like those times when...'

While generalization often makes you feel less resourceful and able than you are, the great thing is that the same process can also work in your favour – provided you generalize from the right things!

How to construct and use truthful and helpful generalizations about yourself.

1. Jot down as rapidly as you can all the favourable comments you can remember having received about yourself as a rider in one list, and about your horse in another.

2. Now scan each list to discover any themes that emerge – for example, *'good balance'*, *'sympathetic riding'*… *'tries hard'*, *'forward-thinking'*.

3. Write a brief sentence about each theme on a separate sheet, beginning:

   I am someone who usually/always…
   My horse usually/always…
   The best thing about my riding is…
   The best thing about my horse is…
   We are good at…

4. Pin these statements in places where you will notice them regularly. If you are embarrassed to put them where other people may see them, write them at intervals in your diary, perhaps one per week, repeating when you reach the end of your list. Choose one as a screen saver; paste one inside your tack box…

5. If you are embarrassed at the thought of anyone else seeing, ask yourself what you are anticipating happening as a result. Is it so likely, or so bad?

Maxim | how you think shapes what you do

- Think back over your riding, and your life in general, and recall at least three times when you felt how you would like to feel more of the time (e.g. calm, confident, in control, having fun, etc.).

- Take a few minutes to sit quietly on your own and remember one event in detail. Make use of as many of your senses as you can (sight, hearing, feeling, smell and taste) to recreate a rich experience in your mind. What differences do you notice in how you feel now, both emotionally and physically?

- Go through this mental experience several times, and find where it feels at its most intense. Is there a detail, or a word or phrase you can give to that peak moment of the experience, that will act as a trigger to bring it back, together with the sense of self it calls up, whenever you want it?

- Practise using your trigger as a short-cut into the experience. To increase the calming and self-enhancing effects, you might find it helpful to start by taking a deep breath, and let it out again slowly as you use your trigger. At first, use your trigger in neutral and non-horsy moments. When you know you can do this reliably and easily, begin to do it just before you ride, when you first get on, at the start of something new or difficult, when things go wrong...

How to build resourceful memories and link them to resourceful and confident mind-body states.

Self-talk

Most people talk to themselves. We may 'talk ourselves through' something complex, encourage ourselves, tell ourselves off, remind ourselves about something, or make a running commentary about what's going on. Often, we do this without realizing it – and that's why we don't realize, either, how profound an effect this self-talk can be having. Because, when we talk to ourselves, we are also the ones listening! You could say that this is the original form of subliminal perception – we take in what we're saying, and it can affect us deeply, without our realizing that anything of the kind is happening. The same goes for the way we see

Maxim | how you think shapes what you do

ourselves. Many competitors will be running a put-down commentary as they ride a test, or watching themselves critically in a corner of their minds. *'Just look at that – what a mess. How unbalanced. Now he's against the hand. Just what our trainer is always on about. I bet the judge just gave that a 4. She's probably wondering why I bother to bring him at all.'*

Where judges have been critical in the past, the wounds they unintentionally inflicted by their comments can be kept open for years in our memories. I say 'be kept' rather than 'remain' because we have a hand in this. Every time we mentally revisit that devastating test sheet and replay the test that gave rise to it, we keep the pain, the self-limiting beliefs and the critical self-talk alive a bit longer. As a judge, I try to remember this possibility when writing my comments – but I also know that riders can and do self-limit without help from me!

One paradoxical reason why people set their sights low, and remind themselves of their limitations, is in order to protect themselves from pain and disappointment. If you have already seen and said the worst about yourself, the assumption goes, you won't be surprised or disappointed by what someone else says. Of course this is true in a way, but the price you pay for not being disappointed is that you less often get to feel confident, or hopeful!

However, you don't have to go on being your own victim like this. When I first met Shane on one of my 'Make a Difference' clinics several years ago, she told me how anxious she became when doing dressage: as an eventer she needed to do it, but she hated being watched and felt very self-conscious. Not surprisingly, she and Ted went through the motions but lacked harmony and fluency, and their scores were disappointing. In doing our case-study sessions together, it was my hope that Shane could come to believe that dressage was no longer an outlandish, ill-fitting garment she had to get into from time to time, but an elegant, comfortable outfit she could put on and feel at home in whenever she chose. Knowing that whatever Shane believed would also get through to Ted, I wanted to help bring about a change in her beliefs about herself. At the end of our seventh session, in which she tried (and achieved) shoulder-in for the first time (see photo on page 256), Shane let slip that she was going to be presented that evening with her Riding Club's prize – not just for having won the most points in the season at showjumping (which surprised no one) *but also for dressage!* And when she talked a few minutes later about her aims for the year, I wasn't surprised that they included achieving fluency in all the basic movements needed for eventing dressage. Shane was still thinking of herself as an eventer – but an eventer whose skills could and would naturally include dressage. She had learnt some new skills in our session together but, even more importantly, she had started to think about herself, and talk to herself, differently.

Maxim | how you think shapes what you do

Learning to talk to yourself more helpfully

Using your head and eye positioning to tune in and tune out

Given that self-talk is so common, perhaps the first step to ensuring that it works in your favour is to learn how to switch it on and off! Within the last thirty years or so it has been discovered that there's a predictable correlation between the way people are thinking and two externally observable things: the way they position their head and the direction in which their eyes are looking. It isn't yet known exactly how this happens, let alone why, but there is plenty of evidence to show that the connection exists reliably. Since looking ahead with your eyes defocused will automatically connect you with your unconscious, broad-beam processing, you can use this as a deliberate way of making that connection. There's another automatic behaviour you can make use of, too. When someone is having an internal discussion with themselves they tend to glance down and to their left and to tilt their head towards their left shoulder (see illustration).

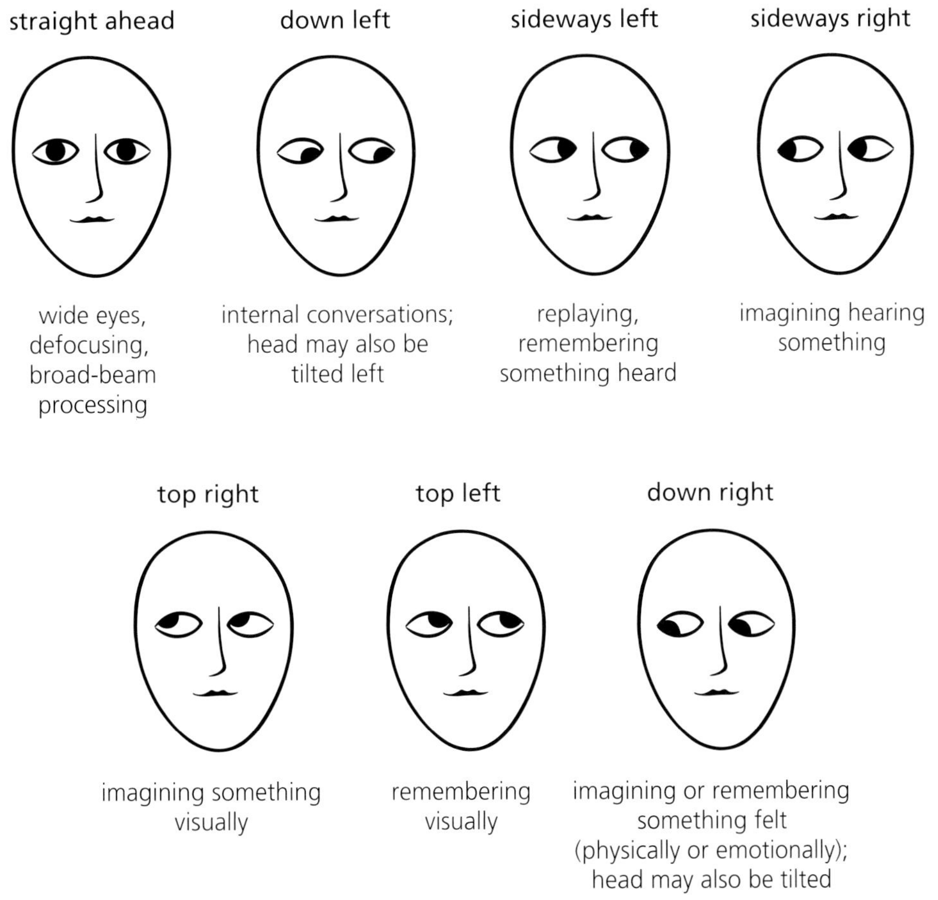

straight ahead — wide eyes, defocusing, broad-beam processing

down left — internal conversations; head may also be tilted left

sideways left — replaying, remembering something heard

sideways right — imagining hearing something

top right — imagining something visually

top left — remembering visually

down right — imagining or remembering something felt (physically or emotionally); head may also be tilted

Eye positioning clues and cues. These eye positions (where you look) reveal the type of mental processing you are using (clues) and can also be used to stimulate particular kinds of processing at will (cues).

Maxim | how you think shapes what you do

If you find yourself in an internal conversation that feels unhelpful, your first step may simply be to change your head or eye position. For example, defocus, or straighten the alignment of your head. As you do so, ask yourself: *'Whose voice am I hearing?'*

When people tune in to internal conversations, they may be listening to their own voice – or to that of someone who is, or has been, important to them. Riders may, for example, be hearing their trainers' comments. If critical, these can have undermining effects: *'You don't seem to remember how important it is to keep your hands level'*; if encouraging, they can be supportive: *'You've improved so much – just go in there and enjoy it and you'll surprise yourself by how well you do.'* Clearly, you want to be able to choose to hear what is useful to you – and you can: it's your private 'radio station' and you can choose which scripts to listen to. It may be important to remember about keeping your hands level – but you want your trainer's reminder to sound as though it's supportive, not belittling.

Perhaps as you've been reading this you have already begun to identify what you're broadcasting to yourself. Or you may find you need some quiet time to think it through. It can be helpful to jot down the comments that you play the most – and then decide what you want to do about them. Comments from the past can often continue to be powerful long after circumstances have changed. You may still hear your Pony Club teacher, or a competitive friend, telling you how stupid you looked when... Or wondering how anyone could be so careless as to... It may be helpful to imagine tuning out internal voices of this kind (drowning them with white noise for example) or, each time you hear them, saying in a firm voice something like: *'That was then, and I know/do better now.'*

On the other hand, you want to make the most of any helpful comments you have stored internally, so that you can benefit from them at will. What have people said about you or your riding that really gives you a glow when you think of them? We all carry other people's voices with us – make the most of those who value and support you and whose advice you cherish and benefit from. Can you hear them saying such things? Do you feel good when you replay them? Play them often!

Positivity or honesty?

I'm not suggesting that you fake the evidence with a false positivity or try to persuade yourself everything's fine when it isn't. Good friends and good teachers will tell you the truth because they're on your side and have your interests at heart. If you need to work on keeping your hands level, or maintaining rhythm, or keeping your lower leg stiller, it does you no favours to let you go on in ignorance thinking everything's fine. What you need is a rich range of feedback on how you're doing: knowing what is good and what has improved gives you the heart to tackle what isn't yet as good as it could be. Replay the encouragement *along with* the points that need improving.

Take your mentors with you

Supportive voices in your head can be a powerful help to you in many situations. You don't have to restrict yourself to the comments of people you know, or even to things actually said. As a coach, I have often been told that in some tricky moment one of my clients asked herself, *'Now what would Wendy have to say about that?'* Through our working together, they have come to know the kind of thing I'd say, to the extent that they can invent the kind of comment I'd make, even in circumstances we have never talked about! What does this tell me? That in some way I have become an internal mentor whom my client carries around with her. It's not really a question of guessing what I'd say, it's a question of having taken my principles and values on board and being able to work from them – *for herself*. Rather than being a form of dependence, it's actually an enriched form of *independence*.

> Who are the internal mentors you'd like to have with you when you're riding and competing? In what ways would their internal presence be helpful to you?

Remember, too, that you will have internalized the way some of your mentors behave as well as how they sound and what they say. Think of the riders you most admire: do you already 'take them with you' when you ride? And if you don't yet do this, how can you begin to feel your horse as they would feel him, react to him as they would react and, as you partner him, produce your own performance – but with the additional qualities they would produce?

Rehearsal

This leads me on to the final theme of this chapter: how you can make use of your own imagination to help 'set up' the best riding you are capable of. Of course, this can have a particular value when you are going to compete, but I'd like you to think of this as something that can help your riding all the time, not just on special occasions.

Many years ago, an experiment was carried out that involved helping basketball players shoot more goals; and it became famous among psychologists and trainers because it demonstrated something very interesting: rehearsing something in your mind can improve your actual performance just as much as 'real-life' rehearsal. The group of basketball players who spent time imagining shooting goals improved just as much as the group who practised with real balls on real courts. Why can this happen? Because, when we imagine something intensely, we are actually creating and then deepening the mind-body pathways that are involved. So after we have rehearsed something mentally, we naturally find ourselves performing the physical actions more fluently and with greater skill and accuracy. Mental rehearsal helps us give our best performances – sometimes better ones than we had thought ourselves capable of.

Many outstanding performers in different sports have discovered this, and it's become a regular part of sports psychology and sports coaching. Annie found this a help in getting the best performances from her spooky partner, Red (see Chapter 16). In her feedback notes she said:

> *My dressage results have improved during my lessons with Wendy. I think about keeping calm and relaxed and not suddenly changing and pulling up the reins as you turn up the centre line! I can concentrate on looking like a dressage rider. Before the competition I ride the test over in my head, visualizing how I'm going to prepare for different aspects of the movements. Red has never been an easy horse: he is very excitable and loses concentration easily, especially at competitions. I now feel that due to me being calmer… he concentrates and listens to me much better.*

'He concentrates and listens to me much better.'
Annie and Red.

Maxim | how you think shapes what you do

- First, you want to build up a really rich, multi-sensory impression of everything that's going to be involved. To start with, begin with something you already know a fair amount about – for example, the kinds of things you are expecting to do and how you would like your horse to go in your next schooling session or lesson with your trainer. Remind yourself of what will be involved: where you'll be, what you'll be doing, what skills you'll be using or developing. It will help you to build a rich, multi-sensory impression of these, involving what you are likely to see, hear, feel (maybe also smell and taste). I'd like you, though, to go beyond these and include some of the things we've been exploring earlier in this chapter. What values and principles will you be working from? What kinds of belief about yourself, your horse, and your abilities will you be taking there with you?

    This kind of information-gathering is your first step. Now you need to get it working actively for you.

- Now, think of this future session/lesson as a scenario. How would you like it to go? Create your own mental 'story-board' as if you were directing a film. This is your chosen narrative. Adjust the sights, sounds, feelings and behaviour, together with your priorities, self-belief and self-talk, until you are satisfied with them. Did you include your internal mentors? Give yourself time to run this scenario more than once in privacy and quiet. Now build in some less-than-perfect moments – together with the coping strategies you'd like to use. What if your horse spooks, for example? Manage that imagined spook better than you ever thought you could.

> How can you use mental rehearsal to improve the results you get?

Run your scenario several times between now and your next riding session. Notice what happens as a result. What was different? What stayed the same? If you are disappointed, ask yourself what you left out, or failed to take into account. Remember, there is no such thing as 'failure': if you didn't get what you wanted, you need to make some adjustments. Maybe you forgot something important. Maybe nobody could have anticipated that *that* (whatever it was) would happen. Maybe you didn't realize just what assumptions you were taking in there with you...

Maxim | how you think shapes what you do

> Use this kind of mental rehearsal for different sorts of everyday or frequent events in your life. Get familiar with doing it, and comfortable with your ability to adapt it and learn from it. Only when you are, will it be fair to yourself to put it to the test with things that are more crucial, such as competitions (or job interviews, or family crises...).

Your mind is an amazing asset – and we all know that it can also be a liability! No one manages their mind perfectly all the time, but we can all benefit from its incredible abilities once we know how to work with it. And the first step we can take is to regard it as a friend we can learn to trust and rely upon.

Tips for trainers

- **Remember that memorable phrases get remembered!** Whether you intend it or not, you are recorded on your clients' mental audiotapes! They will be hearing your voice in their heads – is it saying things that are helpful and supportive? Or critical and negative? This is not about your *intent* but about the *effect* that you have. Try to listen to yourself as you teach, and hear yourself with your clients' ears. If you feel honest and bold, ask a client with whom you have a good rapport which of your comments have been most helpful to her – and which have not. Would you be pleased to hear what you are saying inside her head?

- **Sometimes you will be creating your effect through what you do not say just as much as what you do.** If you mostly draw attention (as some judges do also) to what your client has got wrong and needs to improve, your effect will be negative and could be undermining your client's self-belief, even though your intention is to use your expertise to help her ride better. What effect is the drip, drip, dripping of your comments likely to be having over time?

- **Have you found a way to be honest about what your client needs to improve without knocking her self-esteem?** It's mistaken kindness to tell your client things are fine when they're not. However, make sure you tell her what is good and what works as well as what needs improvement, and be as specific as you can about any changes she needs to make and how she can make them. This kind of honesty earns trust and actually helps strengthen the rapport between trainer and pupil. This way, when she hears your voice in her head it will be informative *and* supportive.

Maxim | how you think shapes what you do

SELF-BELIEF, SELF-TALK AND REHEARSAL • 177

- **Train yourself to notice what kind of self-belief and self-talk your client is operating on.** We all give away our beliefs and assumptions through what we say and how we say it. As a professional, you can develop your sensitivity to this and invite your clients to expand on what they may be *implying* rather than actually *stating*. Sometimes they won't have realized just how much they are limiting themselves – and their horses. *'Of course, since he isn't a Warmblood...' 'Because I'm an amateur...' 'I can't really expect to...'* Asking your client sympathetically to explain a bit more fully what she means will often allow her to realize how her thinking is getting in the way, and to begin to find her own route through. Sometimes you may need to be a bit firmer and actually challenge her: gentle teasing can sometimes be a way to show her you are on her side without accepting for a moment that she's as restricted as she thinks! I often find this is a good way to disarm a client's expectations about what she can and can't do. I might say something like: *'And because I know you can already manage five impossible things before breakfast I'm going to be a perfect pest and ask you to do ... as well. As if I hadn't already given you more than enough to think about!'* There is a powerful 'undercover message' here, which a very slight change of my tone of voice will convey to the client without her even realizing it: ...because **I know you can already manage five impossible things before breakfast** *I'm going to...* The message I want her to receive is that I believe she can do it – because she is already highly capable.

The message I want her to receive…she is already highly capable. My unusually still and composed posture, as much as my words, tells Carolyn how well she is doing. It's a posture that clearly shows admiration. My open chest, upright stance, squared shoulders, 'planted' feet, and 'I could watch all day' arms, just as much as my smile, all say: 'That's it! Well done!' I chose this picture because of its expressiveness: on this occasion my body was naturally reflecting how I was feeling, but as trainers we do need to be aware of how much is communicated through our body language, and learn to monitor and use this consciously as well as unconsciously.

Maxim | how you think shapes what you do

section four

Pathways to performance: the strategic skills

Strategies for managing competition nerves	**180**
'Reading' and choosing tests	**194**

13 Strategies for managing competition nerves

> How many of you have ever thought about something that hadn't even happened yet, and felt bad about it ahead of time? Why wait? You may as well start feeling bad now, right? And then it didn't actually happen, after all. But you didn't miss out on that experience, did you?
>
> **Richard Bandler,** *Using Your Brain for a Change*[1]

I have included this chapter in the 'strategic' section of this book because, for so many people, 'nerves' are something they only feel, or feel most acutely, when they are competing. So what's needed is an effective strategy for managing them at that time. In the first half of the chapter I'll be looking at what 'nerves' are. How does each of us actually construct our own recipe for being nervous? I'll show you how understanding your own unique 'recipe for nerves' can be the starting place from which you can begin to change things for the better. In the second half of the chapter, I want to offer you a strategic plan for managing competition which includes every possible layer of your experience. Taken together, these two will give you a comprehensive map of what competition means to you now, and some guidance that will help you pick your way through this potentially difficult territory more effectively and cheerfully.

What nerves mean

What do competition nerves mean for the individual, and how can one cope with them better? This kind of nervousness is a form of performance anxiety, and it's very physical! Actors – even good and famous ones – feel nerves but often say that, without them, they would not perform so well. This is because the physical sensations you feel are the result of increased adrenalin in your system. Your mind has signalled that you need to be alert and ready to cope with a situation that's special, out of the everyday, and demanding both emotionally and physically, so you have automatically gone into flight/fight mode. For good performance, you do actually need that alertness – you need that edge – but you may not need quite as much as you're getting, and you'd certainly be better without the unpleasant and often debilitating side-effects! So the question is how to have enough, but not too much?

Strangely enough, we often feel much the same sensations when we're really excited about something, but we rarely complain about them then! The difference is an important one, and it usually has something to do with our beliefs and feelings about being judged in comparison with others (more of that later in the chapter).

What do nerves mean for you?

Here are some of the most common things that people experience. How many of them occur to you? (There are spaces for any others that are part of your personal 'nerves recipe' – jot them down because you'll need to work strategically on them, too.)

- Dry mouth
- Butterflies in the stomach
- 'Freezing'
- Mind goes blank
- Irritability
- Keep running to the loo
- Imagining the worst – 'what if...?' scenarios
- Wishing you were somewhere else, had a reason to back out
- _____
- _____

You'll see that some of these items are physical and some are mental: the mind-body connection is very noticeable here. I have sometimes monitored the change in myself from calmness to nerves as an event approaches and wondered just what trigger or time-horizon tips me over that edge! I used to be sick before parties when I was little – and before exams. As a shy child, I both looked forward to and dreaded parties, and as a bright one I knew that once an exam started I would

Maxim | there are always alternatives

enjoy rising to the challenge and probably do well. Even knowing this, I couldn't eat beforehand, was sometimes sick and felt totally wound up. Recently, I noticed that although I felt calm anticipation and great enjoyment when trying out new horses with a view to buying one, I was almost paralysed with nerves the first time I rode our chosen one at home! What starts in the mind ends up in the body.

What do your nerves mean for your horse?

We all know how sensitive our horses are to our moods, and how their behaviour tends to reflect what sense they make of us. All too often, this compounds the problem! Your horse may:

- Pick up your feelings and get uptight himself. He won't understand what's worrying you, of course, but he will sense how you are feeling in your physical tension and posture, in your breathing, and in your altered responses to him and to what's going on.

- He is likely to feel that you have abandoned him because you are not giving him the kind of attention he's used to.

- Depending on his nature, he may become 'difficult' or 'naughty' in an attempt to get your full attention back again; or he may defend himself differently by switching off and becoming unresponsive.

- He may get more anxious and spooky – any fears he has about other horses, flags, flowerpots, bustle and charged atmosphere at the competition venue will seem greater to him because he senses you are not fully 'with him', or are less patient with him than usual.

You now have an unfortunate circuit going:

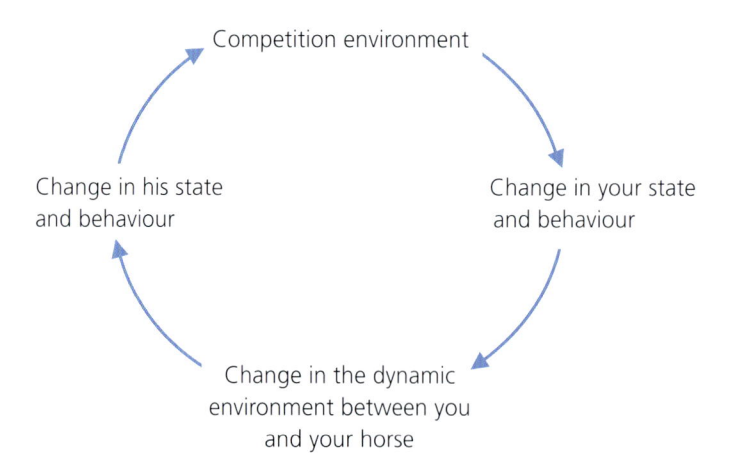

Competition environment → Change in your state and behaviour → Change in the dynamic environment between you and your horse → Change in his state and behaviour → (back to Competition environment)

Maxim | there are always alternatives

What would help you?

Feeling different, of course! Silly question! But unpack this just a bit more, though. Would it help you if you felt more confident? Would it help if you could just stop running those disaster scenarios? Would it help if no one you knew was watching – or if you could remember in the arena all those encouraging and helpful things your trainer says? Or if you could perhaps just mind a little less whether you look like an idiot, or whether you don't get placed...

Since we are all so different, there's no one single answer to this problem. However, the good news is that, once you can understand *how* you construct and run your own personal recipe for nervousness, you will know just where to make the changes you need to improve things. It may not be as simple as taking away the adrenalin-fuelled feelings. For example, in my case exam nerves didn't go away – but I learnt as a teenager that, with the help of dry biscuits, Bovril and a calming gin-and-tonic or two the evening before the exam, I could endure the waiting and feel less sick. Nowadays I'd say that I was able to reframe my anxiety as excitement. I did much the same not long after I started riding dressage, when my riding teacher suddenly asked me one day to ride a young Lipizzaner stallion we had at the yard. On that occasion the sequence went: initial reaction – panic > remind myself this is an amazing opportunity > remind myself that my teacher must think my riding is okay, so why would anything go wrong? > feel really excited > enjoy the ride.

What would help your horse?

Probably the single most important thing that would help him would be if he had your full attention again, so that together you could manage the necessities of the test in the normal way you manage anything else you do together: grooming, lungeing, riding in the school and hacking out. As an experienced duo, you have evolved ways of coping with everyday incidents and environmental encounters (birds flying out of the hedge, tractors, dogs, other horses), so you have a repertoire of coping strategies that work most of the time. It's only when you judge that a situation falls outside the 'normal' that you change – so giving your horse a signal to change in turn.

Charles de Kunffy once said to me that a horse shouldn't think of competition as anything special: '*...even if he's in the Olympics he should think of it as schooling away from home*'. (For more details of our conversations, see my book *Schooling Problems Solved with NLP*.) If you can find a way to think like this and ride accordingly, it will do a lot to restore your confidence and your competence – and it will give your horse the message that, together, you can manage this situation just as you have managed thousands of others in the past.

Maxim | there are always alternatives

As part of this, there will be another important change taking place. If you think of riding in the arena as just another piece of schooling, you will be *riding the horse, not just riding the test*. You will be there with him in the moment but with an alert view both of what's happening around you (that flapping flag, that judge's scribe trying to hold her test sheets flat in the wind, that gaggle of spectators chatting to each other) and to what's coming up next (collect now so he's ready for that transition in the corner, get him stepping under on this half-circle so that he doesn't lose balance and impulsion when we turn to the matching one in the other direction on the centre line). There's no difference, so far as he's concerned, between this and related experiences out hacking. Is that mower going to turn your way when it reaches the end of the field, or is it going to go away from you? Is that cow going to stand up suddenly as you pass? Better slow down and rebalance well before that turn through the gap in the hedge, since the grass is a bit slippery today after last night's rain.

Even when things go wrong in a test – perhaps, *particularly* when things go wrong – having your primary focus on the horse will help you rescue a situation and move on from it better. If he loses balance and breaks into canter – or, being excited, misreads your aid for lengthened strides and revs up a gear – you will be much more effective if you calmly but firmly return to trot again in time to begin the next movement at the right place and in the right gait, than if you're dwelling on the mistake. Compare that with the possible effects of getting caught up in a different kind of thinking: *'That's bound to cost us – probably lose the chance of qualifying – wish I hadn't given such a strong aid – how will we ever get balanced in time for the circle...'* If half your mind is off in the past or the future you've only half a brain left for the here and now. And here-and-now is where it's happening, and where you have the power to influence what happens next.

How you can change things around

However helpless we sometimes feel when our feelings seem to run away with us, there is actually plenty we can do – and the best time to begin turning things around is well before the next time it happens! Here are some skills that people often find helpful.

> **Change your mental and physical state by understanding what goes into your personal 'anxiety recipe'.**

Maxim | there are always alternatives

Though we talk of 'thinking' as if it was the same process for everybody, in fact people do not all do it the same way. Thought involves a number of things: making pictures (visual processing), physical feelings (kinesthetic processing), hearing inside our heads (auditory), sometimes even being aware of smells (olfactory) and tastes (gustatory). If you ever 'hear' a favourite piece of music in your head, picture a place or a face that means a lot to you – or can 'smell' new bread or creosote just by reading these words – you will know what I mean. People tend to favour one or other of these processes more than another: some people find it impossible to make pictures, while easily imagining how something feels. Others produce pictures easily; run mental videos, perhaps even with voice-overs. If you are primarily a picture-maker, your nerves are likely to involve pictures too: movies of past events or visions of what might happen. Telling yourself you shouldn't be so silly isn't likely to change things much, because it's not working within the same processing system. You need to change the pictures, like one rider I worked with who had actually given up riding her horse because she kept visualizing him running away with her. As soon as her internal videotape got to the running away bit, she switched the pictures off – unintentionally reinforcing her own fears. Once she learnt to continue the video, building in some further footage of her stopping the horse and coming safely to a halt again, she was no longer so frightened. And she began to ride again.

Your 'nerves recipe' will also be made up of these components, in your own unique combination. Check which you use most by remembering something you enjoy, like a pleasant holiday or a meeting with friends. Just how are you remembering it? Check out *how* you 'do' nervousness: are you making pictures, hearing a running commentary saying how poorly you are doing, feeling that loss of balance or that hesitation that comes just before he starts to buck…?

Is there a difference between how you do enjoyable thinking and how you do scary thinking? Can you edit in any of the elements that help make the enjoyable thinking so good? Does it help to add in something that isn't there in your nervous thinking – for example, putting an encouraging voice-over on your visual tape?

There is no one recipe that works for everyone – but once you know how you do the bits that don't work well for you and the bits that do, you have the elements to experiment and begin to discover how to make changes for the better.

> **Find, and make more use of, your own experiences of confidence and competence.**

Maxim | there are always alternatives

Virtually everyone feels confident and competent in some areas of their lives. Often, it's something we take for granted. My husband Leo used to say that every woman who runs a home, looks after children's needs and maybe also has a job should automatically be awarded a degree in Business Administration! Yet many women don't think there is anything special in being able to juggle tasks, times and sequencing like this. How would it feel to recognize what a supremely skilled administrator and manager you are – and to be able to carry both the skills and the feeling across into planning for a show and then performing at it? What are your secret skills? Being calm in an emergency? Thinking ahead? Being a problem-solver when you are up against things? Or…? Give yourself a few minutes to appreciate yourself – and a few minutes more to begin to wonder what a difference your abilities might make to your riding, and to competing, if you tapped into them more. Come back to this again from time to time in the next few days, and then on a regular basis.

> **Find a feeling that would really help you when you compete.**

People often tell someone who's tense and anxious to 'relax'. Not only is that very difficult to do (the adrenalin is already in your system and it takes time – even a matter of hours – to disperse), but it isn't actually appropriate! When we ride we need tone, not relaxation, in our muscles! And we certainly don't need to be so cool that we're switched off. We actually need calm alertness – though not hyper-alertness.

Think about your life as a whole. When, and where, do you feel this combination of mental alertness and physical tone? Maybe it's when you are playing other sports. Maybe it's when you are taking the dog for a walk, or cooking a meal, or meeting up with friends… (It may occur in more than one of these, of course.) Imagine that situation now. Get really into it – and notice what characterizes it most. Is it a feeling – if so, what and where? Warmth between your shoulder-blades? A sense of being grounded in your central core? A feeling of connection to the earth? Or is it something visual? Are the colours all bright – or soft and fuzzy? Is the detail sharp and crisp; is it in a close-up focus – or a soft one? Or maybe it involves sound. Is there a phrase or a word that just seems to sum it all up? Something someone said which you hear again in your mind's ear? Something you say to yourself? A snatch of tune…? Perhaps it's the smell of a warm, damp autumn evening, or a crisp winter morning? Or a taste – of buttered toast, or a glass of your favourite wine?

Maxim | there are always alternatives

I hope that these suggestions will have been enough to set you off on an internal search for your own personal 'icon' – something that can act as a short-cut to what that special experience means for you, and to the sense of your calm, alert and competent self that goes along with it. Once you think you have found your icon, practise using it as an instant route to your toned alertness and feeling of competence: do it while you're in the shower, waiting for the kettle to boil, standing in the queue at the check-out... The idea is to make it automatic, so that you know, absolutely, surely KNOW, that you can access that valuable and helpful feeling whenever and wherever you want it. Then put in into your riding... Then put it into the way you compete.

> **Think more like your horse and less like yourself.**

This, too, needs practice, but it is a good way to help you focus on what your horse feels and needs when the two of you are away from home together. Put yourself in his shoes: what is he noticing? What is likely to alarm him? What reassures him? What does he find difficult? Exciting? Try to do your imagining in his terms, as a flight animal with a veneer of civilization! Beware of imputing human motives or feelings to him: horses do not set out to wind up their riders, or test them, or make their lives difficult for them – that takes an ability they don't have; the ability to set aside their own experience and get inside yours! (Which, however, is the very ability that *you* are trying to cultivate.) Think simple, think loud and clear, think cause and effect, think leadership and follower. As his 'top horse', how can you take care of him, direct and protect him – in his terms? There is a growing literature on understanding how horses experience things, which can be really helpful here. You will find some suggestions in the Useful Reading section at the end of the book.

> **Learn how valuable it can be to watch yourself from outside, objectively, with sympathy and concern but without emotion.**

When we can see ourselves from a different perspective in addition to that of our own first-hand experience, we gain a valuable corrective to the alarms and despondencies we may be feeling. If you can see the humour of a situation, if you can honestly applaud yourself for trying hard, or for a small success that you know

Maxim | there are always alternatives

has been difficult for you to achieve (even though nobody else may have noticed it), if you can take criticism or problems as potentially valuable feedback rather than getting lost in a morass of anger or self-pity, then you will have enriched your riding – and, potentially, many other areas of your life as well. If you visualize easily, try watching yourself in an imaginary movie. If you are kinesthetic, imagine how something might have felt, or might feel in future, if you had the skills of your trainer, or of one of your equestrian heroes or heroines. The difference in Roy when I asked him to 'ride like Marion' (see page 267) was truly amazing. Most amazing of all, of course, was the fact that Roy had been able to bring about such a transformation in his riding simply by using information he already had in his mind. What was in his mind shaped his body – first by blocking it, then by liberating it. He stopped limiting himself ('*I'm not as good as Marion*') and, by 'pretending', achieved the real thing! What might you achieve if you dare to tap into *your* mind?

A strategy for effective self-management

The 'layers' concept

So far in this chapter, I've invited you to get involved in a piece of personal detective work in order to answer the question: '*How do I go about making myself nervous about competition – and what might I do to change it?*' Now I want to use the idea of different layers of experience to help you develop a personal strategy for managing the experience of competition that is both comprehensive and practical.

Understanding oneself can be a bit like peeling an onion: as each layer gives up its secrets, further and deeper ones are revealed beneath. Or you might like to think of a Russian Doll: each version seems complete in itself, yet it contains other versions, and other patterns, layered beneath. Each of us contains, and yet is more than, all the layers of our experience: the metaphor of layers can help us not only to understand ourselves better, but to work with ourselves to manage our lives more effectively. Unlike the onion, we do not need to destroy or discard any layer of ourselves as we work with what's beneath. As with the doll, we may examine the versions separately, yet put them back together again afterwards. The whole is always more than the sum of its parts.

Each of our experiences in life begins on, or initially relates to, one of five layers of meaning. Starting from the outside and working inwards, I'm going to explore how we can use each layer to develop a comprehensive strategy for managing competition. I shall return to this idea of layering again and explore its wider implications in Chapter 15.

Maxim | there are always alternatives

Outer layer: environment – what's happening around you

Your environment – in its broadest sense – can be an important element of competition nerves for both you and your horse, so managing it with that kind of toned alertness I talked about earlier in this chapter can be very useful. Animals – including human ones! – are creatures of habit, so change can stress them. Often, it's the change in routines before a competition that helps make you edgy and signals to your horse that something important and possibly scary is about to occur. For seasoned competitors, and horses who enjoy competition, it can signal that a fun day is in the offing – for example, when some horses see a horsebox, they're really keen to get on it. Others, as we know, go straight into fearful or stubborn resistance.

Strategic tips:

- Get yourself and your horse used to competition – if possible without actually competing! If you have a youngster, take him out with older horses so that he can get used to the atmosphere and to being around strange horses and strange places.

- Anticipate and plan for possible problems. If you tiptoe around at home, don't be surprised if your horse reacts to noise when he's out. Put flower tubs around your yard. Get him used to prams and umbrellas. Play music. Hang up a sheet or two as a preparation for those flapping flags.

The behaviour layer – what to do and what not to do

Behaviour is what you do within your environment and how you act upon it.

Strategic tips:

- Plan and organize beforehand. Leave as little as possible for the day itself.

- Allow yourself plenty of time – and then plenty more than you first thought of! Things you do every day, you do quickly; things you don't, often take much longer. Allow for this in estimating how long it will take you to get ready, and how long it will take you to get there, get tacked up, warm up, etc.

- Ask yourself honestly whether you find it more, or less, helpful to have other people with you. If family and friends give you courage – drum up your supporters! If you find them a distraction, if their advice is just what you don't want when you're anxious, if they get in the way at all – *don't take them!* Be honest and tell them why.

Maxim | there are always alternatives

- Many people have to share transport when competing. Talk this over beforehand with the others involved, so that you avoid getting frazzled by the sense of pressure created by your different times and different classes. Some people like to talk their anxieties through as they go along; others prefer to stay quietly inside their own space. Try to match yourself with someone who manages things like you – if this is not practical, then agree not to get in each other's hair on the day! The last thing you want is to add someone else's anxieties and sense of pressure to your own!

- Use your competition warm-up just like your warm-up at home – for the loosening and stretching and going forward and let's-pay-attention-to-each-other. Even though other people may be practising their leg-yields or half-passes beside you in the warm-up area, it's really best to concentrate on simple stuff and leave the fancy stuff out. You have either done enough at home, or not! Now is too late to make a real difference, and may only create just the sense of pressure for both you and your horse that you'd rather avoid immediately before a test.

The capability layer – what you know and what you can do

Your capability is your knowledge and your skills. Capability shapes your decisions and your choices about your behaviour in your environment.

Strategic tips:

- Compete at a level below the level you are working at when you're at home. That way, you minimize the pressure on yourself and your horse. If you do what you both already find relatively easy, you will have energy and attentiveness to spare for managing the extra demands of working away from home, after a journey, in a busy environment.

- Take what happens in the test and the judge's comments on your sheet as specific hints for future training, not as general comments on how 'good' or 'bad' you and your horse are. Comments and marks are snapshot reactions to specific moments – keep them that way!

The beliefs and values layer – what competition means to you

What we believe and what we consider important directs the way we apply our knowledge and skills to direct our behaviour and operate on our environment. We can hold beliefs about any of the other layers, including the innermost one,

Maxim | there are always alternatives

identity, and they can have profound effects because beliefs and values direct the *choices* we make.

I want to ask you a very important question: *Why are you competing in the first place?* When I asked this question at a local Riding Club, I could see by some members' reactions that this was the first time they had ever thought about it! Afterwards, I overheard someone say: *'I always assumed I should compete. Now that I think about it, I'm not really sure that, for myself, I actually want to!'*

I'm not trying to put you off – simply inviting you to take ownership of competition as *your choice* for you and your horse: owning it may make all the difference! A personal commitment at this level drives a very different kind of intent and will certainly be picked up by your horse and reflected in his commitment. When you are tackling something difficult, a commitment that is positive and shared can be essential!

Strategic tips:

- Be clear whose agenda are you working to. Is competing your idea – or your trainer's? Is it something that everyone else at the yard does and thinks you should do?

- Get clear about what competing means to you. When I asked Roy how his horse came by the name, 'Corinthian Spirit', Roy explained that it was the belief of the Corinthian Greeks that what was important about competition was *to take part*, not just to win. With this belief, he will find it easier to enjoy and be satisfied by competition than someone whose heart is set on winning.

- Ask yourself what winning would mean to you. A reward for all the hard work you and your horse – and your trainer – have put in? A recognition of your quality? A proof that you are worth something as a person? A badge of your skill? We can have beliefs about any of the other layers, too: from my questions you can see that, because of what you believe, winning may tell you something about what you do on the day, what your level of skills are, or even who you are as a person (the innermost of the layers, coming next). Your beliefs will certainly shape your interpretation of what happens on the day – and they may also shape what actually happens, too!

- What does it mean to you if you don't get placed, or if you get low marks – or lower marks than usual? What layer does this connect with for you?

- Do you believe that the judge's marks and comments tell you whether she 'likes your horse' or not? If you do, you may be hooking into issues of identity, not performance – and giving yourself cause to feel upset or depressed if she 'doesn't like him'. (Liking him, of course, is not part of her job.)

Maxim | there are always alternatives

- Beliefs and fantasies feel very real in our minds, so what you believe will tend to shape your feelings and thus affect what happens in the arena (the layers of capability, behaviour and environment). If you are dreading forgetting your test, the very dread you feel will take up some of the mental and physical attentiveness you need, and make it more likely that you will go wrong. If you are frightened that your horse will spook, you are likely to become jumpy yourself, and react edgily at potential terrors rather than keeping your focus and giving him a clear message of 'that's nothing to worry about – let's get on with the job'. So then he spooks – surprise, surprise!

- Do your beliefs make it easier for you to do your best, or harder? Are you someone who focuses more on that 2 marks by which you 'lost' the class to someone else – or on the fact that you actually got over 65% for the first time? And how does that affect you next time you go out to compete? It is admirable to set yourself high standards; but when you focus more on the details of how you are *not* living up to them than on how you are being guided by them and making steps in the right direction, you deprive yourself of satisfaction as well as adding pressure. Effectively, you keep moving the goalposts – thereby ensuring that you never feel as if you are really achieving anything. In the eyes of the perfectionist, there is always something not quite right and something more to do. This can create a permanent state of edgy self-driving – and of course it will be passed on to your horse. If you allow yourself to be realistic about how far you fall short – and yet to delight in doing the best you can on the day – you will put yourself in a much more relaxed frame of mind – strangely enough, one that is also more focused and thus likely to help you achieve even more! When Roy began to regard competition as part of a training process, rather than an end in itself, he discovered that both he and Cori became more relaxed. Not only was this more pleasant at the time, but it also earned favourable comments from the judges!

The innermost layer: identity – what's at stake for you personally

The core of ourselves is our individual identity: who we are; what we are worth; how we are different from others; what makes us special. So it's incredibly important to each one of us. It's where we feel extremes like pride and confidence, worthlessness and vulnerability. It's where criticism whangs right in between the joints in the armour. It's where we are warmed to the cockles of our hearts.

Is this what's on the line for you when you compete? *I hope not.* You have a right to put this kind of pressure on yourself as an individual, but because riding involves another living creature who is unlikely to share this agenda, you owe it to your horse to consider how your drive and ambition may be affecting him. Some horses, of course, do enjoy competition, and some, like racehorses, are bred for it; but I think it's unlikely that their very sense of identity stands or falls on the results. Even though it may feel good to experience winning at an identity level (and why not, it seems), it will put pressure on you the next time you go out, and the next time. And you will put pressure on your horse. Try using the concept of the layers to move the consequences of success or failure in competition further out to layers such as behaviour or capability, where they matter less crucially. Let me remind you of Charles de Kunffy's view (cited earlier in Chapter 2), that: *'No serious riders ever believed the training goal was to compete.'*

Here are some statements that I believe, and that I think can help us ensure that our identity doesn't become the prize we are really competing for.

- What happens when you compete is *not* a statement about your essential personal worth, or that of your horse. (It's interesting that jockeys – who obviously have a vested interest in winning – will often say of a horse not good enough to get involved in the finish: 'He ran a nice race.' I think we could all benefit from looking at competition in this generously appreciative spirit.)

- It is *not* a 'final account' – just a snapshot of what happened on the day.

- It reflects many things at lower levels: take it at the right level and you'll find it helpful for future progress and future performance.

Using this layered approach for managing yourself and competition has many benefits. From the outermost layer of managing yourself in your environment to the innermost layer of protecting and enhancing your sense of identity, it offers a powerful tool for allaying your fears. Working with the practical strategies, you have ways to avoid those things that could go wrong and cause you stress on the day. Working with the issues of your beliefs and values about competition gives you a way of keeping it where it belongs – away from being a decisive factor in affirming or denying your identity and the degree of your personal worth. And in doing those things, it gives you a way to set aside anxiety, calm your competition nerves and have a fun day out in the big world with your horse.

Maxim | there are always alternatives

14 'Reading' and choosing tests

> There is only one correct way of riding. That is, riding for the good of the horse and not for the expectations of judges… However, and not coincidentally, when a judge knows his science and commands the necessary crafts and skills, he will recognize in the horse the physical and mental manifestations that document how well schooled he was for his own sake. Expert judges appreciate riding that benefits the horse…
>
> **Charles de Kunffy,** *Dressage Principles Illuminated*[1]

There is all the difference in the world between stringing a list of movements together and creating the impression of an effortless flow – and that is the difference you'll need to aim for if you are going to improve your scores. To do this, you need to learn how to 'read' the tests and understand what they are asking for overall, not just what movements they specify and in what order you have to perform them. Once you know the answer to this question, you can decide whether this or that test will bring out the best in your horse or, on the other hand, make it difficult for him to show his unique qualities. You wouldn't expect a sprinter to perform well in a marathon; a large, relatively unschooled horse will have difficulty balancing in some tests but plenty of power and flow to carry him through others; a horse who's supple and well-balanced will stand out in a test that involves changes of direction and variations within the gaits.

In the long run, of course, you will be aiming to help your horse become as much of an all-round athlete as he can be; but why put unnecessary pressure on yourself or him in the meanwhile by failing to 'match' him as best you can with the tests you choose to enter at any particular point in his development?

Maxim | there are always alternatives

Learning to 'read' the tests

When I first began judging, I learnt a test much as a rider does – as a string of commands. But as I got familiar with different tests I started to notice that they had different flavours to them, and so I began to ask myself a bigger question: *'What is this particular test asking for? What is it **about**?'* Understanding what a test is really testing helps you prepare for it both intelligently and effectively and, at the same time, gives you an in-built check on how your schooling at this level is progressing. I have used the word 'read' in the heading to this section because it's a common way of describing searching for meaning at a level deeper than the mere surface; but I could also have used phrases like 'getting the feel for', or 'mapping out the territory that this test covers'.

What helped me to realize that there was more to a test than learning a sequence of movements was drawing out my own diagrams of the different tests. Judging relies on vision and I found that, when riders went wrong, it was more helpful for me to be able to see instantly where they had deviated from a drawn-out 'map' of the test than to have to compare what they were doing with a set of instructions I had learnt and memorized through my internal ear. (You will understand from what I've said in earlier chapters that this second alternative involves 'translating' from one sense to another, which takes fractionally longer and also occupies a degree of attention that it's better to have available for making the judgements themselves.) Once I had a set of movements mapped out, I started to become aware that different tests had slightly different emphases. I found myself asking, *'What questions is this test asking?'* In thinking this through, I began to get a feel for how the horse would have to be moving – and what this would require in terms of rider preparation and support. I hope that this chapter will help you learn to do this, too.

If you don't already make visual maps of tests for yourself, I'd strongly suggest that you do so. You will achieve much more by making your own than by buying ready-made ones (or looking at them again if you have them already) because making your own gets you to go over the test in all three major sensory systems at once: as you read the words you are scanning *visually* and also probably *hearing* the instructions in your head. As you draw out the patterns you are recapping the information *kinesthetically* (your hand is going over the patterns and helping to ingrain them). And then, as the patterns appear on the paper in front of you, they are repeated again *visually*. This is a pretty comprehensive way to take your learning forward!

Maxim | there are always alternatives

Taking the test from your horse's perspective

As I imagined my way through different test patterns I found that something I hadn't expected was happening. *I began to think as if I were the horse.* Doing this can really help trainers teach, and riders learn, what is physically involved in performing movements (for example, lateral ones) correctly, and I think you will find it also helps you to gain a different perspective (and a different handle) on riding tests. As Charles de Kunffy puts it: *The rider's commitment is to ride the horse, not to just ride the pattern.*

So let's examine some test sequences from the horse's perspective. I'm going to look at examples from British Dressage tests: if you are reading this in another country I'm sure you will find similar sequences, and similar issues, coming up in the tests you are faced with. Even if you are familiar with a test, imagine now that you are going through it, not as yourself, but as your horse. To do this you will need to tap into your kinesthetic way of imagining (what he is likely to be experiencing in his body), and link this with some visual cues (looking out through his eyes). Don't forget that, as him, you are aware not only of your gait, direction and balance but also of feelings in your mouth, on your back and sides, which are trying to tell you what she – that rider of yours – wants. Remember, you don't know what she's going to ask you to do next. What signals and what support do you need? Are they coming at the last moment, or enough in advance for you to respond smoothly and easily? Is she making it easier for you do something (e.g. make a transition) by warning you in good time? However, given your ability to remember things, you may well be anticipating what's coming, either from tests you've done before or from practising this one. You might be right – or not! How will your rider react?

Your horse doesn't think of a dressage test as something made up of a number of movements, with specified starting and finishing points, even if you do. It might be more helpful for you to think of it in a more connected way, perhaps as a thread or string, with beads or knots on it, or a video sequence, or a path with various features and directional changes en route. This puts you closer to your horse's way of experiencing it. He may have learnt to expect a 'stop' signal at X or G if he has done a lot of tests, but it's more likely that he will be experiencing the movements he is required to do simply as actions in a kind of perpetual present. Horses go through life in the moment and, though your horse is affected by memories and emotional associations from the past, the one thing he doesn't do is think strategically ahead. He does what seems important to him at the time and, hopefully, quite a lot of the time and owing to your partnership and shared history, that means he does what you're asking. So you are the partner who needs to take responsibility for thinking ahead – and that means using your ability to 'read' a test in every sense to plot the smoothest and most delightful way through it, so that both of you experience it as a continuous flow. If you do this, your judge is likely to see it in that way, too.

Let's examine how this can work in practice. First, let's look at a test that is all about *engagement* and *balance*: BD Novice 24. See pages 198–201.

How does it come across to you? Imagine doing it *first* from your horse' viewpoint, then from your own. *Note how doing it first from his perspective affects your own run-through.*

By contrast, let's look at another test that looks simple, often rides flowingly, and for high marks requires *suppleness* and the ability to *engage and bend*; BD Novice 21. Again, run through it as your horse, then as yourself. How do you feel about this one? See pages 202–204.

To a rider, BD Novice 33 (see pages 205–208) looks at first as though it's going to be easier, because you have a long arena and this offers you more time between any changes of gait, balance and bend. However, the 'hidden requirements' if you are a horse are that you carry yourself in balance over those longer distances and that you have learnt to be independent of the 'moral support' of the wall: you have to make loops off the track and show medium strides across the open arena both on the diagonal and, in canter, on a curved line. This asks you to engage well with your hind legs in order to carry your shoulders, and also to listen attentively to your rider because on one canter half-circle (movement 5) you will need to stay 'through' and in self-carriage while she takes away your rein support but on the very next movement (6) you are not to assume that the same is required: this time you have to engage enough to produce a rather different result – the increase of power, lengthening of stride and 'uphill' carriage of your shoulders that add up to a medium canter.

I hope that imagining your way through these examples as your horse rather than as a rider will have given you a sense of how different even tests of the same level can be. Higher number tests are not automatically more difficult, nor are long-arena ones. It all depends...

Now let's take an example of a Medium test; BD Medium 71 (see pages 209–212). Initially, run through it as your horse. If you are good at lateral work and can collect your walk when asked, you'll probably enjoy and shine at this one. You need to be pretty well balanced and 'sitting' in your canter, too, because your rider's going to ask you to show medium strides and then collect again at the end of the long side – and immediately after that you'll be asked for half-pass and then right after that 10-m half-circles in canter with a simple change over X to alter direction. This test has what I think of as 'cascading' sequences, rather like what

continues on page 201

Maxim | there are always alternatives

NOVICE 2002 — 24

Arena 20m x 40m
Approximate time 4½ minutes

			Max. Marks
1.	A C	Enter at working trot. Proceed down centre line without halting. Track left	10
2.	HE E	Working trot Circle left 20 metres diameter	10
3.	E X	Half 10 metre circle left to X Half 10 metre circle right to B	10
4.	BF between F & A	Working trot Transition to walk (2-4 steps), and immediately proceed at working trot	10
5.	A	Circle right 20 metres diameter with a transition to working canter right, over X	10
6.	AKHCM	Working canter	10
7.	MXK K	Change rein. Give and retake the reins over X Working trot	10
8.	KAF FXH H	Working trot Change rein and show some medium trot strides Working trot	10
9.	CMB B	Working trot Circle right 20 metres diameter	10
10.	B X	Half 10 metre circle right to X Half 10 metre circle left to E	10
11.	EK between K & A	Working trot Transition to walk (2-4 steps), and immediately proceed at working trot	10

Maxim | there are always alternatives

			Max. Marks
12.	A	Circle left 20 metres diameter with a transition to working canter, left over X	10
13.	AFMCH	Working canter	10
14.	HXF F	Change rein. Give and retake the reins over X Working trot	10
15.	FAK KXM M	Working trot Change rein and show some medium trot strides Working trot	10
16.	MC between C & H	Working trot Medium walk	10
17.	HXF F	Change rein at free walk on a long rein Medium walk	10 x 2
18.	A D G	Down the centre line Working trot Halt. Immobility. Salute.	10

Leave the arena at walk on a long rein at A

COLLECTIVE MARKS

19.		Paces (freedom and regularity)	10 x 2
20.		Impulsion (desire to move forward, elasticity of the steps, suppleness of the back and engagement of the hindquarters)	10 x 2
21.		Submission (attention and confidence, harmony, lightness and ease of the movements, acceptance of the bridle and lightness of the forehand)	10 x 2
22.		Rider's position and seat; correctness and effect of the aids	10 x 2
		Total	**270**

© **Published by British Dressage.** All rights reserved. No part of this Publication to be reproduced, stored in a retrieval system or transmitted in any form or by any means, electronic, mechanical, photocopying, recording or otherwise without the prior permission of British Dressage.

Maxim | there are always alternatives

The movements of BD Novice 24 (reading from left to right)

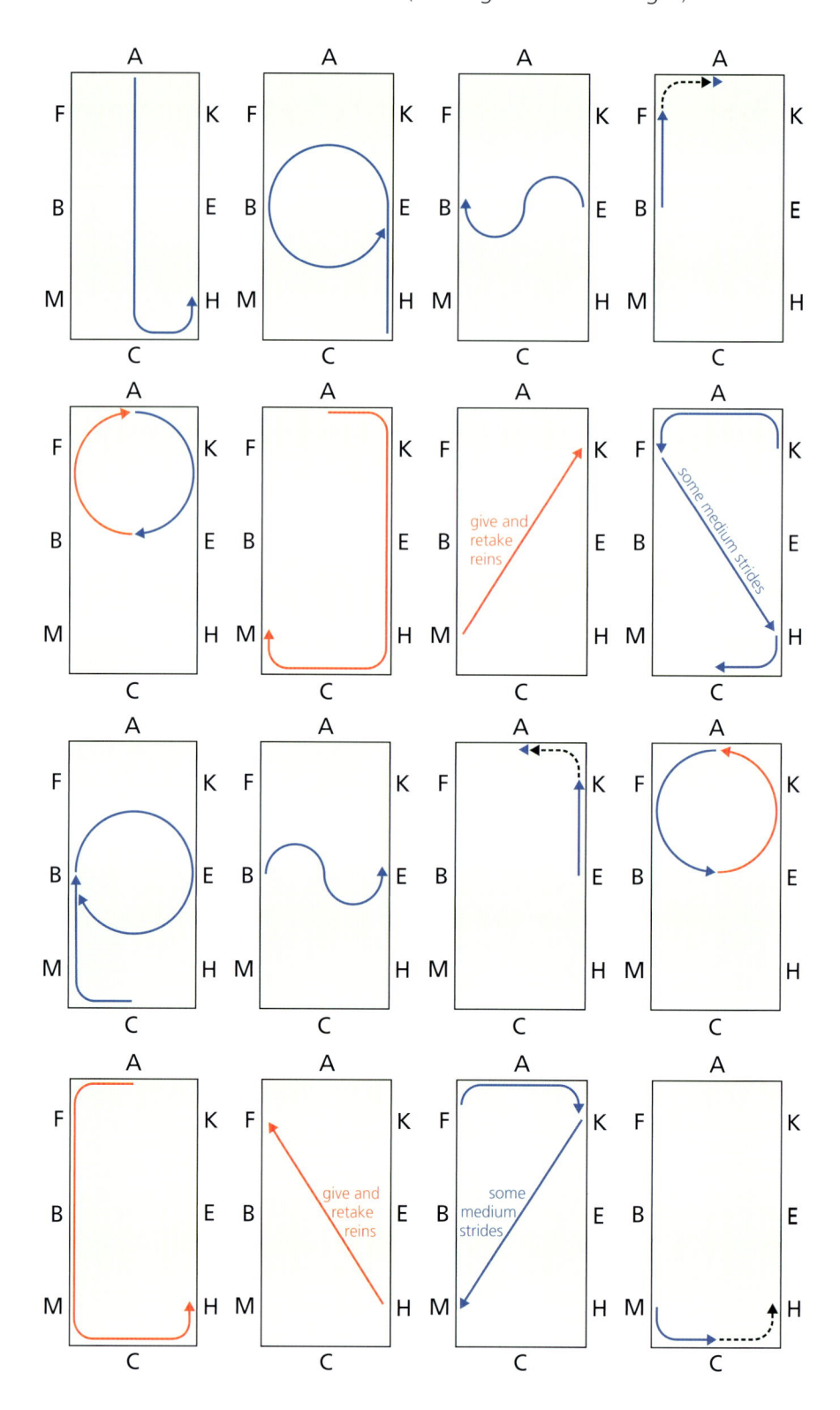

Maxim | there are always alternatives

The movements of BD Novice 24 continued

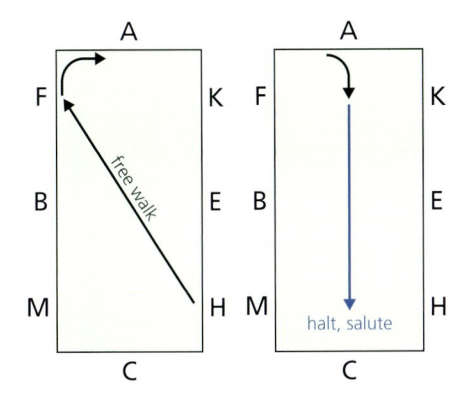

happens in a series of showjumping or cross-country fences: if you do one movement correctly it will set you up for the next – but if you haven't got what it takes you will start the following movement at a disadvantage. And the dominoes will continue to topple… Let's take a sequence and track it through.

Trot work – Medium 71 movements 2–5.

2.	E	Half circle left 10 metres diameter to X
	X	Half circle right 10 metres diameter to B
3.	BF	Travers
4.	KXM	Change rein at medium trot
	M	Collected trot
5.	HD	Half-pass left
	A	Track right

Doing these half-circles well means that you need to step under, especially with your inside hind leg, and swing your rib-cage outward to create bend round your rider's inside leg. If you are engaged and bent like this, your inside hind leg will be able to deliver its thrust upward and forward rather than delivering it outward through your shoulder. Then your quarters won't swing out and your shoulder won't fall out and you'll find it easier to straighten over X and change your bend when asked. With you in good balance like this, your rider will find it easier to help you make the two half-circles equal size. The second half-circle then sets you up with the correct bend needed for the travers – your rider's left leg keeps pressing your quarters in while she straightens your forehand and tells your forehand ' go straight ahead'. At F she'll ask you to finish off the travers by straightening briefly, and then you'll need to step under actively with your hind legs (especially the

continues on page 212

Maxim | there are always alternatives

NOVICE 2002

21

British Dressage

Arena 20m x 40m
Approximate time 4½ minutes

			Max. Marks
1.	A	Enter at working trot and proceed down centre line without halting	10
2.	C	Track right	10
3.	A	Serpentine 3 loops, each loop to go to the side of the arena finishing at C	10
4.	Between C & M B BAE	Working canter right Circle right 20 metres diameter Working canter	10
5.	Between E & H K	Half circle right 15 metres diameter returning to the track between E & K Working trot	10
6.	A	Serpentine 3 loops, each loop to go to the side of the arena finishing at C	10
7.	Between C & H E EAB	Working canter left Circle left 20 metres diameter Working canter	10
8.	Between B & M F	Half circle left 15 metres diameter returning to the track between B & F Working trot	10

Maxim | there are always alternatives

			Max. Marks
9.	FK	Working trot	
	KXM	Change rein and show some medium trot strides	
	M	Working trot	10
10.	C	Medium walk	
	HXF	Change rein at free walk on a long rein	
	F	Medium walk	10 x 2
11.	A	Down centre line	
	D	Working trot	
	G	Halt. Immobility. Salute.	10

Leave the arena at walk on a long rein at A

COLLECTIVE MARKS

12.	Paces (freedom and regularity)	10 x 2
13.	Impulsion (desire to move forward, elasticity of the steps, suppleness of the back and engagement of the hindquarters)	10 x 2
14.	Submission (attention and confidence, harmony, lightness and ease of the movements, acceptance of the bridle and lightness of the forehand)	10 x 2
15.	Rider's position and seat; correctness and effect of the aids	10 x 2
	Total	**200**

© **Published by British Dressage.** All rights reserved. No part of this Publication to be reproduced, stored in a retrieval system or transmitted in any form or by any means, electronic, mechanical, photocopying, recording or otherwise without the prior permission of British Dressage.

Maxim | there are always alternatives

The movements of BD Novice 21 (reading from left to right)

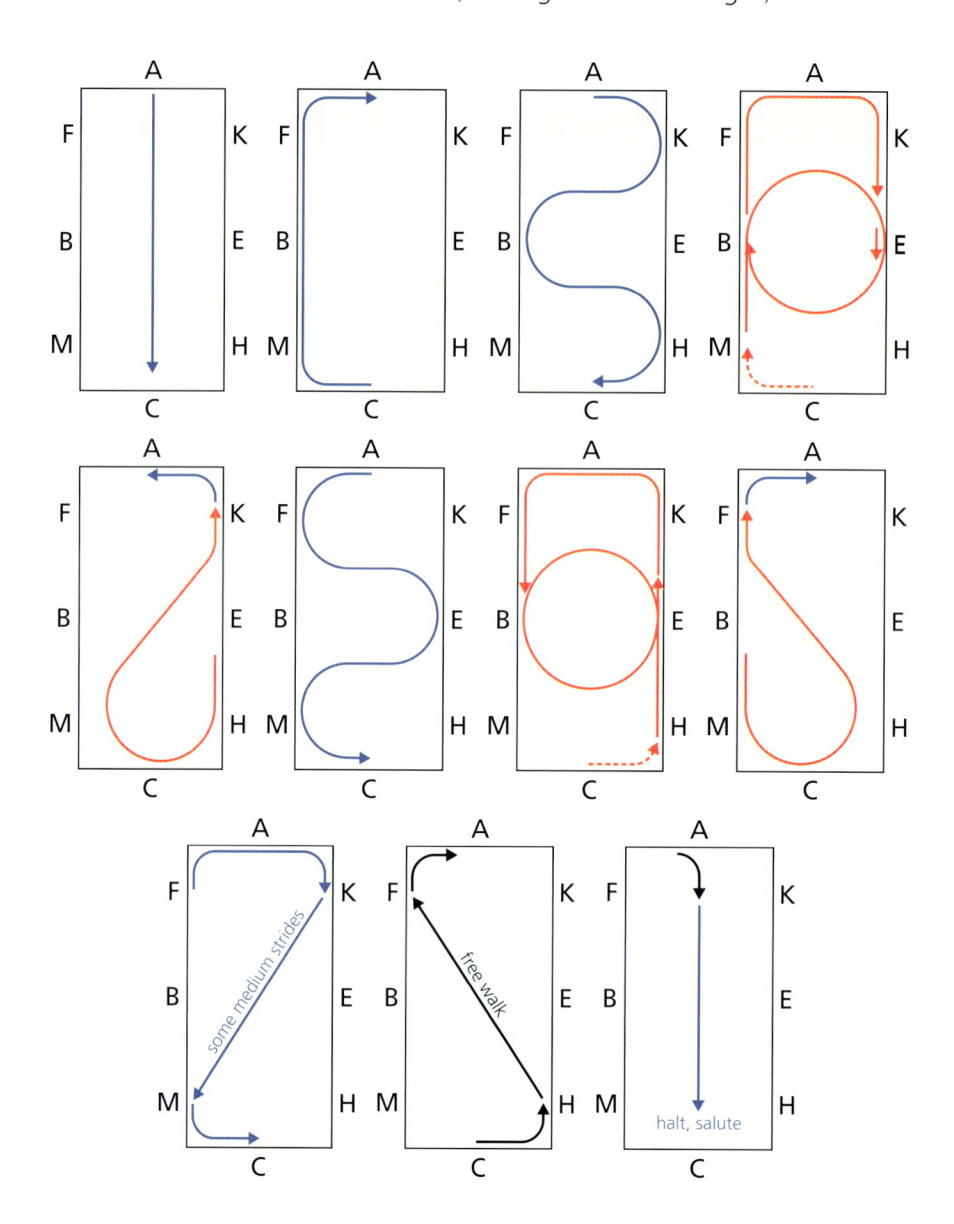

Maxim | there are always alternatives

NOVICE 2002

33

Arena 20m x 60m
Approximate time 6 minutes

			Max. Marks
1.	A	Enter at working trot. Proceed down centre line without halting.	
	C	Track right	10
2.	Between M & F	One loop 10 metres in from the track	10
3.	A	Circle right 15 metres diameter	10
4.	Between A & K	Working canter right	10
5.	KS	Working canter	
	S	Half circle right 20 metres diameter to R, give and retake the reins when crossing the centre line	10
6.	RP	Working canter	
	P	Half circle right 20 metres diameter to V and show some medium canter strides	10
7.	VH	Working canter	
	H	Working trot	10
8.	MV	Change the rein and show some medium trot strides..	10
9.	V	Working trot	
	A	Medium walk	10
10.	FEM	Free walk on a long rein	10 x 2
11.	M	Medium walk	
	C	Working trot	10
12.	Between H & K	One loop 10 metres in from the track	10
13.	A	Circle left 15 metres diameter	10

Maxim | there are always alternatives

			Max. Marks
14.	Between A & F	Working canter left	10
15.	FR R	Working canter Half circle left 20 metres diameter to S, give and retake the reins when crossing the centre line	10
16.	SV V	Working canter Half circle left 20 metres diameter to P and show some medium canter strides	10
17.	PM M	Working canter Working trot	10
18.	HP	Change the rein and show some medium trot strides	10
19.	P A	Working trot Down centre line	10
20.	X	Halt. Immobility. Salute.	10

Leave the arena at walk on a long rein at A

COLLECTIVE MARKS

21.	Paces (freedom and regularity)	10 × 2
22.	Impulsion (desire to move forward, elasticity of the steps, suppleness of the back and engagement of the hindquarters)	10 × 2
23.	Submission (attention and confidence, harmony, lightness and ease of the movements, acceptance of the bridle and lightness of the forehand)	10 × 2
24.	Rider's position and seat; correctness and effect of the aids	10 × 2
	Total	**290**

© **Published by British Dressage.** All rights reserved. No part of this Publication to be reproduced, stored in a retrieval system or transmitted in any form or by any means, electronic, mechanical, photocopying, recording or otherwise without the prior permission of British Dressage.

'READING' AND CHOOSING TESTS • 207

The movements of BD Novice 33 (reading from left to right)

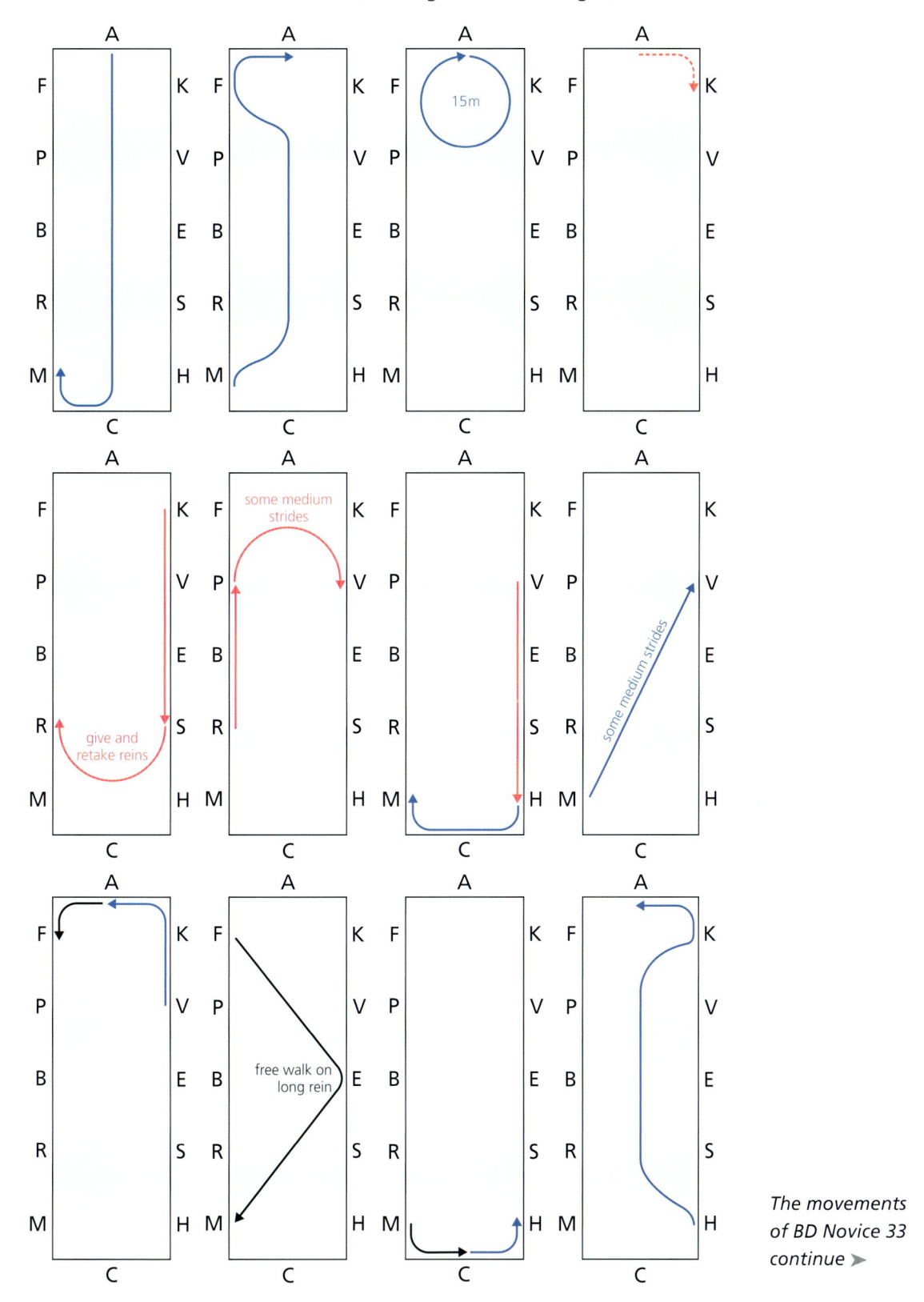

The movements of BD Novice 33 continue ➤

Maxim | there are always alternatives

The movements of BD Novice 33 continued

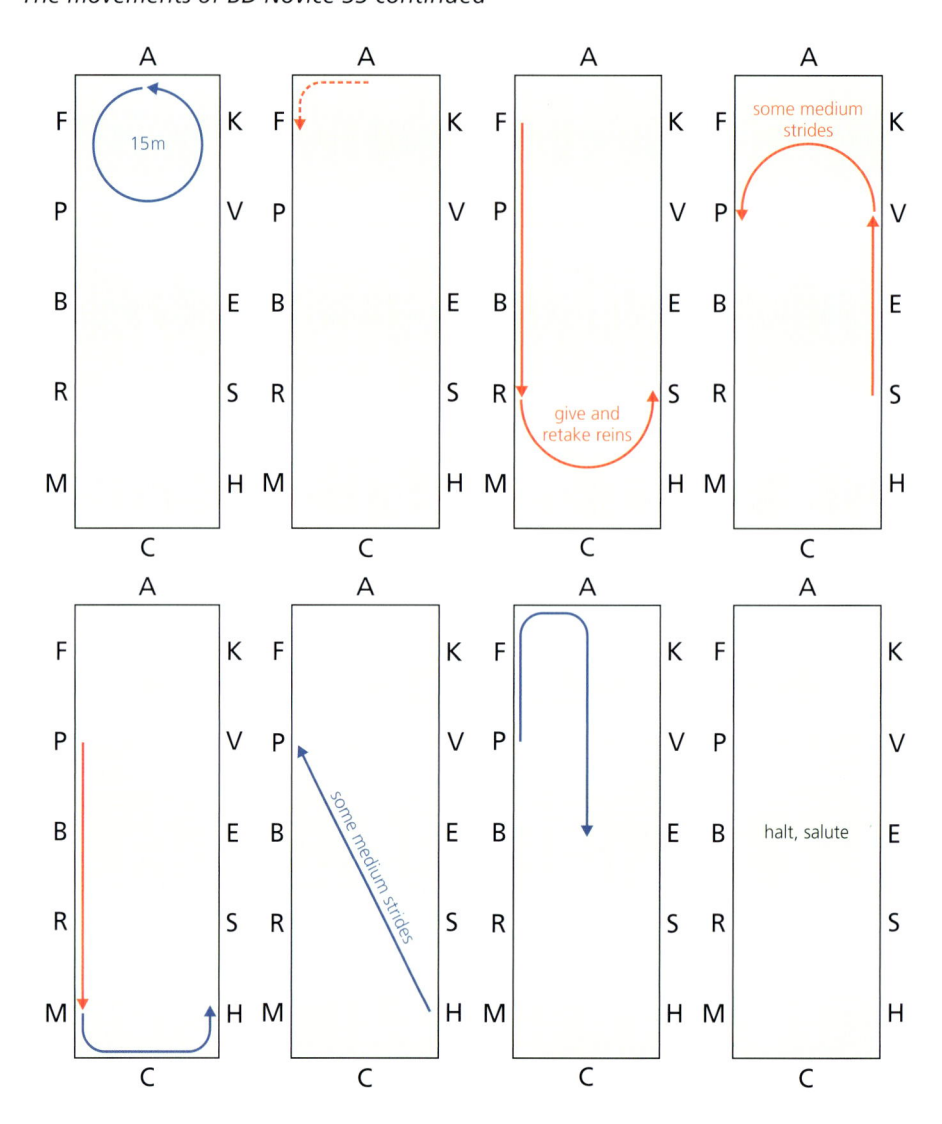

MEDIUM 2002

71

BRITISH DRESSAGE

Arena 20m x 40m
Approximate time 5 minutes

			Max. Marks
1.	A X C	Enter at collected trot Halt. Immobility. Salute. Proceed in collected trot Track left	10
2.	E X	Half circle left 10 metres diameter to X Half circle right 10 metres diameter to B	10
3.	BF	Travers	10
4.	KXM M	Change rein at medium trot Collected trot	10
5.	HD A	Half-pass left Track right	10
6.	E X	Half circle right 10 metres diameter to X Half circle left 10 metres diameter to B	10
7.	BM	Travers	10
8.	HXF F	Change rein at medium trot Collected trot	10
9.	KG C	Half-pass right Track right	10
10.	MXK K A	Extended walk Collected walk Down centre line	10 x 2
11.	X	Collected canter left	10
12.	C HEKA	Track left Collected canter	10

Maxim | there are always alternatives

			Max. Marks
13.	FG C	Half-pass left Track left	10
14.	HK K	Medium canter Collected canter	10
15.	FXH	Change rein with simple change of leg at X	10
16.	MBFAK	Collected canter	10
17.	KG C	Half-pass right Track right	10
18.	MF F	Medium canter Collected canter	10
19.	KXM	Change rein with simple change of leg at X	10
20.	MCHE E	Collected canter Collected trot	10
21.	A X	Down centre line Halt. Rein back four steps. Proceed at collected trot	10
22.	G	Halt. Immobility. Salute. Leave arena at walk on a long rein at A	10

COLLECTIVE MARKS

23.		Paces (freedom and regularity)	10 x 2
24.		Impulsion (desire to move forward, elasticity of steps, suppleness of the back and engagement of the hind quarters)	10 x 2
25.		Submission (attention and confidence, harmony lightness and ease of the movements, acceptance of the bridle and lightness of the forehand)	10 x 2
26.		Rider's position and seat; correctness and effect of the aids	10 x 2
		Total	**310**

© **Published by British Dressage.** All rights reserved. No part of this Publication to be reproduced, stored in a retrieval system or transmitted in any form or by any means, electronic, mechanical, photocopying, recording or otherwise without the prior permission of British Dressage.

Maxim | there are always alternatives

'READING' AND CHOOSING TESTS • 211

The movements of BD Medium 71 (reading from left to right)

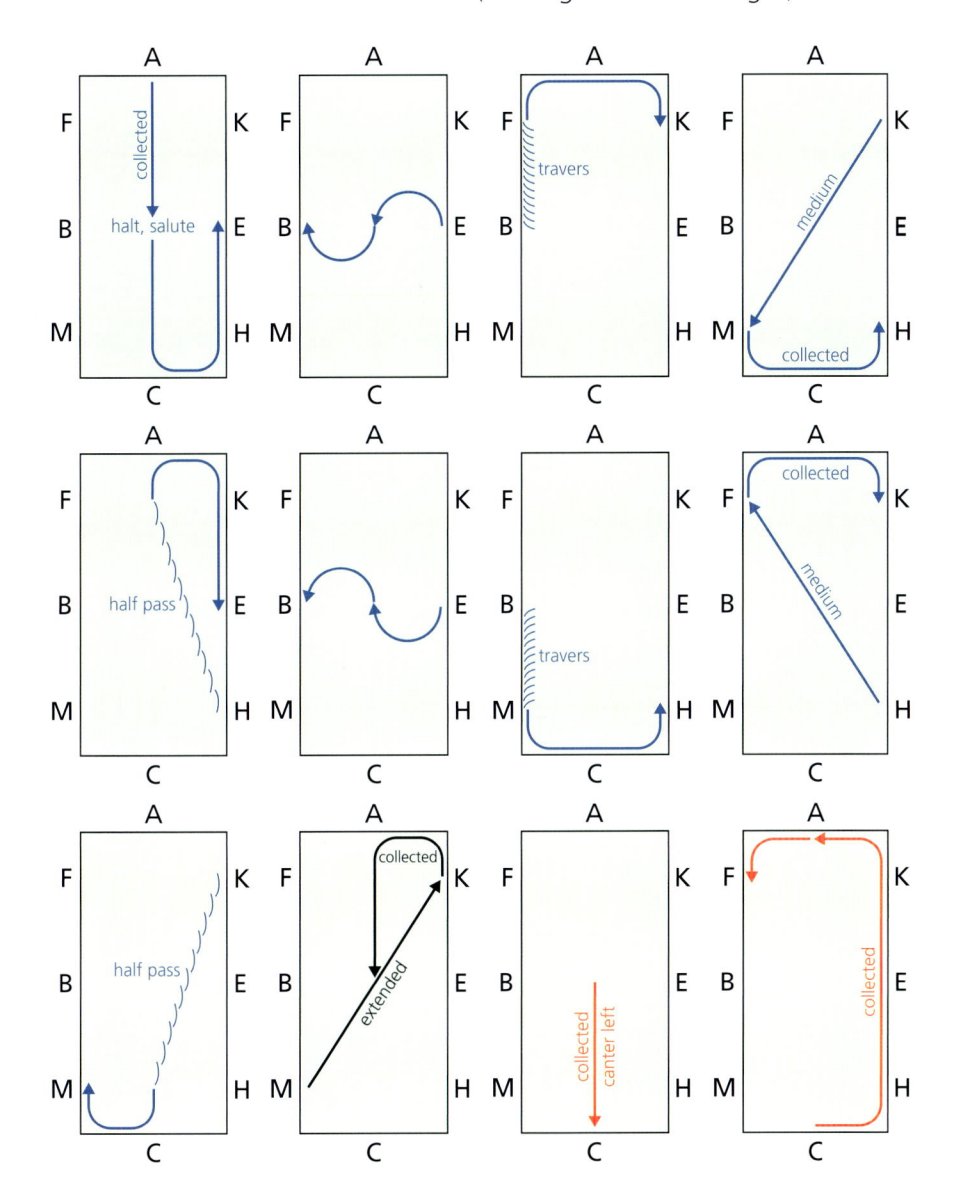

The movements of BD Medium 71 continue ➤

Maxim | there are always alternatives

The movements of BD Medium 71 continued

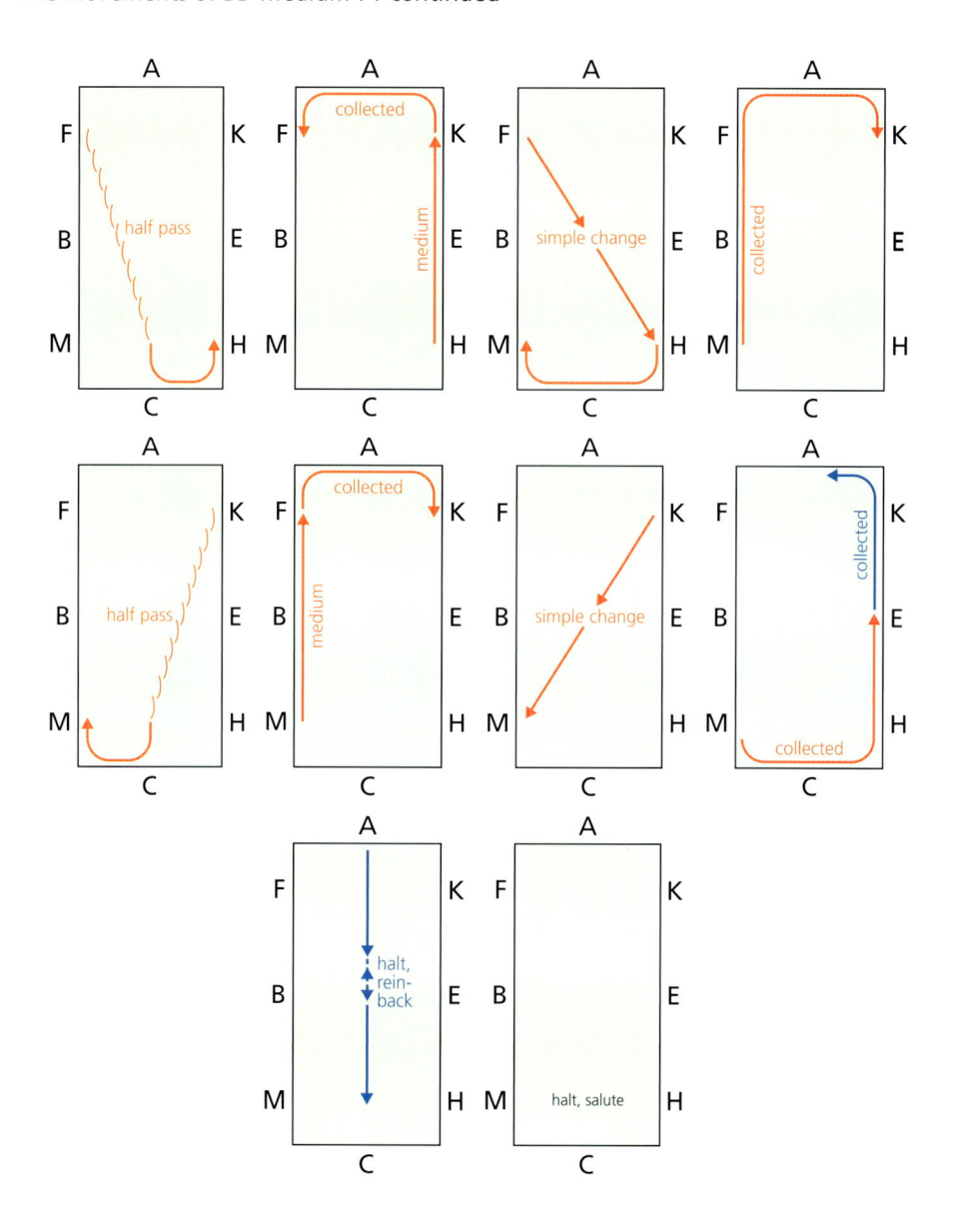

right, inside one) and use the short side to rebalance so that you are then ready at K to power off in an 'uphill' posture across the diagonal in medium trot. You need to be 'uphill' so that you can lengthen the reach of each stride (cover ground) without falling on your forehand: if you achieve this, it will be relatively easy for you to collect again when you are asked to at M. The short distance between M and H will then allow you to confirm your balance and collect again by bending your hind legs more and delivering their thrust upward into increased suspension rather than partly upwards and partly forwards in the ground-covering way they

Maxim | there are always alternatives

needed to do for the medium strides. Then, when your rider puts her right leg back at H to ask you for the bend and the sideways tracking of half-pass, and her left leg on your girth continues to ask for your forward energy, you will have enough balance, bend and engagement to simply flow across the arena...

Or, on the other hand, you could:

- Fall round the half-circles on your shoulder and maybe spin your quarters out because your inside hind isn't stepping under and taking your weight enough...

- Fail to straighten again from the second half-circle onto the long side so that your rider needs to shove your quarters in again (a bit late) for the travers…

- Not be able to bend your body enough because, as your rider tried to shove your quarters in, her weight fell to the outside and upset your balance so your inside hind had a hard job taking your weight and it fell out through your left shoulder instead…

- So when you got to F she had to straighten you by pushing your quarters out again…

- So the short side wasn't long enough for you to rebalance, step under and get your hocks bending…

- So when you got to K you couldn't do a proper balanced 'uphill' medium trot – all you could do was propel yourself and either flatten or drive onto your forehand…

- So that, in turn, made it difficult to get your balance back at M and you drifted into a working sort of trot rather than being able to make a clear transition from a proper medium trot to a true collected one…

- So that when asked for half-pass at H your left hind wasn't engaged and you pushed off rather than lifting and carrying yourself, ending up with your quarters trailing on a diagonal line rather than doing a proper half-pass.

Compare the two versions of this test. As the horse, did you get the feeling from the first that you were being offered thoughtful help and guidance – and from this second version that you were being inadvertently push-pulled about? As the rider, did the first seem like one of those concentrated yet strangely light-hearted and relatively effortless experiences, and the second rather a distressing – and expensive – sequence? Even if you are relatively inexperienced and your horse is relatively 'ordinary,' it is within your power to make performing a test more like the first, if you approach it thoughtfully and strategically.

Maxim | there are always alternatives

> As if you were your horse, let your rider take you through the following canter sequence, from BD Elementary 45:

12.	H	Proceed in working canter right
	C	Circle right 20 metres diameter
13.	C	Collected canter
	CMB	The collected canter
14.	B	Volte right (8m)
15.	BF	The collected canter
	F	Half circle (8m) returning to the track before B
16.	(B)MC	The counter canter
17.	C	Simple change of leg

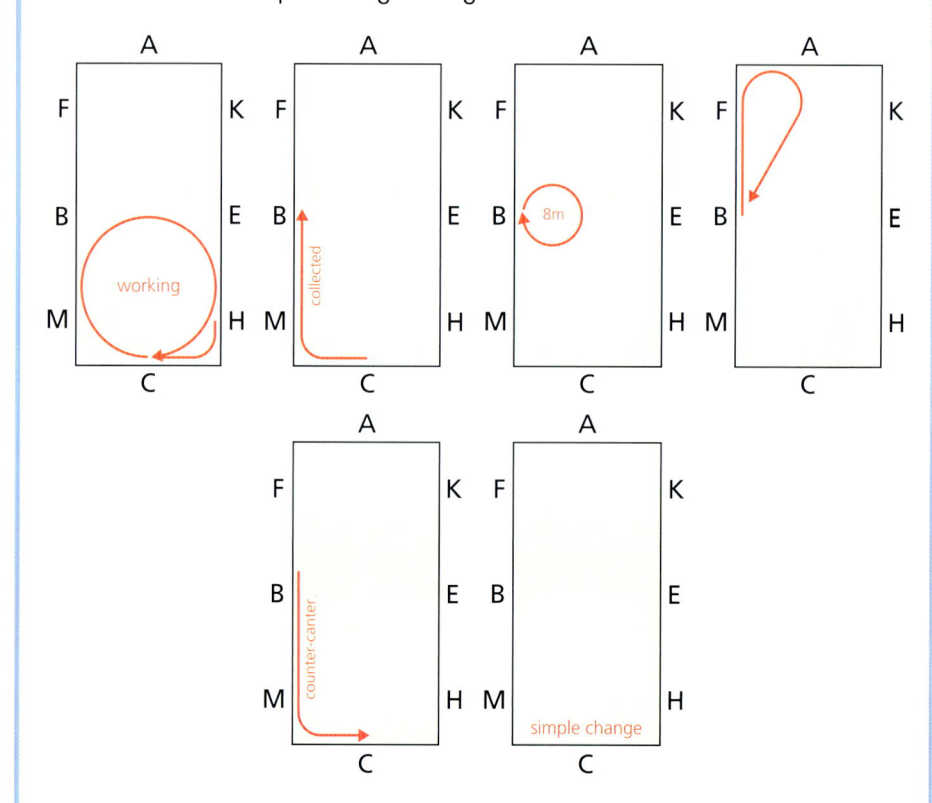

Don't be afraid to have a go at this, even if you and your horse have never worked at this level – it's only in your head! In fact, the relatively high order of difficulty can help you assess even better what you'd need to do and how timely your aiding would have to be. (For anyone contemplating riding this test, the reason why the test sheet stipulates 'For use on an artificial

continues

Maxim | there are always alternatives

> surface only' is that it contains movements that an Elementary standard horse would be likely to perform with more assurance on a good all-weather surface than on potentially wet/slippery grass.)
>
> As your horse, what would it take at each stage for you to carry out this sequence easily, fluently – and correctly?
>
> As the rider, what help would you have to give your horse to make this possible?
>
> What knock-on effects might there be if you didn't?

Thinking ahead

I once attended a course which involved participants in two relatively simple yet thought-provoking exercises. The first was long-reining a horse between a series of road markers in a simple bending pattern, and the second was to lead a horse on a slack metre-long rope through a 'maze' made of poles on the ground. Doing these exercises – especially with a horse I didn't already know – made me aware of the time interval a horse needs between receiving an instruction (turn right, slow down, etc.) to being able to complete the movement. In the case of the maze, yet more time/distance is needed for the horse's full body-length to go through any one part of the pathway: while the front end may have nearly reached a corner and be needing to turn, if the back follows naturally and begins to swing round and out, the hind legs will almost certainly step sideways over the pole and so fall 'outside' the maze. The handler has to be thinking ahead the whole time and trying to make the right decision about when to give the next instruction! Sometimes I felt as though my horse was as long as the brontosaurus in London's Natural History Museum – I wondered how long an instruction received at the front end would take to get through to the tail!

Timing instructions may seem simpler, and the time interval needed seem shorter, when you're on the horse rather than leading or driving him, but this can be something of an illusion. When I judge, I can often see more experienced test riders preparing their horses sympathetically and effectively by giving early aids, and less experienced ones waiting until the last moment. Which group would you rather be in?

You don't have to get it right all at once, even if that were possible. Start small and build up your competence bit by bit. As you do so, you'll also be building the confidence your horse has in you, both in the 'special' situation of competition and in your everyday activities as a partnership.

Maxim | there are always alternatives

> In your schooling and hacking out, take simple sequences involving two or three movements/components, look ahead, choose where you want to start and mentally 'nominate' a point where each movement has to flow into the next. As you ride along your chosen route carrying out this short sequence, experiment with different aiding distances until you have discovered how much notice your horse needs to be able to make the changes you have in mind easily, gracefully and in balance. (Different distances may be involved for different gaits, or as 'warning time' for movements of different difficulty, and they can also vary with your horse's physique and level of training.) Memorize what the successful distances look and feel like so that, when you are running through a similar sequence in competition, you can confidently and accurately give your horse the advance warning time he needs.

Choosing the right tests – a strategic approach

You can think of tests in two main ways: either as benchmarks of your existing level of skill and a source of feedback that can help you in training, or as a stretch for you and your horse towards the next level up. You could, as some riders undoubtedly do, think of them as an end in themselves; but I hope and believe that if you have read this far you will be convinced that this is the one thing they should, and need, never be. Paul Belasik puts it neatly – and brutally: *'Choosing the path of the winner, will make you the loser.'*[3] The ironic truth is that in having a narrow focus – winning – you lose the greater vision, which, as Carolyn put it, is *'being the best we can be and enjoying getting there'* (see Chapter 16).

Competition as benchmark and feedback

If you want to use a competition as a benchmark of how well your training is progressing, choose a test that you feel you and your horse can manage comfortably. If you are getting 6s and some 7s, you know that you are working competently at this level, though you are probably not feeling competent – or confident! – enough yet to have a go at the next level up. If you have some 5s, they will either tell you what went wrong for you on the day, or what specific things you need to address in your training before you can consider this level as your 'home-base' at the moment. For example, I recall judging a horse at Novice who got 6s

Maxim | there are always alternatives

and 7s for much of his work – but when it came to downward transitions (canter-trot, trot-walk, walk-halt) he was only getting 5s. Since he tended to stop in front rather than step into the transition from behind I knew that his rider needed to use her seat more to help him engage and stay 'through', and to make less use of her hands as a way of limiting his forward progress. As a partnership, they needed to approach these transitions differently.

If you find patterns like this cropping up on your sheets, resist the temptation to query individual marks or comments and, instead, consider honestly what this pattern tells you about your stage of progress up the training spiral. A horse who has to be stopped by the hand out hacking because you and he don't know how to stop him by rebalancing from behind could be one who ploughs onto his forehand, can't stop easily in an emergency, is 'heavy' and tiring and for any of these reasons could, given the wrong circumstances, be unsafe. Some work on the basics that underlie faults like this will pay enormous dividends in performance in the longer term.

If you are getting quite a lot of 7s you will no doubt be pleased – even though the verbal description attached to 7 is only 'fairly good', a full score of 7s would, at 70%, usually be enough to put you among the placings! If you are already working on the skills required for the next layer of your training spiral, the feedback you get from using your competition as a benchmarking exercise will probably encourage you to have a go at the next level. You are ready to stretch yourselves.

Competition as stretch

In my book *Solo Schooling* I discussed the 'zone' model and explained that we don't learn, only reinforce our learning, when we're in our 'comfort zone'. That's why it's a good zone for test riding: as a partnership, you are both likely to feel comfortable with what you're doing. Learning comes from excursions into your 'stretch zone'. That's why we usually reserve this more taxing work (physically, mentally, and often emotionally) for work at home, where we are less visible and where mistakes are part of the learning. But sometimes it's a good idea to forgo that safety net and deliberately use a test situation as a chance to stretch. This kind of stretch can sometimes give you a pleasant surprise: having a go at something you thought beyond your reach may show you that you had it in you after all! This was Carolyn's experience with Ambrose:

> Before, I'd feel I couldn't progress from Preliminary level until I was really doing well in competition. Since working with Wendy my confidence has built, I've entered Elementary tests, achieved some good percentages and had some positive comments from judges. I enjoy the more advanced work and can do some of it,

Maxim | there are always alternatives

now I have more of a 'let's try it' attitude. My best Elementary has been 67%, which I'd have been pleased with in a Preliminary test.

You do need a safety net in place when you go for this kind of stretch – but it's a mental/emotional one, not a physical one! Roy's experience of doing his first Advanced Medium tests with Cori draws our attention to something it's very important to bear in mind when you start competing at a new level in this stretching way – you need to take a different attitude to judges' comments:

…difficult to say about judges' comments…judges can't really tell if I'm happy about attaining a movement well or with more expression. I know the differences that have been made, i.e. the medium and extended trot and canter; now they are coming from the right places, not all in front but from behind, with more balance and softer. I'm looking at this phase as something of a transitional phase, so not too worried about marks, but more about trying to do things correctly! I'm far happier about the way Cori goes and I know what has improved.

This is one place where it is really important to take a comparative view, because it gives you a more realistic picture. Judges, of course, have to mark what they see on the day, even if they have judged your horse before. You, on the other hand, know how he is developing, and it's important that, like Roy, you take pride and satisfaction in his progress, even when the mark given in that particular test on that particular day isn't so special. For Roy, moving up from Medium, where he and Cori were comfortable performers, into Advanced Medium was this kind of a stretch. It was really important at this stage that Roy had a strong sense of how they were progressing to help him create a realistic context in which to place the marks and comments they got early on. Taking any negative marks or comments on board without referring to the context as Roy did could lay you open to disappointment and dent your self-esteem: in context, you will have the right to feel pleased, without in any sense being defensive or unrealistic about how much you still need to do to become secure performers at the new level.

Showing your horse at his best

Throughout this book I have emphasized that we need to see short-term competitive test riding as a by-product of something much more fundamental and long-term: the progression of your horse's training up the spiral of learning and skill that enables him to be, at every stage, the best athlete he can be. So it's only on this basis that I'd accept that, if you are going to compete, you have every right to showcase your horse's special abilities by choosing the tests that allow him to shine. This is so long as you don't let the results of that skewed evidence blind you to a realistic evaluation of his work and progress as a whole. At heart, you know what he finds difficult. You know where you and he need to improve. Given that fundamental honesty, why not enjoy doing what you do well and having it appreciated! There can be an additional benefit, too: if you spend time concentrating on things your horse is doing well, this (correct) work is likely to improve his suppleness, balance, engagement, etc., in a way that will also help him with more difficult or advanced work.

> When you are thinking of entering a competition, first look through each of the tests you could enter in the way I've outlined earlier in this chapter. Will it come easily to your horse? Does it ask for abilities he's got in spades? If you are competing for fun, why not choose tests he can shine at and enjoy? If you are competing in order to benchmark his progress, choose tests that have a mix of what he's good at and what he finds harder. Or pick one of each – and afterwards 'read' your sheets according to what you knew when you made the decision to enter. That way, you won't inflate and be blinded by the appreciation you expected – and you won't be disappointed and disheartened by criticism that is fairly deserved.

Maxim | there are always alternatives

section five

Working together

Are you on target?	**222**
Coaching centaurs	**236**

15 Are you on target?

> The object is not to get someone to give you the answer, the idea is to figure out your own answer…
>
> **Paul Belasik,** *Riding Towards the Light*[1]

A homeowner called an engineer because the central heating had broken down. The engineer took only the briefest look at the system before tapping just one radiator. The system started working again. When the bill arrived, the homeowner was horrified, and phoned the engineer to complain that his fee was extortionate. 'You're asking me to pay you hundreds of pounds! Yet all you did was tap one radiator', he said. 'That's right', replied the engineer. 'I charged you five pence for tapping the radiator: the rest is for knowing where to tap.'

Good riding can look as simple as this tap in the right place – and it involves just as much hidden expertise. As you try to communicate better with your horse, refine your position and your aiding, and score more in competitions, you can invest enormous amounts of energy and dedication. But are you investing them in the right place? Are you aiming them for the right target?

Improving performance in dressage competitions is usually thought of as a matter of learning new skills and honing technique. I'm sure that by now it will have become clear to you that I see it as involving much more than this. Many of the great equestrian teachers and writers, including in recent times Erik Herbermann, Paul Belasik and Charles de Kunffy, emphasize the mental and spiritual dimensions of riding. They are clearly passionate about the educative power of horses and the role of dressage as a form of absorption almost akin to meditation, yet I don't think they have been able to offer a structure for developing these other dimensions of the rider that even begins to touch the sophistication and practical usefulness of their technical advice. These writers share a fundamental philosophy about what it means to be a rider, which has been handed down for hundreds of years, and this is part of what makes their work truly inspirational. They can, and do, tell us about the ideal frame of mind in which a rider should approach riding – but not exactly *how* to go about having, or getting into, that frame of mind. That's what I intend to explore in this chapter.

The need for mental strategy in riding

Until relatively recently we have lacked the groundwork for understanding just how people *inwardly* go about making sense of their individual experience of the world and how this translates *outwardly* into the way they seek to shape and influence it. We have lacked the how-tos of the mind. So far in this book, I've only referred briefly to Neuro-Linguistic Programming (NLP), though that is the body of knowledge that helps me understand how human beings function and gives a strategic underpinning to my work as a coach. I find NLP an extremely valuable tool-box for working on my own riding and for helping other riders, and it is NLP that I believe provides us with the missing 'technology' that can help us to understand and manage the mental and emotional dimensions of our riding more effectively.

In Chapter 13 I explained how you can develop a comprehensive 'layered' strategy to prepare for competition and manage your personal version of competition nerves. I was drawing on one of the most powerful and versatile NLP tools: the model of the neurological levels. This model, often expressed in NLP as 'Neuro Logical', or 'Logical Levels' arises from the common awareness that experience is multi-layered and that experiences on different levels (layers) can be linked to each other. Like everything else in NLP, this system of categories was identified through observing and talking to many, many people, so it's grounded in proven experience rather than just proposed as a theory.

The words 'layer' and 'level' both indicate that, in order to make sense of their experience and work with it both mentally and in practical terms, people make use of an (often unrecognized) organizing system that they have implicit in their minds, that seems to come naturally to most other people as well. I want to return to this naturally occurring mental organization of experience more fully now and to use the model NLP offers us to show how it can be applied in an even more far-reaching way, ensuring that you and your horse both get the most out of your time together.

The neurological levels model offers us a clear and simple way of unpacking our instinctive appreciation of the multi-layered way we think about the world, and gives us real leverage not only for understanding its complexities better, but also for becoming more effective in practical terms. It gives us a comprehensive way of working with ourselves and others. It helps us make sure that we focus our energies where we need to and yet, at the same time, leave nothing important out. It's a multi-tool that covers both thought and action, helping us to analyse what's happening (mentally or externally), to act appropriately and to ensure that what we do fits with who we are.

I believe that the neurological levels model can help us extensively and profoundly in every aspect of our riding. In my earlier books (*Schooling Problems Solved with NLP* and *Solo Schooling*) I briefly explained some ways in which this model can be used. Though, as mentioned; it's often referred to as just 'Logical Levels', I'm going to keep to its original title here because that helps to remind us of the body-mind connection so essential in riding: we're not just talking about logic and thought, but about how these interconnect with the body, affecting a person's energy levels and mind-body states as well as their actual behaviour.

Exploring the neurological levels model

Human beings seem to categorize things quite naturally: we learn quite young in life that our friend *Fluffy* is a *cat*; later on we may come to understand that a cat is a *mammal*; that *mammals* are *vertebrates* and that *vertebrates* are *living organisms*. In expanding our view outward from one personally-known cat into this series of ever-widening groups, we are making use of a 'nested' system of categorization. It's quite likely that children will also be taught how this works – and how it doesn't work – in reverse: not all living organisms are vertebrates... not all mammals are cats... The nesting principle of categories is one that most people understand quite readily. The neurological levels system is also one that seems to come naturally, in fact people use its distinctions *without having been taught them;* it seems to have a mentally 'built-in' or 'hard-wired' quality. This means that, though its different levels are part of the very fabric of the way we think and talk, we make use of them instinctively rather than consciously and deliberately. But this also means that, until we have a fuller awareness of how the levels relate to each other, we haven't got the fullest access to all their potential *as a system*.

There's a very simple way of remembering what the different neurological levels are: each one of them gives you the answer to a common everyday question.

Where? and **When?** take you into the area of surroundings, context and ENVIRONMENT (e.g. 'Where do you ride?' – 'I ride on bridleways and farmland'.)

What? takes you into actions and BEHAVIOUR (e.g. 'What kind of riding do you do?' – 'I go out hacking.')

How? takes you into methods, skills and knowledge, ability and CAPABILITY (e.g. *'Can your horse do flying changes?'* – 'No, but he can do simple ones.')

Why? points you towards reasons, explanations, BELIEFS AND VALUES (e.g. *'Do you do anything apart from dressage with your horse?'* – 'Yes, I think it's important for him to do things that freshen his mind and exercise his muscles differently, like jumping and hacking.')

Who? directs you towards IDENTITY (e.g. *'What kind of a rider are you?'* – 'I am a bold/timid rider.')

If you think carefully about these questions, you can see that the sequence they occur in is not just random. There's a principle at work, just as there was in the sequence that began with *Fluffy* and led to *living organisms*. The underlying principle of the neurological levels is different but, in its own way, just as progressive. In Chapter 13 I described the system of layers as being like the layers of an onion, and this system of concentric circles is one way in which the neurological levels model is often presented, emphasizing the gradations of difference between 'innermost' and 'outermost' layers. However, in this chapter I want to use the other version of the model, which emphasizes a hierarchy (top-bottom) of importance. Each version offers us a slightly different – and therefore differently useful – 'take' on the same essential concept.

Think of a pyramid with **identity** at the top and **environment** at the bottom:

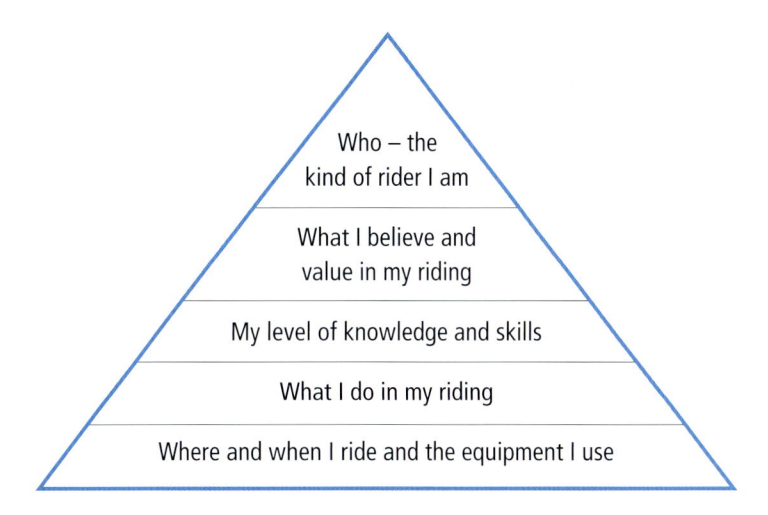

```
                    /\
                   /  \
                  / Who – the \
                 / kind of rider I am \
                /─────────────────────\
               /   What I believe and   \
              /    value in my riding    \
             /───────────────────────────\
            /  My level of knowledge and skills \
           /─────────────────────────────────────\
          /        What I do in my riding         \
         /─────────────────────────────────────────\
        / Where and when I ride and the equipment I use \
       /───────────────────────────────────────────────\
```

If you look at the list like this, **identity** clearly seems more important than **environment**. It sits naturally at the top. You will obviously feel more strongly about problems, conflicts, concerns and triumphs that involve your sense of identity – who you are – than you do about your surroundings and equipment

Maxim | you've got what it takes

(**environment**) because who you are is closer to your heart and thus more precious to you. The rider whose horsebox broke down (yet again) on the way to a competition (**environment**) is unlikely to be in tears because of her broken clutch cable! It's much more likely that she will be disappointed, frustrated or furious because an environmental glitch prevented her from showing her ability to perform (**capability**) or perhaps winning that class she needed to prove her ability in the big league by qualifying for the National Finals (**identity**).

Often, in trying to deal with a problem, we try to fix it in its own terms – that is, on its own level – but this rarely helps. Finding a solution can often be more complex than simply identifying and matching the right level because there can be important influences and knock-on or cascading effects *between* the levels. For example, the kind of environment (mental as well as physical) chosen by the individual will, in part, be determined by who she is, and the environment she's in could also affect how she expresses her identity. For example, if you are an anxious, careful rider, or lack confidence, you may play safe by choosing a reliable rather than a particularly talented horse, operating from your comfort zone rather than taking risks. One knock-on effect of such a decision might be that you don't get the competition scores you could perhaps have achieved with a 'riskier' partner. You may be sentencing yourself to safe mediocrity and thereby fail to discover that you are actually more talented than you think. You'd be missing out on a potential aspect of your identity. By contrast, however able you are and however able your horse, if you can ride only twice a week and have to keep your horse at grass (environmental issues), neither of you may be able to attain the level of fitness you need to excel in competition and therefore may not achieve the fullest expression of your athletic identity that you could do if the circumstances were different.

The point I'm making is that none of the neurological levels should be taken in isolation: you need to consider the interplay between them as well as what may be going on at any individual level. Every level is potentially linked to every other level. The effects are sometimes trivial and sometimes of great significance. Becoming aware of how they can affect you, your horse and your relationship as you progress up the learning spiral gives you much greater understanding and greater leverage when you need to make changes, as I shall go on to explain.

How the neurological levels model can help us

In writing about this model in my earlier books I was drawing briefly on its power to help us work out what kinds of problems we are dealing with, and how we can best approach and solve them. However, the neurological levels model offers us much more than this: it can help us in a number of different ways:

- It gives us a way of understanding the huge complexity of thought, feeling and action involved in all of our experience.

- It provides the base for devising very practical strategies which will work for us individually.

- Because the model allows you and me to map out our unique way of experiencing the world, it can also help us, as unique riders, to identify which of our difficulties are more than they seem on the surface, what they are really about and where we can most effectively intervene to fix them.

- It can get us out of conflicts, with ourselves or with others, and help us develop and tailor-fit solutions and strategies which will enhance that uniqueness of ours.

- It can help us pick goals and find ways to achieve them.

- It allows us to learn more about our own ways of learning.

- It can help us become more competent at what we choose to do – and more fulfilled in doing it.

In short, it's a tool that can lead each of us to a treasury of personal resources, helping us both as riders and as individuals living our unique lives.

Using the model

When I came to read the notes that my case-study riders had written about our work together, I was struck by the fact that the learning and change they were talking about was occurring on a number of neurological levels, and was not restricted to behaviour and capability. Here are some examples:

*'…when things slip, just thinking elbows, and thinking **proud**, makes an **immediate** difference'.* (Roy)

(**Behaviour** plus **beliefs and values** eliciting greater **capability**)

'…made me more aware of what I can achieve by being more positive myself'. (Roy again)

(**Beliefs** influencing **behaviour**)

'Before I'd feel I couldn't progress from Preliminary level until I was really doing well in competition... Since... I've entered Elementary tests...' (Carolyn)

(**Beliefs** influencing **behaviour**)

'I had lost confidence owing to a fall. I had started to convince myself that Ambrose had a stumbling problem: whenever I cantered, be it in the school or out hacking, I thought he was going to stumble and fall over... You understood why I felt that way and encouraged me to accept that I needed a great deal of canter practice to rebuild the confidence I'd lost. Now I'm riding and thinking about the quality of the canter, sending it on and bringing it back... Enjoying canter!' (Carolyn)

(**Behaviour** influencing **beliefs**, then changed **beliefs** bringing about a change in **behaviour** – and **beliefs**!)

Though I could take a very wide view of how the neurological levels model can help us, here I'm going to focus specifically on how it helps with learning and problem-solving.

Learning and problem-solving

What does learning involve? Many people would answer this question by talking about acquiring or developing their *knowledge* and *skills*. What kind of skills? In riding, various physical skills, such as mastering rising trot and learning leg-yielding, or mental skills such as knowing what to feed a horse that will keep him fit without having him jumping out of his skin. Maybe some other people's answers would refer to getting the best **environment** for learning to take place: in a riding context this might include things like finding a good riding school or a different livery yard, getting access to gallops or a cross-country course. It could even include things like choosing the right bit, or knowing whether a trainer offers lessons in the evenings. The answers they'd be seeking would help them select the right environment (very broadly defined) for their riding.

    Riders and trainers spend a lot of time on issues like these. Lessons, books, videos and magazine articles all focus on them. In your ongoing development as a rider, your learning will be greatly affected by where and when you ride, by what you do and how you do it, by the way you are taught and the level of understanding and physical proficiency you achieve. These things are important but, as we know instinctively, there's a lot more to riding than that – and so there must be more involved in learning to be the best kind of rider you can be than simply gathering information, honing physical skills and getting the context of your riding right. So what's been left out?

In beginning to answer this question, I should explain that I've chosen to focus on learning rather than on performance because learning underlies and shapes performance and also because it's my belief that every ride is a learning opportunity, for us and for our horses, whether or not we take it as such. Riding is never finished, because it involves a relationship between living creatures that has to be negotiated and renegotiated every time we ride. It involves mind, body and spirit, and the interaction between distinctly individual beings. That's why these often-left-out areas are of such vital importance. When we look at the layers of human experience identified by NLP in the neurological levels model it becomes very clear that our understanding of riding will be limited (and therefore limiting) when it leaves out those most important elements – that is, **beliefs and values** and **identity**. As I've explored earlier in this book, what you **believe** about your horse, about training and about competition will affect what you think is important (and therefore **value**), the choices you make and whether you are able to perform to the best of your ability. And your very **identity** – who you are – which includes what you **believe** about yourself – is of huge significance. It can make all the difference to your confidence; it can limit your ability to succeed and achieve; or it can help you make the very best out of your partnership with your horse.

I've argued earlier in this book that we can make more progress – and feel less anxious, guilty or inadequate – if we take problems, not as obstacles to overcome, but as diagnostic feedback about where we need to refine how we go about things. And it's in this spirit that I think we can gain most from using the neurological levels model. Any problem, on whatever level, is a valuable signal. However, the best place to take action may be somewhere else, and the model can help you discover where that is.

Learning and change – don't stop too soon!

It's clear that learning a physical skill such as riding will involve you in learning about environment, behaviour and skills. But learning happens in a context – not just one involving these lower levels in the neurological levels model, but one that involves the higher levels as well. If you confine your skill-development, your questioning, your experimenting and adjusting to feedback to the lower levels, you will be in danger of missing out on learning that is much more comprehensive and satisfying, and solutions that really work instead of ones that just put a cosmetic gloss on the situation. You will be stopping too soon.

Let's look at why this is. As part of our regular lessons and the 'riding weeks' that our first teacher, Kimberley, organized for us as a family in our early days of dressage riding, we learnt about feed, shoeing, tack and stable routines as well as about what to do on a horse. We learnt about conformation and breed types. We did exercises on the lunge, and learnt how to lunge. We learnt leg-yields and turns on the forehand. We rode with and without stirrups. Sometimes we rode with our eyes closed to develop our feel and (eventually!) our confidence. But we didn't stop there. From the outset, Kimberley set all our learning in a context of beliefs and values: those of classical horsemanship and classical dressage. Believing that this way of riding offered greater gymnastic value to the horse in his training, and greater pleasure and finesse to the rider in communicating with him through the aids, meant that whatever we did and whatever we learnt was within a distinctive framework of beliefs and values that made even quite small things more meaningful. Riding without reins and stirrups on the lunge was an achievement not just of knowledge, behaviour and skill but also one that contributed to a new sense of our identity: we weren't just riders, not even novice dressage riders, but *classical* riders. This belief that we were working within an important and admirable tradition helped set our less-than-perfect attempts in a framework of being 'apprentices' to that great tradition: instead of blaming ourselves for any 'failures', we were much more inclined to mentally pat ourselves on the back for knowing what we were aiming at and for working patiently to improve each attempt to live up to those high standards that we valued.

It's interesting that Paul Belasik draws on the same metaphor of learning – that of the ancient Guild system – when he talks in several passages of *Riding Towards the Light* of being an 'apprentice' and 'journeyman'. From apprentice to journeyman to master craftsman… How would it be to think of your own riding in the light of that patient and systematic progression? Some trainers in the classical tradition even give their pupils the courtesy title 'Master', not because they have attained mastery, but in recognition of their determination to progress down that path. If we take riding in this way, it helps us to put our learning in a context that actually brings the different neurological levels together in a meaningful way. The notion that riding is an ancient art, to be handed down from generation to generation, means that its knowledge and skills – and the hard work, dedication and discipline that are involved in acquiring them – are underpinned by an appropriate system of beliefs and values, giving a sense of meaningful identity to each and every participant who works at their riding in that spirit. There is only a dwindling number of great equestrian academies left, but if you adopt the values and practices of classical equestrianism as your own you are volunteering to make yourself a member of the same 'guild', serving the same values they serve.

When you underpin your riding like this, there's another very important consequence: you will find a sense of one-ness in your learning that can sustain you through its difficulties as well as enhance your sense of its achievements. You will be experiencing a sense of *alignment* or *congruence* between the neurological levels.

The where-and-when, the what, the how, the why and the who of your riding will all work harmoniously together. Think of times when you have felt stressed in your riding; in conflict with others at the yard, not in tune with your trainer or out of synch with your horse. If you think back on these times now, from the perspective of the neurological levels, I think you'll find that there has been a lack of 'fit' somewhere in the hierarchy. Write the levels down in their hierarchical order…

Identity
Beliefs and Values
Capability
Behaviour
Environment

…and the problem areas are likely to feel as though they should be off to one side or the other, rather than in a clean, straight line with the rest.

For example, if you take a poor competition mark as 'evidence' that you are no good as a rider, the lack of alignment will be between your capability (as represented by the marks you achieved) and your sense of identity:

                                                          Identity
              Beliefs and Values
Capability
                   Behaviour
                 Environment

A misalignment of a different and more complex kind would arise if you felt that your trainer was bullying you to take a firm line with your horse because she thought he was being lazy, while you thought his reluctance to go forward really stemmed from finding the work difficult. In this case, the conflict at first seems to be between what you are actually doing and what she thinks you should be doing (behaviour). However, there's more to it than this: the real conflict is not between values (hers) and actions (yours) but between the different beliefs you each hold about why your horse is behaving as he is – a lack of alignment on the level of beliefs and values. So there are actually two misalignments operating at once:

                        Identity
Beliefs and Values
(hers and yours)   Capability
                                          Behaviour (your horse
                                          and you)
                      Environment

Maxim | you've got what it takes

Once you have identified the lack of fit that's distressing you, you can begin to work out how to restore alignment and harmony. If one of the higher levels is involved, that's usually the level you need to work with. Take the first example again: openly discussing your ideological differences with your trainer may mean that the two of you are able to find a point of agreement. In the course of talking things through with each other, you may find that either or both of you can modify the way you see the situation, restoring your harmony and giving you a common ground for working with your horse. Even if your original trainer is technically 'right' in her diagnosis, for so long as you can't go along with her at such a high neurological level you will not be able to benefit from what she has to offer you – and your horse will be a victim of your tensions and conflicting approaches. If the case is extreme and talking things over just hardens your differences, you may have to find another trainer who sees things more as you do. If you are struggling to make such a decision, remember that you are not the only one whose alignment is involved: your trainer – and your horse – will also be suffering. It's not necessarily selfish, or a 'cop-out', to make that break.

As a rule of thumb, when you are having difficulties, be ready to look beyond the obvious level on which they are occurring, and to explore what other levels may be involved.

The neurological levels model isn't just for problems and crises, though. When you are having successes, it will pay you to ask yourself the same questions: where's the success showing up – and where's it stemming from? Maybe you are a really quick learner. Is that just because you are able intellectually, or have good coordination (both features of your equestrian capability)? Or is it because you are willing to experiment, to take feedback and try to use it in a positive way? The underlying value you cherish here may be 'the principles of classical riding', and your underlying belief may be something like, 'I can learn from the feedback my horse and my trainer give me.' Or maybe your underlying platform for success is at an even higher level: it's to do with how you think of yourself (your identity): 'I'm someone who loves learning and enjoys using feedback of all kinds to challenge myself and refine what I can do.'

It's a curious fact that, though it's common for riders to think well of their horses (at an identity if not always capability level!) they are much more reluctant to think well of themselves. (Where the situation is reversed, of course, the way is open for treating the horse as an object rather than a sentient being, often with unpleasant consequences for the horse.) How would it be to accept who you are – just because that *is* who you are – as wholeheartedly as you accept your horse for who he is? Years ago we took on a youngster, Hawkeye, with a snatching hind leg action that had resulted from severe muscle damage: if we hadn't taken the risk, he would have been shot. Backing and training him classically under our teacher

Kimberley's guidance, and in so doing helping him build up strength to compensate for that damage, was one of our most exciting achievements as a family. A horse who in one judge's view 'should never have been brought into a competition arena' was the gentlest of giants and the most reliable of friends. Another horse we had, our much-loved and valued Lolly, had a dramatic sway back – but he also had a generous nature and an enthusiasm for life (as well as a lightness off the leg and a balanced self-carriage) that were infinitely more important than his strange shape. Why can we extend warmth and generosity to our horses on this most important of levels while we sometimes find it difficult to extend the same acceptance to ourselves?

Improving your dressage scores can be taken as an end in itself; but I hope that by now you will be convinced that the best route to this achievement is one which will bring you so much else besides. If you care for your horse, and your riding, on every one of the neurological levels you will be on a journey of exploration and discovery that never ends, and yet always offers you rewards and satisfactions. You will be on a journey that has been travelled over the centuries by all the great horsemasters, and many, many discerning riders. You will have the means of recognizing when things are out of alignment, and tools for restoring harmony. You will enjoy this amazing centaur-like partnership with your horse, and keep discovering how to refine it – and be refined by it. Problems will suggest avenues for further learning, and deep down you will know just how you have gone about creating your successes.

Like the spiral of training, riding itself is never finished. It is always going somewhere – in every moment. I believe that its frustrations and its rewards stem from the same thing: riding can involve us at every level. Riding a cherished partner in this spirit also gives us a way to be true to ourselves.

Tips for trainers

Coaching the whole person – finding the most effective level for leverage

In teaching as in riding, the aim is to get the best result for the least effort on the part of both teacher and learner. To achieve this, you need to know about leverage. Think of a paving stone: it may be heavy but it can be lifted relatively easily if you have the right kind of lever applied in the right place. The neurological levels model gives you, not one lever, but a whole set of them! Here are some suggestions as to how you can apply them most effectively in your teaching.

- When your client runs into difficulties, use the model to identify the level on which she is experiencing the problem and then to check whether the origin of the problem may be on another level. Problems at the levels of behaviour and capability often have their origin at the level of belief. I remember, for example, having a jumping lesson in which I successfully coped with several increases in the height of the bar. Then suddenly I 'just knew' I couldn't manage the next height – a rise of only an inch or so. This was not about out-there behaviour, but in-here belief! To assist me, my teacher would have needed to help me find a way to change the belief that was limiting my behaviour and preventing me from developing my skill. (Maybe something like this issue of belief prompts horses to refuse sometimes: in their own way they may believe they have reached a limit. As with riders, it can be important to try to determine whether the problem is one of self-belief rather than physical capability. The training need – to build the individual's confidence in ways that work for them – is much the same.)

- When you offer criticism, offer it at the lowest level that you can. It's easier for someone to take on board the idea that they need to make a change in environment (*'Try it without stirrups'*), behaviour (*'Put your lower leg further back'*) or capability (*'You'll get better at that with more practice'*) than it is for them to accept a change in beliefs (*'You need to understand that horses are lazy and try every evasion they can'*) or identity (*'You'll never be a bold rider'*). Essentially, it's the way you offer feedback that makes it constructive or destructive: going in at the lowest level that respects the usable truth of the situation is the secret.

- When you offer praise, on the other hand, offer it at the highest level you can, so that it has the most impact in terms of enhancing self-confidence. Without self-belief, even the most talented rider will under-perform: with it, even an average rider will be able to do her best more of the time. Remember, too, that your pupil's self-confidence is what supports her horse – or erodes his confidence, not only in her, but in himself and the situation. *'You are such a quick learner'* (identity) means so much more than *'You picked that up fast'* (capability). And a rider who's told: *'You're working on the right principles'* (beliefs and values) will be much more ready to work on enlarging her knowledge and refining her behaviour.

What would it be like to coach a centaur?

The classical myth of the centaur possibly arose out of the sheer marvel of seeing a human being apparently at one with a horse. Even now, when we have centuries of familiarity with that marvel and so much knowledge about how that apparent

Maxim | you've got what it takes

unity is created and maintained, the image offers us an ideal of how we would wish riding to feel: as though we and our horse were one being. I think it can also give us a new aim in our teaching: what if we were working with a single, unified pupil – a centaur – rather than with the rider or the rider-and-horse? I think it might also focus our attention more on developing the mutual flow of attention and harmony between the 'top-half' and the 'bottom-half' of this creature.

I think it might save us from the potential damage we can cause when we ask the human half to demand that the equine half do something, or tell her he's cheating on her. Would you tell someone that her own legs or back were cheating on her? Of course the centaur is a myth, but it can inspire us to be more sensitive in our teaching and to help our pupils become more receptive to each other in their learning. What differences would thinking about your partnered pupils like this make to what you say to them, or about them to each other? Would you feel quite so free to get on someone's horse 'just to sort him out' for her, as you have done in the past? How would it affect your understanding of the difficulties they get into with each other? How would it impact on your understanding of the way they can best learn together? How might it help you become the kind of teacher who enhances their integrity and helps them display their shared uniqueness?

There are no simple answers to these questions – but then the questions aren't simple questions. They are questions at the levels of beliefs, values and identity. They are worth asking, and worth trying to answer. They are the kind of questions I found myself asking when I worked with my case-study partnerships – which is why the next chapter has headings composed of four paired sets of names. I realize now that was how my husband Leo and I thought of them, when we booked sessions with them in our diaries, when we made notes about what happened in each session, and when we talked about them to each other. We never talked about 'Annie and her horse', or 'Carolyn and her horse', but always about Annie and Red, Carolyn and Ambrose, Shane and Ted, Roy and Cori. Perhaps, in our minds, we even saw these entities as single forms with no spaces between the names, e.g. 'Annie&Red'. This wasn't deliberate: it just seemed to happen naturally. I'd like to think it happened because, at heart, our work together was aimed at developing four living, multi-talented creatures rather than eight separate ones.

Maxim | you've got what it takes

16 Coaching centaurs

Working with an established horse and rider partnership is rather like trying to help the right hand understand what the left is doing, or trying to be helpful to the partners in a marriage: there are unrecognized or even hidden dynamics, powerful loyalties, shared history and tender feelings to be respected. Any change in one partner will inevitably affect the other, and so a ricochet effect can develop: when you ask the rider to make a change, it will inevitably affect not simply her horse but also the intangible but nonetheless real entity that she and he make up together. Coaching the centaur is hugely complex, hugely exciting – and a huge responsibility.

When I started planning this book, I assumed without thinking too deeply about it that I would need 'case-studies'. I would try to help some riders 'score more'. When I've done this in the past, it's provided first-hand stories to illustrate what I'm saying and bring it to life for the reader. I assumed that this would happen again, and that, in working together, we would be able to explore and demonstrate the kinds of things that inhibit and enhance progress in competition dressage. But it worked out much better than that. It just so happened that I started planning the case-studies and wondering who to work with as spring was beginning, and so it seemed a good idea to begin our training sessions almost at once so that we could take advantage of the longer days and (hopefully) better weather. We began, in fact, some months before I was free to begin the actual writing. This hands-on-first timing was an accident that turned out to be a true blessing, because the questions that arose, the discoveries we shared and the achievements we celebrated together each time we met did far more than illustrate an argument: they effectively shaped and directed the whole course of the book. In the best traditions of any practical endeavour (including, of course, NLP itself) the 'hows' – both physical and mental – came first: the refinements of understanding and practice – the recipes for what works and why – were distilled and refined later.

My contribution to our work was two sets of tools: an understanding of classical equitation and my skill in NLP coaching. My hope was that whatever we did 'on the day' would make a contribution to the case-studies' progress around the spiral of learning and, at the same time, enrich them on a number of the neurological levels. Each rider-horse combination had its characteristic strengths and challenges, and these themes will emerge as you read through the notes Leo made during the working sessions. The riders brought their love of their horses, their commitment to doing the best they could by them, and their curiosity, openness and commitment to learning. Between us, we had not just the basic ingredients for learning and improvement, but the best possible ones.

An additional, unplanned, aid to the riders turned out to be the photographs that Leo took of each session. These were originally intended to document our work and their progress, and after each session we gave each rider a set as a record. As it turned out, the riders all found more practical value in the photos than we had anticipated: they scrutinized what they had done in relation to the discussions we had held in the sessions, and used them as aids to memory for practice between sessions. They were deeply pleased by having their 'good moments' recorded – and willing to look at and learn from the less good ones.

To my mind, the best place to begin describing how we worked together is with the riders' own words (which are then followed by the notes Leo made of each session). It's an axiom of NLP that 'the message means what the receiver receives': in other words, it's not what I *intended* that counts but what they *understood* by it. The experiences that the riders talk about affected them and their equine partners on many of the NeuroLogical levels and, as a coach, I believe that we were able to achieve more just because we were willing to make jumps and connections between them.

Annie and Red

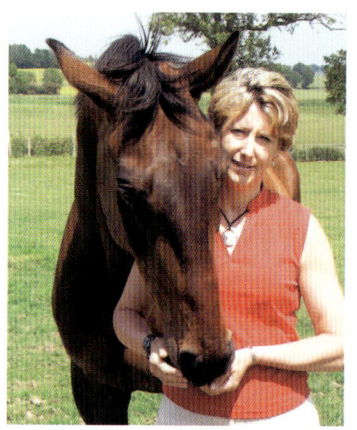

Red is a 12-year-old Trakehner x Thoroughbred whom I bred myself. He lives out along with our other horse and pony. I work full-time in the family business, and also have two children, so Red doesn't get worked as much as I would like. When I was younger I worked part-time and could spend more time on my riding. Now, at 40 and with full-time work and my family needing more of me, I find that my weekend riding usually has to be done early in the morning! My daughter also wants to ride and Red is too spooky to be a reliable lead horse. Red and I compete in most activities offered by our local Riding Club, though nowadays the pressure of juggling all my commitments often means that I have to ask myself if I have enough time to prepare properly.

What Annie said about the sessions

I was thrilled when I received an e-mail from Wendy inviting me to take part in her new book. The added bonus of the photographs was fantastic too. I have been riding for many years, being taught by people who were obviously good riders, but not so good at relaying their knowledge.

I had just had a year's fortnightly lessons with a teacher who had managed to make me appreciate how to *feel* what I wanted to achieve. This, I realize, was the most important first step.

With Wendy we worked on those feelings which improved all my riding; not only the gaits but the transitions up and down. A lot of teachers concentrate on individual gaits but not how to move up and down through them.

Wendy explains how the horse is going to tackle a movement, which order the legs move in, how he bends his neck and body and how I can give aids and when, to help him understand.

I have noticed that when mistakes are being made, mostly you have no idea that you are doing them. If my hands are in the wrong place or moving too much, instead of repositioning them which most teachers do (this doesn't help because as soon as the teacher isn't there they go back to the wrong place), she makes you *feel* them keep still, by placing them on a fixed spot, thighs or pommel. This makes you aware of how much movement you were making. You can slowly adjust them back into a more correct position, keeping the elbows in and keeping them relaxed back. Wendy then gives you mental pictures, which help you maintain this – rise through your hands – carrying your tea tray.

My dressage results have improved during my lessons with Wendy. I think about keeping calm and relaxed and not suddenly changing and pulling up the reins as I turn up the centre line! I can concentrate on thinking about looking like a dressage rider. Before the competition I ride the test over in my head, visualizing how I'm going to prepare for different aspects of the movements.

Red has never been an easy horse. He is very excitable and loses concentration easily, especially at competitions. I now feel that me being calmer has helped him and, although he has also grown up (Trakehners take a long time to mature), he concentrates and listens to me much better.

In his favour, Red is a very willing horse who tries hard for you most of the time. I tend to feel frustrated when I'm not managing or achieving something, which I blame onto him (e.g. breaking in canter) and call him lazy. Wendy has explained that this may be owing to him not being balanced enough and that I should change his pace [either 'speed' or 'gait' as appropriate – author] and make a transition before he breaks so that he can build up his strength.

below left **'Wendy explains how the horse is going to tackle a movement.'** In this case I seem to be demonstrating with my legs how we want Red to move, while using my torso and arms to show Annie how she should orchestrate the leg-yield she is about to try. Multi-messaging – no wonder Red looks so quizzical!

below right Annie and Red showing good balance in the canter.

What we did together

First session: off-horse

Annie's aims:

- Move on from Preliminary to higher levels.
- Improve the skills I've got.
- I'd like to feel at the end of a test that I've achieved something and be able to use it for benchmarking progress.
- Know I'm giving him the correct messages (e.g. for shoulder-in) and be able to do it each time.
- Keep focused.
- Not get angry when we go wrong, because it annoys Red.

Annie says that, when learning tests, she visualizes and remembers the test as a pattern. This can easily get blanked out if she is doing more than one test.

Second session

Exercises to get Red listening to the leg.

Helping Red to stretch and take the contact.

Making Annie's elbows a part of her seat: closeness and bend.

Sitting more upright, softening her lower back to absorb movement.

Annie needs to straighten her left wrist and grow taller in her left side, which tends to collapse.

Using the slope to encourage Red to carry himself and adjust his balance without Annie 'carrying' him.

Third session

Annie wanted to do lateral work.

Has been practising keeping her elbows in and helping Red work towards the bit. Wendy comments that her elbows are following softly in the canter.

Using inside leg to help Red engage through corners, and keeping legs against his sides more of the time to support him.

Shoulder-in and leg-yielding. Preparation of balance and engagement through the corner before asking.

Fourth session

Annie got 66.4% and 69.2% in competition the previous week.

Different saddle – gave her a better leg position.

Working on compressing and lengthening the stride in trot – making use of the changing slopes in the field. Increases confidence in being able to produce correct work in different terrains (useful for an eventer!) Does a trot have a halt ready in it? Or a canter? If you ask?

Annie reports she finds it harder to keep her right leg on – Wendy suggests off-horse strengthening exercises to help even up.

Fifth session

Rain stopped play! Went indoors and looked through the photos from fourth session. Minute analyses of balance, engagement and 'throughness'.

Annie reported that a recent test had gone badly: Red was spooky and she grabbed him to pull him together. She said it was a reminder to ride him more softly and less aggressively in future.

Analysis of the photos shows that Red is more together and 'through' when Annie's legs are in the correct position, stretched back and down, and when her shoulder-

above left Annie's habit of collapsing to the left (a very common one amongst kinesthetic riders) is allowing Red to overbend and fall through his right shoulder in this shoulder-in.

above right A more upright posture from Annie produces better balance and control from Red.

Maxim | you've got what it takes

hip-heel alignment is good. She now needs to make sure this happens more of the time!

Talked about rising trot – going forward from the hip with weight on knee rather than up-down with shoulder pulling/leading. Annie could see this clearly and we all practised it in the kitchen, lifting from chairs.

Wendy suggested leg swings and calf pressures to strengthen Annie's right leg, plus calf-raises to help deepen heel stretch.

The issue of shoulder-hip-heel alignment. As we can see from the *left-hand* picture, a 'disengaged' rider produces a disengaged and 'hollow' horse. When Annie engages her seat by bringing her legs back and down and growing tall in her spine (*right-hand picture*), Red is able to engage (note the closed V-shape in his trot) and to lift his back and connect through.

Sixth session

Annie reports that when Red is calm in tests judges' comments tend to say *'could do more'*. Talked about increasing his activity behind with more stepping under, less pushing forward. Using corners to increase engagement and concertina-like lengthening and collecting on the long sides.

Shoulder-in and leg-yielding. Annie says: 'Very helpful: gave me the feeling of what should happen.'

Encouraging Red to move through the back more. Annie found the suggestion to 'rise through your elbows' helpful – so did Red, who softened in response as she softened. Annie said this was 'one of those times when I felt the trot was balanced enough to have a halt – or a canter – ready in it'.

Making sure Annie doesn't curl over to the left with inclined head and collapsed waist.

Seventh session

Annie's elbows bent and placed correctly, but 'held' so that her hands are rising and falling. Reminder to rise through her elbows. Tried some work with hands touching pommel to steady them.

Red carrying himself more elastically – looking short for a long horse.

Annie reports 70.5% in Horse Trials dressage – same mark at two different venues.

Lengthening and collecting the canter from the seat (larger and smaller movement) rather than relying on the reins. Red finds it difficult to shorten his stride – tends to fall into trot – so we know more practice is needed. His near hind is weaker – more shoulder-in to help strengthen it.

Red **'looking short for a long horse'.** This silhouette photo shows clearly how Red is stepping under and carrying himself with balance and elasticity.

Eighth session

Working on self-carriage.

Transitions within the trot, aiming to get Red more elastic and suspended.

In the canter Red drops out on left rein and loses balance. Asked Annie to scuff down her inside heel on every stride to encourage him to keep his inside hind active. Suggested keeping bursts of canter brief and returning to trot before he falls out of balance. Gradually aim to lengthen canter bursts.

More work on Annie's uprightness, especially on the left rein.

Homework: more of this and to be thinking towards higher levels of competition, where she will be asked for more advanced work. Push the boundaries a little.

Maxim | you've got what it takes

Ninth session

Red has lost condition in the cold winter, so less energetic work today.

Spiralling in and out at walk to help bend and build ability to carry himself more with the inside hind.

Trot standing (i.e. light seat) to reward and loosen him through after concentrated work. Emphasis on soft elbows opening and closing as Annie rises and sits – keeps the hands level and contact constant.

A little canter work – aim is to get Red carrying himself more rather than relying on eventing forwardness and propulsion.

Walk to canter for two or three strides then trot again or ask for walk. Annie to bring her inside shoulder back in rhythm with the stride for two or three strides to deepen her inside seat-bone and help Red's collection, then make the transition itself with the outside shoulder: give with the hand the moment he obeys. Annie says, 'It feels gratifying knowing you are doing it without being told.'

Tenth session

Let's see what emerges from the warm-up. Nice stretch and activity in trot.

Canter plié [a shortish leg-yield that requires the horse to balance in an unsupported space, often ridden from the quarter line to the track, or across a corner] from A or C to increase engagement and suppleness. Also canter shoulder-fore [halfway to shoulder-in] on the long side. Red found both movements harder on the left rein and offered to overbend the neck to avoid engaging and sometimes fell out

Red stretching and taking the rein.

of canter. Annie felt this was inviting her to skew over to the left again and draw up her left leg. More practice needed! Annie says she can feel Red using himself when he's doing it right; 'Like a resistance almost but not in the mind' – pushing his physical boundaries.

Balance is improved. Some really elastic work when Annie shortened the trot. Red is really willing now to stretch and take the rein – contrast how he was when we started. It now happens automatically.

A well-managed canter plié.

Annie's hard work on bending her elbows and keeping them close is paying off in this controlled leg-yield. She is also holding herself much more upright, which helps her control Red's right shoulder. If she had kinked to the left as she often used to, he would almost certainly have overbent his neck and fallen out through his right shoulder.

Carolyn and Ambrose

Ambrose, a.k.a. Double Venture, is a black 12-year-old, 16.3 hh Thoroughbred x Irish Draught. I'm a single parent of two teenage boys. Like many people I juggle horse care and riding with working, parenting and a hectic life. Though riding since childhood, my skills were quite basic when I bought Ambrose four years ago. Training with classical principles, partnered by a horse with ability and a kind, honest temperament, we continue to learn together. We affiliated last year and compete successfully in Riding Club teams at Novice level, now moving up to Elementary. A high was winning the British Riding Clubs' Pairs to Music Championship with my riding partner, Wendy Ducker.

What Carolyn said about the sessions

The following are notes about 'then and now.'

- I started my sessions in a positive frame of mind, open and excited about trying new things.

- I've enjoyed being less structured about my schooling sessions, letting things happen more naturally. It's encouraged me to try things that may not work but accepting it's still okay and that it's still useful.

- Before, I'd feel I couldn't progress from Preliminary level until I was really doing well in competition.

- Since working with Wendy, my confidence has built. I've entered Elementary tests, achieved some good percentages and had some positive comments from judges. I enjoy the more advanced work and can do some of it, now I have more of a 'let's try it' attitude. My best Elementary has been 67%, which I'd have been pleased with in a Preliminary test.

- I had become disheartened with some aspects of my previous training, feeling that I was never going to progress further than a basic level. Now I'm developing more self-belief: from the start Wendy made me feel that I had a good grounding in training, that I *could* work alone with my horse, that I *could* school and develop him and *progress*.

- I'd become stuck in a way of riding that I didn't feel able to get out of: trainer tells me exactly how to ride; leg here, hands there, weight there, I do it and hey presto it works! Then wait until next week's training session to be able to get it again. Now I'm more selective about my training. I still want and need it but no longer feel I have to cling to it. I have less training but consider it more; use it as an aid, not a crutch.

- I had lost confidence owing to a fall. I had started to convince myself that Ambrose had a stumbling problem: whenever I cantered, be it in the school or out hacking, I thought he was going to stumble and fall over. Wendy helped me to understand why I felt as I did about the issue; allowed me to feel that way, understood why I felt that way and encouraged me to experiment with canter, not to be afraid of it and to accept that I needed a great deal of canter practice to rebuild the confidence I'd lost. Now I'm riding and thinking about the quality of the canter, sending it on and shortening it up. Thinking about softening my position and making my aids clearer and more effective. Enjoying canter! Being brave enough to sit back in canter, which is really sitting up straight!

- I used to school Ambrose thinking that I had to get everything right by the end of the session. I used to want to get Ambrose 'together' as quickly as possible in a session. Now I think just work on one thing and see where it takes us. I like to have a plan for my schooling sessions but now I'm more open to changing the plan. I often use the holding the stick in both hands exercise, which helps me stabilize my elbows and keep both hands level and more still. I'm less in a hurry to get Ambrose 'together'; now I spend much more time stretching in all gaits to get him really warmed up. I also school far more in rising trot.

Conclusion

I feel able to look at myself, see where I am and where I want to go. To think about what I want to achieve, have a go, be more experimental and enjoy, have fun with my horse and my dressage.

There are better horses and better riders but what I want to focus on is being the best we can be and enjoy getting there. To continue learning, training in a classical way and to have a happy, healthy horse.

Enjoying canter. These four canter pictures, starting with Carolyn's first ridden session and finishing with her tenth, clearly show how the effects of their traumatizing fall were eroded by a combination of Carolyn's courage and sheer 'canter miles on the clock'. Carolyn's tense, 'perching' seat and Ambrose's hollow back (1) both responded to their growing confidence and connectedness (2 and 3) and finally changed to a state of real mutual enjoyment and relaxation (4).

'I often use the holding the stick in both hands exercise which helps me stabilize my elbows and keep both hands level and more still.'

What we did together

First session: off-horse

Carolyn says her confidence was knocked about cantering – the fall where she and Ambrose both slid along the ground.

At a recent unaffiliated competition she had a mark of 51% – very disappointed and couldn't work out why the mark was so low.

She and her dressage partner (another Wendy) won the RC Pairs Dressage at Addington – she feels this is a pressure to live up to. Has a 'little voice' that's worried she will let partner Wendy down when they next compete.

Lot of internal dialogue, much of which isn't positive. 'What ifs…' Dwells on past mistakes, has anxieties about letting self and Wendy (trainer) down.

Wendy encouraged her to monitor her self-talk and change it when it's negative.

On the other hand, make use of self-talk to run an internal commentary to help her remember the test and keep focused when competing.

Second session

Test sheet comments on Ambrose's canter along lines of: *'bit lazy – no jump in it'*, *'some small resistances'*. Carolyn feels that Ambrose doesn't have a consistent rhythm – she has to keep adjusting it.

Maxim | you've got what it takes

Wendy asked her to give Ambrose a longer rein and encourage stretch at the start of working sessions. Experiment to discover what Ambrose's natural rhythm is in different gaits.

When asked for trot, Ambrose offered canter. Carolyn says, 'Got to make myself do it – I need miles on the clock in canter. I do 30–40 circuits at trot for every one in canter.'

Wendy invited/encouraged/persuaded her to do a number of circuits in canter on each rein – Carolyn found it (emotionally?) tiring but was pleased with herself for having done it.

Third session

Carolyn's left wrist often kinking down – Wendy suggested she abandon whip for the moment. Explained how riders are often less connected to the left side of their bodies. Asked her to do a serpentine in walk, paying particular attention to changing position, weight and seat – without relying on, or really using, her hands.

Some cantering – focus on keeping left hand still, elbows still, becoming more aware of when Ambrose isn't quite 'through' and using her shoulder to deepen her seat and bring him to this state.

Collecting trot on short side, opening it out on long side.

Homework – do lots of canter!

Asking Ambrose to produce a collected yet impulsive trot on the short side (*below left*) allows Carolyn to generate enough energy for a bigger trot on the long side (*below right*). Because Ambrose is balanced and active, he can produce a truly 'uphill' yet still rounded medium trot rather than – as so often happens – getting faster and flatter.

Fourth session

Area festival – competing at Preliminary and Novice next week. Pairs Final a fortnight away.

Carolyn has been enjoying watching a video of Arthur Kottas. Discussion about lifting the shoulders and then letting the shoulder-blades slide down into the right position.

Trotting – bringing her pelvis forward between her elbows towards her hands.

Canter, using inside shoulder to help Ambrose gather himself. Carolyn notices that she is a bit stiff – Wendy says,'Yes, but think about the progress you have made in just three months – at the beginning you didn't feel able to canter!' Discussion about adjusting ourselves on three planes as horse moves in canter, and how complex this is.

Lateral work – leg-yielding. Carolyn finds it hard to keep weight central and inside leg in correct position (it comes up and forward).

Canter plié [as with Annie and Red], A–E and A–B.

Shoulder-in – start with small circle in corner then coming off on long side in shoulder-in. Concentrating on sitting straight and tall, not kinking in or dropping inside shoulder. Watch out for inside hand creeping across the withers.

Carolyn and Ambrose in shoulder-in. Carolyn's inside (right) hand is creeping across Ambrose's withers, her left arm is straightening and her left hand has become heavy, creating a 'false bend' in Ambrose's neck rather than a 'true' one throughout his body.

Fifth session

Carolyn's outside elbow straightening and hand dropping. (Carolyn had also noticed this in the photos.)

How to offer practical help without nagging? Wendy suggests hold whip across the body in both hands (see book jacket!) – this makes it easier to keep hands level and monitor when they stray.

Did trot to canter transitions, canter on both reins, 5-m loops from the track, all with whip held like this.

Carolyn says she is getting a more consistent feeling and having to use her upper body more to aid, rather than relying on her hands. Wendy notices she's not fiddling to get Ambrose's head down.

Why not try leg-yielding holding the whip? Carolyn is feeling for the moment when Ambrose's inside hind lifts so that she can time her leg aid at this moment of most influence.

Finished with a stretched, energetic trot: very 'through'.

All very pleased with ourselves and each other!

Sixth session

Carolyn says she has been doing a lot of hacking and not much schooling recently, but schooled yesterday using the horizontal stick.

Doing Elementary 41 next week: 'I feel we lose balance in downward transitions.'

Wendy suggests preparing for downward transitions by allowing ankles to flex deeper and deeper with the last few strides – down, down DOWN into the transition. Transition is about using soft vertical pressure. Slowing Ambrose down into a more suspended, not-quite-passage trot in preparation.

Carolyn wants to get Ambrose lighter in front in the canter – Wendy says: 'Make sure you are not behind the vertical, stroke downwards with your inside leg to encourage each stride. Bend elbows, keep hands closer together.'

More difficult for Ambrose on the left rein – this is also where Carolyn's left hand tends to pull back and down. There is a ricochet pattern – she pulls back > he hollows > she pulls back. This pattern needs to be interrupted.

Seventh session

Carolyn wants to practise some movements from Elementary 41 – simple changes and change through trot. These both require her to be able to collect the canter before the transition – collection is the building block. It's also needed for balance when giving and retaking the reins in canter.

Carolyn also wants to work on getting a better transition from free walk to medium. We start with this – Wendy reminds Carolyn of the aiding sequence that helps prepare the horse for any changes: seat, leg, rein. If you alert the horse with seat and leg at the end of the free walk he will gather himself together and bring his head up naturally – then all you have to do is gather up the slack in the rein that he has already offered you!

Carolyn says she is reluctant to collect the canter because Ambrose tends to drop out of the gait. Wendy reminds her that, as they progress, they will need to be able to do collected, medium and extended canter – better begin playing around with these now!

Wendy reminds Carolyn that, when you are aiming to do a movement that is new to you, (and/or the horse) think about what it involves and 'chunk down' to find something that you can do relatively easily that helps build towards what you're after longer-term: 'If that's the desired movement, what are its component parts?'

Noticeable today that Ambrose is staying in collection more consistently. Carolyn's hands are better, though the left hand lets the rein slip more and so she has to gather it in more often.

Carolyn says she has not had any lessons since we last met – has felt 'more grown-up and independent working on her own'. There's a direct connection here between environment/behaviour and identity.

Eighth session

Carolyn had attended a demo by Kyra Kyrklund. Horses should halt square – Ambrose doesn't! Rider needs to be able to feel which leg is doing what. We do some halts, but not too many adjustments as this tends to get horses shifting about – the opposite of what's wanted.

Decide to look at transitions in general – halts are just one sort. Work on getting Ambrose off the seat in upward transitions by clenching buttocks rather than relying on heaving, or solely on leg aid. Get Carolyn to soften her lower back and lift her pelvis up and forward to allow Ambrose room to continue swinging through whilst shortening his stride and collecting – a kind of soft 'trampolining' effect on the saddle. Talk about bouncing a ball and changing its trajectory and height depending on how you do the bouncing – horse a bit similar.

Trot work is really lovely now; canter needs to be softer and more 'through'.

Canter on left rein. Ambrose still tends to brace his neck – Carolyn works on giving the inside rein to help him soften his neck down and come through. Carolyn says she is expecting him to not get around corners without rein aids! She is left-handed and still feels her left hand is too strong – even out hacking. More experimenting needed to find the lightest contact she can manage, and remembering to use upper body position, seat and weight aids for steering, rather than relying on reins!

One good halt is enough – though in the arena a horse often moves as soon as his rider leans forward and lifts her seat to pat him like this!

Shane and Ted

Ted is rising 9; an Irish horse whom I bought, just broken, when he was 4. I breed and show sheep, and also teach riding. I keep Ted at home, and he helps out by taking me around the farm to check on the sheep! We compete in affiliated eventing at Introductory and Pre-novice level, and at showjumping in British Novice and Discovery competitions. We do Riding Club dressage, and have also done some side-saddle and ridden hunter showing.

What Shane said about the sessions

1. We worked on many things over the last six months. Some of them are proving very difficult – my hand, elbow and upper body position being amongst them. I'm seeking even, consistent contact with Ted; correct use of the arena; straightness, in me and in Ted, and 'preparation' in transition, movements, etc.

2. Changes I have made to my riding and my attitude, other than being really conscious of where all the parts of my body are (especially my elbows) are more the thoughts and feelings of how I am when I'm riding: trying to keep a positive attitude when things go wrong and not dwell on the mistakes I've just made. I seem to be asking myself what I can do to improve this more. Have a plan in mind of how to turn in the next corner and stick to the plan (even if the horse is being distracted by something going on elsewhere).

3. Changes I have noticed in both Ted's and my way of going are that we seem to be working more as a team. We've become more balanced. He understands my leg a little more. It's not just for going forward, but sideways as well. We have both become softer in our bodies, especially Ted through his neck.

4. Listening skills have developed throughout the sessions. Ted always seems to be waiting and listening. Sometimes I find this harder to ride as I have to be very precise in what I am asking him. We still sometimes think opposite things from each other.

'We've become more balanced.'
In the picture above, taken during our first session together, Shane is behind Ted's movement and Ted's weight is on his shoulders. In the lower picture, taken in a much later session, Ted is in self-carriage, stepping well under himself and connected through his top-line. Though she is looking down, Shane's seat and lower leg position are much more effective and her close, bent elbows are connecting her rein aids, via her unified upper body, down into her seat. She and Ted are, as she says, 'working more as a team'.

Maxim | you've got what it takes

5. Comments have changed on my sheets. Riding marks are on the up. There are more positives than negatives on them, but still room for great improvement.

6. At the moment I still find it hard to stay chilled at the competitions, so we are using them as schooling sessions to practise staying soft, relaxed, calm and rhythmical, with impulsion. We're improving but not enough to feel I could be reasonably competitive.

7. I have changed the ways I prepare for a dressage competition. The day before is very important to me. Ted needs to have a good workout as well as running through my test once, working on accuracy and activity. At this stage I should know it. In fact I make sure I know my test inside out so that I can plan how I ride

left **'We have both become softer in our bodies'.** This shoulder-in shows Ted bending calmly to the right while remaining soft through the neck and listening to Shane's aiding. She is helping him understand what she wants by turning her shoulders and upper body parallel to his, and she is controlling his outside (left) shoulder with a bent, close, yet soft left elbow. Her hands are held level, with thumbs correctly uppermost, and the impression is rather as though she is 'carrying her horse on a plate' in front of her.

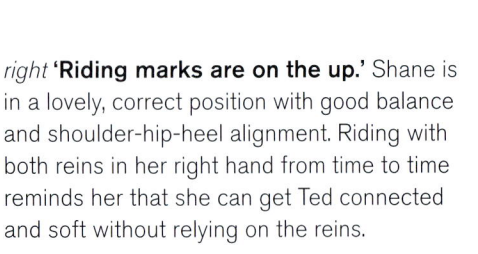

right **'Riding marks are on the up.'** Shane is in a lovely, correct position with good balance and shoulder-hip-heel alignment. Riding with both reins in her right hand from time to time reminds her that she can get Ted connected and soft without relying on the reins.

it without worrying where I am going. At the competition Ted can be quite sharp, so I've always rushed my warm-up. We went straight into trot; we never seemed to chill. I think I just wanted to get the test over and done with. I am now taking a different approach and it seems to be working. Walking and relaxing beforehand, even if it's walking up the lane if the warm-up area is busy. This has helped us both not to get so uptight and the tests have become more accurate, with a more consistent rhythm throughout the movements.

What we did together

First session

Warm-up at walk in long stretch. Shane says they usually get 7s or 8s for walk.

Wendy asking Shane to bend her elbow to connect Ted to her seat through her hands – even on a long rein.

Walk seems a bit plodding: Wendy asks: 'What happens if you think about how he walks when he's coming home to his dinner after hunting?' Walk improves immediately.

Shane stretching long and tall.

Serpentines using weight aids and turning of the upper body rather than reins to guide Ted in walk and trot.

Wendy suggests that Shane does side-bends to increase her flexibility in the waist, and carrot stretches for Ted (especially to the left) to increase his.

Second session

Shane reports they got 8s for their entry and final halt last time out!

Ted seems to be drifting to right – work on straightness.

Wendy helps Shane to keep her position in canter, especially making sure that her legs don't come forward.

Encouraging her to control Ted's speed with the outside elbow, rather than using both reins. She needs to soften on inside rein and especially on left rein. Left hand tends to drop – work on keeping it soft and checking its height periodically.

Focus on Shane's riding rather than on Ted.

Wendy asks her to get a 'kneeling' feeling in trot – helps her balance better and keep her legs back and down.

Using a squeeze of her buttocks to signal upward transition, rather than major leg aids.

Shane says, 'He feels as if he's soft enough to put him where I want.' Ted's hind leg separation in canter improving.

Third session

Shane reports her dressage scores have gone down (NB this is an *improvement* in event scoring!) though they could still improve. She feels she is now getting a better tune from Ted at home, but not yet when out in competition.

'Rattling' the left bit ring to soften contact and at the same time 'talking' to Ted on this side.

Shane asks: 'How do I ride a corner?' Wendy asks her to ride squares, with small quarter-circles between the sides, making sure to ask for engagement and bend through each corner, first in walk, then in trot. Asks her to 'anchor' her outside elbow to her hip so that her arm doesn't straighten and throw away control of Ted's outside shoulder.

'How do I ride a corner?', Shane asked one day – so we worked on her turning from the waist, deepening her inside heel with weight to the inside, and getting Ted actively forward from her inside (in this case, left) leg with a gently shaping outside (right) leg to ask for a bend in his body. Ted is kinking a little in the neck because Shane has allowed her right hand to give forward, which means she is losing control of his right shoulder.

Fourth session

Shane reports that she came second in her most recent test – beat somebody else on her collective marks. She wants to practise upcoming test (Novice Horse Trials). Working-in aimed at softening Ted through – long rein to stretch.

Ted stepping under himself more than when we started – closer leg-V in trot.

Wendy says: 'If his head comes up, check what your left hand is doing – offer it forward.'

Spiralling in and out on circle to help develop more flexibility in Shane and Ted, then practised doing the half-circle from long side to X, followed by half-circle from X on new rein to opposite long side.

The work on turning is paying off! In this later session Shane and Ted are practising spiralling in and out to develop flexibility and control. Shane has an inviting, slightly 'open' left hand, but this time she has not given away her right elbow, so Ted's balance and carriage are better and he is more 'through' in the neck.

Serpentine in walk on the buckle to test effectiveness of weight and turning aids they had been practising.

Ted sometimes kicks out against the canter aid. We discuss whether this could be over-reaction to leg-aid? Wendy suggests experimenting with using buttock squeeze instead of leg pressure. Worked 'brilliantly'.

Shane and Ted can do brilliant halts just by 'thinking about them'. For homework, Wendy suggests Shane tries extending this to other downward transitions. Work on anchoring the right elbow and softening the left hand up and forward. Continue with waist flexibility exercises.

Fifth session

Whilst warming up, check stability of Shane's left hand.

Wendy says: 'See how floppy you can make the small of your back – trot and canter.'

Ted seems really stiff behind, so we cut the session short. Discussion on maybe using more light-seat work to help him get into the habit of swinging through more. Use hacking for this – school him a little when going out to check on the sheep. Do little jumps to improve bascule.

Sixth session

Ted was 'on holiday' with their jumping trainer, so Shane rode her sister's horse. He is 7 and can be flighty at the start – then, once he has got going, he isn't really forward enough. How can we help Shane ride him effectively today?

He holds himself with a very short neck, so Wendy asked Shane to offer a longer rein and work him forward into it from seat and leg. At first, Shane felt her stirrup leathers were long (different saddle) but then she discovered that the extra length enabled her to put her legs further back and stretch them down – more effective too!

By the end of the session the horse was beginning to trust the longer frame and work into it quite readily.

Wendy's note (written just afterwards) reads: 'At the beginning of the session I noticed smoke from the grounds of the house next door. This rapidly developed into quite a serious fire – their barn got well ablaze. Shane's sister called the fire brigade – four fire engines came with sirens wailing. Shane managed to keep the horse focused despite the noises of crackling, crashing and sirens, and despite the fact that in

In these two pictures, Shane is riding Stringer, her sister's horse. Early in the session (*above left*), Stringer has plenty of energy but is holding himself short and tight with a hollow back, raised head and quarters trailing. Shane's arms are straight and her lower legs are forward. In the second picture (*above right*), though Stringer is still rather short in the frame, he has now lifted his back and connected much more. Shane has helped him make these differences by lengthening the reins, bending her elbows and 'picking him up' from behind with a better leg position. His calmer and more attentive expression, as well as his wet mouth, let us know how much more comfortable he finds this way of being ridden.

certain parts of the school he could see the flames. Good rapport to create and maintain this concentration!'

Seventh session

Shane has identified that some of Ted's stiffness problems are the result of ill-fitting saddles. This means that she has to get new ones! For the time being, she has borrowed one – still not quite right, but better. It also helps put her legs in a better place.

We talk about the difference between speed (tempo) and energy. Ted's tempo is fine; energy needs improving.

Shane feels that Ted is carrying himself much better in trot, but canter is not so balanced. Wendy suggests short bursts of slowish canter with trot in between to encourage him to step under and increase self-carriage.

Lateral work will also develop engagement – they haven't really done any. Ted hasn't felt light enough in the hand before. Wendy explains what's involved in shoulder-in. It's unfamiliar for Shane – 'I'm so used to him moving in front of me, not doing movements I can't see behind me.' They do it on the long side then on the circle. Then travers. Ted listens and responds to unilateral leg-aiding. Great! We are really pleased! It's about learning to work both ends of the horse now!

In this early attempt at travers, Shane is kinking in at the waist, but she is placing her outside (left) leg back correctly to ask Ted to bend around her inside (right) leg and to control his quarters. She is controlling his outside (left) shoulder through her close, bent left elbow. Ted's expression shows that he is really listening, and he is responding softly and obediently.

Shane reports that they have won the Riding Club showjumping trophy (expected) – and also the 'most dressage points' one. Not expected! 'I would never have got that before.'

As we are talking, Shane says: 'Ted is 9 now – by the end of this year, when he's rising 10, I'd like to be able to do all the movements we need for our unaffiliated dressage and begin to do some affiliated.' There's a dressage future out there!

Eighth session: off-horse

Ted has a sore from his new dressage girth, so can't work today. We sit in the kitchen and work off-horse.

Shane reports that, at one competition, Ted had spooked and reared on the centre line. So the next time (the day before this session) she had said to herself, 'I'll go and sort it.' Of course, she was thinking differently so he didn't do it.

The previous day she had come third in Novice 24, fourth in Preliminary 4 and won Preliminary 18! Fabulous. Moreover, it was the very first time they had done a Novice test!

She said she had prepared differently this time. She did more walking and chatting instead of trotting in the warm-up. She was much calmer herself, so Ted was calmer too. He was lovely in the warm-up but still a bit tight in the ring.

We talk about ways to help Ted learn to lengthen his stride without just getting faster – the need to develop engagement so he lifts into an upward trajectory instead. Ask for just a few longer strides, not a whole side. His ability to carry himself 'uphill' can only be developed gradually.

Wendy explains how to do canter pliés (fresh from just having done them with Red and Annie).

Shane and Ted's first one-day event is coming up in April.

Roy and Cori

Cori: Born 1991. Roy: born 1951. Work in family business, but able to make time for riding. Bred Cori, registered part-bred Trakehner, myself: sire Downlands Cancara (16.1hh Trakehner); dam Pure Chance (14.3 hh New Forest x Thoroughbred). Cori is short for Corinthian Spirit which means *the taking part, not the winning*. I've always been taught by Marion, who broke Cori when he was 5 years old. I always wanted to event: won first ever one-day event, went on to compete in two- and three-day events. Show-jumping not my strong point; always placed at dressage. Concentrated on dressage for the last four or five years, need now to improve on impulsion and collection for more advanced work. Currently competing at Advanced Medium and Advanced; want to do Prix St Georges within the year.

What Roy said about the sessions

Initially work started with my position: elbows, neck, leg, back, heels, etc. This did have an immediate difference in the way Cori went and just went to show the importance of my balance and position. Even now, when things slip, just thinking *elbows,* and thinking *proud* makes an *immediate* difference. Most notable differences have been to make me think more about my position; what I can do to make things easier for Cori, not always doing 'big' movements, but lots of changes within the gaits.

Went to watch Charles de Kunffy – *inspirational.* Couldn't wait to get on Cori to try out all the different things I saw. Every horse and rider he coached made an improvement within the half-hour. Proved even more that 'improve your

> 'Thinking **elbows,** and thinking **proud,** makes an **immediate** difference.'

Maxim | you've got what it takes

'Working towards canter pirouettes.' Cori is really tucking his pelvis and connecting through his back, but he is overbending. Roy needs to soften the curb rein and 'invite' Cori to lift his head and take the contact more.

As a short-term training measure, Roy is using an upward movement with his hands to help Cori learn to work with a higher head-carriage. Note that Cori's neck is still round and 'through', and the 'invitation' offered by the reins is clearly upward, not backward.

position, etc., and the horse's way of going improves instantly', because as my way of going improved Cori responded – softer, more rhythmical. We now find that we're more relaxed in the approach to competitions, because we believe and know that we are more consistent and rhythmical.

Can now canter at *walking* speed. Working towards canter pirouettes. Flying changes improving, more in balance.

It's difficult to say much about judges' comments. Cori has generally gone well with good natural gaits, but judges can't really tell if I'm happy about attaining a movement well or with more expression! I know the differences that have been made, i.e. the medium and extended trot and canter; now they are coming from the right places, not all in front but from behind, with more balance and softer. I'm looking at this phase as something of a transitional phase, so not too worried about marks, but more about trying to do things correctly! I'm far happier about the way Cori goes and I know what has improved. I'll now try for more, and not worry so much about judges' comments, because I know it's better. I'm still not relaxed in competition, so I'm trying to get myself and my mind more relaxed, which I know improves the way my horse goes.

I no longer just hack, I work on transitions, leg-yielding, shoulder-in, half-pass, flying changes, lots of changes within the gaits, because I realize it's not fair to climb on your horse once a fortnight and say, 'Just for this 5½ minutes I want you to go correctly, but for the rest of the time just slop around and go however you want.'

Key Points

Think *proud* of my horse and his way of going.

Think about my position all the time.

Allow Cori to *carry himself* – not hold him up.

Made me more aware of what I can achieve by being more positive myself.

Making sure that when you want a reaction you get one. An occasional 40- or 60-pounder [strong leg aid] is kinder in the long run.

Don't try too hard – *less is more!* Trying too hard causes tension: if it's not working one way, try another!

Enjoy everything you do together. Realize how lucky you are; just think how many people would love to do what you're doing.

Realize how lucky you are to have someone like Wendy take enough time and trouble to work with and improve you and your horse (return that faith).

What we did together

First session: off-horse

Met Roy and his regular trainer, Marion. Marion and Wendy have known each other for some years: she is a fellow judge and has also been involved with the TTT, (an educational trust for trainers and riders, based in Surrey) so they are coming from the same place with the same values. She is happy for Wendy to work with Roy, and will come to some of our sessions when she can. Cori is soft and fluent – but now they need to make the transition to Advanced Medium, so more engagement and oomph are required.

Roy's wants to work on:

Canter pirouettes

'Uphill' lengthening into medium and extended

Developing engagement

Concentration.

A really lovely 'uphill balance' in the canter. Ideally, the contact with the curb rein could be a little lighter.

Second session (with Marion)

Roy has just come back from Spain – watching the caballeros sitting proud and tall, hand on hip. A powerful image; powerful impression to work towards.

Roy is inclined to look down, and heels creep up – partly because he is rather tall for Cori.

Marion feels he needs to get Cori going more forward into the contact. Roy says, 'If only I could ride him like Marion.' Wendy asks him to go off round the arena for a few minutes and ride like Marion. Total transformation! Wendy, Marion and Leo all stand there amazed.

Rider is transformed – so horse is transformed! Cori was on the seat, so Roy could reorganize his reins without interfering with Cori's balance. Roy got more activity, produced some lovely pirouettes and a couple of fantastic transitions walk>canter, canter>walk.

Discussion about this. Roy is just as astounded as the onlookers – reports that when he 'rode like Marion' he got all the aids flowing without thinking about them separately. Wendy explained that, when we draw upon an internalized 'model' of excellence, all the different features translate unconsciously into external expression. The model we have stored is a template for unconscious competence. That's why it flows.

Roy says, 'It was a "we've cracked it" moment.'

A caballero in Sussex. Roy had just returned from Spain – and I had also asked him to 'ride like Marion' (his trainer). This produced some soft and impressive trot work and this lovely walk pirouette – 'seated' behind and light in front.

Third session

Sculpting Roy's leg to improve his position. Wendy asked him to shorten his stirrup leathers – long leathers have to be 'earned' and Roy is reaching for them with dipped toes (which means raised heels).

Working on transitions. Two reasons: in higher level tests they are marked separately. More importantly, they can be used to increase engagement, which is what Cori needs. Walk>trot>walk every few strides.

Wendy got Roy to do a TTT exercise for increasing engagement – canter transition from walk pirouette. Worked really well.

Collecting and lengthening in trot – will need to do more of this as they are not yet making enough difference.

Ride a square, using deepish corners to shorten and increase engagement, then lengthen on the sides. Cori found this difficult – swung quarters.

Roy says he has discussed and reviewed the photos with Marion – found them really helpful to benchmark how they are doing and what needs to be worked on.

Fourth session

Roy went to watch dressage at Hickstead – compared/contrasted English and German riders, looking out for what's classical. We are looking forward to spending a day together at the TTT next week, watching Charles de Kunffy training.

Wendy asks Roy to stretch and tone his lower legs more back and down. They tend to be rather flaccid and not as effective as they need to be.

Gets him to warm up 'like the Germans', alternating Cori's length of frame for flexibility, 'throughness' and swing.

Play with medium trot – 'fire him from the hip', canter in self-carriage, flying changes. These don't work so well because Roy is trying too hard. Then playing with the beginnings of piaffe and passage.

Fifth session

Start by checking Roy's leg position again.

Roy found the TTT 'inspirational'. We do one of Charles de Kunffy's 'ribbon exercises' – shoulder-in to quarters-out – to get Cori off the leg and bending whilst working the same inside hind in both movements.

Roy has been 'wriggling' his shoulder-blades up-back-down. Says this has improved his half-passes.

Good suspension coming in the trot.

We worked hard to improve Roy's leg positioning. Roy is rather tall for Cori, and in order to contact Cori's sides he had tended to bring his lower legs and heels back and up, as the first picture shows. It also makes it clear how doing this weakens his whole posture and makes his seat ineffective, which is why Cori is dropping onto his forehand with his hind legs trailing out. The second picture (different day) shows me lifting Roy's leg away and helping him rotate it back and inwards from the hip, so that his thigh becomes flatter and closer to the saddle and his heel and seat both become deeper. The third picture shows how, with stretched and 'draped' lower legs and more vertical thighs, as well as a more upright posture, Roy's seat becomes deeper and more effective. Stretching his lower legs down into his heels produces tone in his calves, which means that he can use them to give 'inward' aids rather than backward ones. So Cori is now 'on the seat' and 'in front of him'.

Wendy reminds Roy that, when he looks down, his heels come up and his toes go down – the ankle-bone is connected to the neck-bone!

Roy says, 'Now I realize how much hand I was using in the past.'

Rhythmical canter on left rein. 'Working pirouettes' – i.e. small circles well engaged and 'uphill'.

Flying changes – Cori tends to be late in front. The last of the series happened effortlessly because Roy gave them a little breather and then wasn't thinking about it. He says: 'If I don't have time to think and stiffen, then it happens.' Wendy talks about moving from conscious competence to unconscious competence.

They are both pleased that Roy is now able to keep Cori soft in a slow, balanced trot – 'It's come on so much in such a short time.'

Sixth session

Roy says he has been working on keeping himself more still, with his heels well down. He's been writing down what's happening. We notice that, as he puts his heels down, his head comes up and he straightens.

Cori is softer earlier in the session today.

Roy has been doing lateral work whilst out hacking. 'You have made me think more about each movement.'

Canter: very tight circles; some counter-canter; lateral work in canter.

Seventh session

Roy says that he has been writing notes for Wendy – has found it helpful. He has been working on concertina exercises (lengthening and shortening) and keeping his inside hand more 'alive'. This has helped Cori come and stay 'through' more.

Time for a shorter rein to provide a shorter frame – but still keeping hands soft and contact live.

Eighth session

Stirrups need to go up (Roy had forgotten when cleaning tack and put them at old level).

Roy needs to get his toes in more – get him to rotate his legs in from the hip. Hard!!!

But the trot is much better and he is rising more from the thigh, with better balance over the knee.

Roy says that, when reviewing his notes, he keeps coming back to the importance of elbows. Even thinking about them is enough to bring Cori down and through!

Roy has really mastered the weight-into-the-ankle aid for downwards transitions, from trot and canter. Wendy tells him about the buttock squeeze for upward ones. Magical effects immediately!

More flexibility needed in Roy's waist and more upper body participation in aiding. Wendy suggests 'centre line serpentines' (shallow ones crossing the centre line) with minimal use of hands. Then European serpentines with counter-curving and tighter loops. Fun.

Wendy notices that Roy is putting too much pressure on the curb rein, especially when he re-gathers the reins after they have slipped. Then Cori overbends and drops onto the forehand. Time to pay attention to this for a bit – more leg and more contact on the bridoon. Wendy suggests Roy plays with small versions of the more advanced movements – leg-yielding, shoulder-in – moving fluently with minimal aiding – relying more on seat and shoulders, not hands. Roy says, 'This feels more like riding – it's not so lumpy.'

Then same again in canter.

Homework: bridoon, not curb. Shorter frame, but soft. Weight and waist for turning. Flow, flow, flow…

above left Centre line serpentines.
above right European serpentines.

The difference the curb rein can make.

above left Here Roy has equal pressure (weight) on bridoon and curb reins, and so Cori is beginning to lean and overbend.

above right Roy has given a lighter contact in the curb rein, and Cori's face is nearer to the correct vertical position, with a slightly less open mouth. The fact that his poll is still not the highest point and his mouth is open at all tells Roy that he needs to soften that curb rein still more!

Maxim | you've got what it takes

How we worked together

Environmental level

We met for a single three-quarter hour session roughly every four weeks. Initially, I intended that we would stop after six sessions, but when we talked about it at that point it seemed unnecessarily arbitrary to call a halt: we all seemed to be enjoying ourselves (horses included) and finding it useful for our different purposes. So we continue...

Carolyn, Shane and Roy all had access to an arena. In the summer and autumn, Annie worked in her field: in the winter, when the field surface deteriorated, she brought Red to Shane's nearby arena. As Roy explained in his notes, he also 'did dressage' out hacking on the farm and around quiet lanes nearby.

Behaviour

As the riders have implied, we worked both informally and serendipitously rather than to a fixed plan. Each session started with warming up as I believe this is a very important part of the work and it tells the coach a great deal about the rider's relationship, not just with the horse but with themselves. Sometimes the rider had an issue they wanted help with, or a movement they wanted to learn. At other times we watched and felt for a bit and then decided what would be useful. In coaching, I believe that it's worth taking a lead from what comes up on the day: far from being 'accidental', this normally reflects typical strengths, weaknesses, difficulties and challenges that the client is facing generally. So, though it might seem random to work on transitions one time, lateral movements another, and on the rider's position on another occasion, if the coach's observation is good and the aims are classically correct, any of these will offer an opportunity for relevant work that helps the partnership in its progress round the training spiral. It was my job to think on my feet and select exercises and strategies to support this longer-term aim as well as addressing the immediate issues – in my experience, this is usually the best way of coaching. Often, I got the rider to sum up at the end what they felt they had learnt and needed to play with before the next session. This gave me a check on what the rider had actually taken from the session (how their 'received meaning' related to my 'intended one') – a procedure that usually provides a more valuable check on my coaching and teaching skills than on the rider's understanding!

There was one very important thing I did not do in any of our sessions: *I did not ride any of the horses!* I would have loved to, mainly because their willingness, honesty and delightful attentiveness was so inviting. But there were two important reasons for depriving myself of this pleasure. First, even if I had had the skill to sort out a problem or demonstrate something new, what really mattered in coaching was that *the rider* achieved those things – which meant that they had to do every bit of the work themselves. And, second, so often when someone does something for you instead of helping you to do it for yourself, the hidden message you receive is one of inferiority: you feel less able, or even unable – certainly at the level of capability and quite possibly at the level of identity. This can happen even when the trainer is supportive and when this is the last message she would wish to convey. Riders draw their own conclusions, and often seeing someone else get more from your horse than you do can be profoundly dispiriting and debilitating. I believed that it was my job to help them discover, themselves, how much more they could achieve than they expected. *They have what it takes*. So I felt that doing it for them would be a short-cut that would actually hinder more, and more profoundly, than it could help.

Capability

As we worked together, I began to realize that one of the things the riders found helpful was my multi-dimensional way of explaining things. (Annie's written reflections, for example, also draw attention to this.) When correcting something or explaining a new movement I tend to follow the same pattern and it's only recently that I've realized how comprehensive it is – and, therefore, both how and why it's helpful:

- First I explain in words. The rider *hears* and processes information *auditorily*. Then I show what's involved. The rider processes *visually* by watching, and then reprocesses *kinesthetically* by imagining what the positioning or movement will feel like.

- As Annie explains, and as the photo sequence illustrates, I try to get the rider understanding what movements are involved, not only for herself but also for the horse. I want her thinking and feeling as though she and the horse are one and the completed movement is *hers* in this broader sense, not something produced by one separate being on the instructions of the other. I want the rider to experience mentally a movement or way of going in a unified, centaur-like way.

- After the rider has used all three major senses to process the information vividly within her mind, she usually finds it much easier to translate her understanding into actual behaviour and help her horse *do* the movement. This often means that, even when they are attempting a movement for the first time, they do it correctly and with a real sense of togetherness. Though this includes their individual behaviour – is the rider offering the aids that the horse needs; is the

'I try to get the rider understanding what movements are involved.'

top left You keep your elbows in...

top right ...he puts his left leg forward...

left ...and between you, you make a leg-yield. Right?

horse actually doing what's needed (e.g. dropping his inside hip as he steps under his body in shoulder-in)? – this approach gets the rider thinking, feeling and behaving like part of the centaur. And so the messages she sends elicit a corresponding centaur-like response from her horse.

- In order to 'own' any new skill, rider and horse have to be able to tap into it again on their own. Carolyn's account reminds us how often trainers (especially the instructional kind) miss out this essential step. In order to achieve this independence, we usually focus on a relatively small number of things in any one session. That way, there's time for mental and physical understanding, for experimenting and refining and for getting it good-enough-for-now – as well as for knowing what extra refinement will be needed in the future. Shane's first lateral work was amazingly correct in positioning, angle and rhythm. Even though, in future, Ted will need to bend more around Shane's leg, that was less essential at this point. The important part of Ted's learning this first time was that leg on meant 'move away' not just 'move forward'. In moving his quarters in response to Shane's leg aids he showed us that he had enlarged both his understanding and his physical ability. Learning how to bend around her leg as well as angling his quarters will help him to develop his flexibility and will qualify for higher marks in future tests. But it would have been quite inappropriate to ask them for that in a first attempt.

Beliefs and values

When I'm working with someone I start with a number of important beliefs, and one of my aims is to share and reinforce these in the rider through the way we work together.

I believe that:

- The rider and horse have what it takes to learn and grow, become better athletes and enjoy being together even more.
- They can become more at one with each other if they learn to pay attention to each other more sympathetically and accurately.
- Dressage isn't a special form of riding – it is simply good riding.
- Riding according to classical principles respects the rider's love of the horse whilst helping them both to develop their mental and physical potential.
- Working up the training spiral provides appropriate experiences for both comfort and stretch.

- Riding with these values in mind produces better competition marks 'on the side': aiming for better competition marks does not automatically produce better riding! Shane illustrated this shift in beliefs perfectly when she said: *'We are using [competitions] as schooling sessions to practise staying soft, relaxed, calm and rhythmical, with impulsion.'*

- Even committed, intense riding can be good fun. Roy put this priority clearly when he said, *'Enjoy everything you do together.'*

Identity

One of the reasons why riding matters so much to us is, I believe, that we invest so much in it on the level of identity – both our own and our horse's. The essential miracle in riding is the coming together of two individual creatures who are so different yet who are prepared to cooperate and, beyond that, can come to feel deep comfort and enjoyment in each other's company. Most of us have experienced enough moments like this to sustain us through the times that aren't – and I'm sure from horses' body language that they share some of these deep satisfactions with us.

As a coach, I try to be mindful of this important and vulnerable area whenever I work. As a judge, I salute it when I see the attentiveness and centaur-like harmony it can produce from any kind of pony, horse and rider. I would like to think that some of this deep-level involvement and satisfaction inspires: Roy's reminders to himself to think 'proud', Shane's sense that she and Ted were more often feeling like a team, and her new belief that the full range of event skills would be within their grasp, Annie's increased empathy both with Red and with herself, and Carolyn's goal of 'being the best we can be'. There is a deep enrichment in giving yourself in a relationship: I have been privileged to witness and share, just for those brief times, in what that can mean.

Centaurs (*opposite page*)
top left Annie and Red.
top right Carolyn and Ambrose.
bottom left Shane and Ted.
bottom right Roy and Cori.

COACHING CENTAURS • 277

Maxim | you've got what it takes

What could be more dramatic than to realise that I would never know an ending in riding, that I would always be beginning?

Paul Belasik, *Riding Towards the Light* [1]

References

Introductory quotation
1 Charles de Kunffy, *The Ethics and Passions of Dressage*, Half Halt Press (Middletown, MD) 1993, p.29

Chapter 2
1 Charles de Kunffy, *Dressage Principles Illuminated*, J.A. Allen (London) 2002, p.51
2 Charles de Kunffy, *The Ethics and Passions of Dressage*, Half Halt Press (Middletown, MD) 1993, p.29
3 Paul Belasik, *Exploring Dressage Technique*, J.A. Allen (London) 1994, p.9
4 Paul Belasik, *Riding Towards the Light*, J.A. Allen (London) 1990, p.95

Chapter 3
1 Paul Belasik, *Dressage for the 21st Century*, J.A. Allen (London) 2002, p.8
2 Paul Belasik, *Riding Towards the Light*, J.A. Allen (London) 1990, p.34
3 Paul Belasik, Ibid., pp.70–1

Chapter 4
1 Paul Belasik, *Dressage for the 21st Century*, J.A. Allen (London) 2002, p.66
2 Üdo Burger, *The Way to Perfect Horsemanship*, J.A. Allen (London) 1986, p.72

Chapter 5
1 The *Official Instruction Handbook of the German National Equestrian Federation*, Threshold Books (London) 1987, p.146
2 Ibid., pp.143–6
3 Paul Belasik, *Riding Towards the Light*, J.A. Allen (London) 1990, p.72
4 The *Official Instruction Handbook of the German National Equestrian Federation*, Threshold Books (London) 1987, p.159
5 Ibid., p.160
6 Ibid., p.161
7 Ibid., p.166
8 Ibid., pp.171–2
9 Ibid., p.173
10 Ibid., pp.174–5
11 Ibid., p.146

Chapter 6
1 Wolfgang M. Niggli, *Dressage: A Guideline for Riders and Judges*, J.A. Allen (London) 2004, p.10

Chapter 7
1 Kurt Albrecht, *A Dressage Judge's Handbook*, J.A. Allen, (London) 1988, p.1
2 Ibid., p.123

Chapter 9
1 Timothy Gallwey, *The Inner Game of Tennis*, Pan Books (London) 1986, p.11

Chapter 10
1 Guy Claxton, *Hare Brain, Tortoise Mind*, Fourth Estate (London) 1998, p.128
2 Ibid., p.187
3 Charles de Kunffy, *The Ethics and Passions of Dressage*, Half Halt Press (Middletown, MD) 1993, p.44

Chapter 11
1 Robert Dilts, *Changing Belief Systems with NLP*, Meta Publications (Capitola, CA) 1990, p.xi

Chapter 12
1 Charles de Kunffy, *Dressage Principles Illuminated*, J.A. Allen (London) 2002, p.9
2 Paul Belasik, *Riding Towards the Light*, J.A. Allen (London) 1990, p.124
3 Ibid., p.30

Chapter 13
1 Richard Bandler, *Using Your Brain for a Change*, Real People Press (Moab, UT) 1985, p.9

Chapter 14
1 Charles de Kunffy, *Dressage Principles Illuminated*, J.A. Allen (London) 2002, p.27
2 Charles de Kunffy, *The Ethics and Passions of Dressage*, Half Halt Press (Middletown, MD) 1993, p.16
3 Paul Belasik, *Exploring Dressage Technique*, J.A. Allen (London) 1994, p.140

Chapter 15
1 Paul Belasik, *Riding Towards the Light*, J.A. Allen (London) 1990, p.124

Closing quotation
1 Paul Belasik, *Riding Towards the Light*, J.A. Allen (London) 1990, p.127

Useful Reading

There are hundreds of books on riding and training to choose from. I have found the following authors and their books both inspiring and practically useful, because they share some very important perspectives: first, they assume that riding is essentially a *process of communication*, and, second, they help us learn how to dovetail the biomechanics of our own bodies with those of the horses we ride to make that communication clean, elegant and effective. In addition, these writers take the standpoint that the rider both can and should take responsibility for helping her horse become the best athlete he can be, whatever his breeding, age or previous experience. In so doing, she will inevitably find herself enhancing her own mental and emotional learning as well as her physical skills. This is the slow, taxing and incredibly rewarding – and never-ending – journey that each of us can take.

Books on Classical Riding

Paul Belasik

Riding Towards the Light, An Apprenticeship in the Art of Dressage Riding, J.A. Allen (London) 1990

Exploring Dressage Technique, Journeys into the Art of Classical Riding, J.A. Allen (London) 1994

Dressage for the 21st Century, J.A. Allen (London) 2002

Üdo Burger

The Way to Perfect Horsemanship (English translation by Nicole Bartle), J.A. Allen (London) 1986

Charles de Kunffy
Training Strategies for Dressage Riders, Howell Book House (New York) 1994

The Athletic Development of the Dressage Horse, Manege Patterns, Howell Book House (New York) 1992

The Ethics and Passions of Dressage, Half Halt Press (Middletown, MD) 1993

Dressage Principles Illuminated, J.A. Allen (London) 2002

Erik Herbermann
Dressage Formula, J.A. Allen (London) 1993

A Horseman's Notes, Core Publishing (Crofton, MD) 2003

Books on how horses experience the world

Stephen Budiansky
The Nature of Horses, Phoenix Illustrated (Orion Publishing Group) (London) 1998

Michael Peace and Lesley Bailey
Think Like Your Horse, David & Charles (Newton Abbot) 2001

Lucy Rees
The Horse's Mind, Stanley Paul Ltd (Random House) (London) 1993

and finally, one of the most fascinating explorations of animal and human experiencing I've caome across

Temple Grandin and Catherine Johnson
Animals in Translation, Bloomsbury (London) 2006

Books on NLP and mental strategies

Steve Andreas
Transforming Your Self, Becoming who you want to be, Real People Press (Moab, UT) 2002

Steve Andreas and Charles Faulkner
NLP, The New Technology of Achievement, Nicholas Brealey (London) 1994

Ian McDermott and Wendy Jago
Your Inner Coach, Piatkus (London) 2003

And, finally, you might want to explore the overlap between NLP, coaching and classical riding in my previous books, *Schooling Problems Solved with NLP* and *Solo Schooling, Learn to Coach Yourself when You're Riding on Your Own,* both published by J. A. Allen (London).

Useful contacts

Wendy Jago wendy@jagoconsulting.eclipse.co.uk

TTT
website: www.ttttrust.com
email: secretary@TTTrust.com
tel: 01483 272445

Index

Names of horses are given in italic

'against the hand' 40
aiding
   repetitive 47–8
   timing 215–16
Albrecht, Kurt 88
Ali 18, 36, 38, 41, 42–3, 55, 57, 66, 97, 101–3
Ambrose 32, 79, 86, 161, 217–18, 246–53
anger 26
Annie 71, 115, 118–19, 174, 238–45, 273
anxiety
   horse 44
   rider 32
   see also competition nerves
arena
   lack of formal 114–15
   long (60m) 197
arms 52
association 47
assumptions 148–50
   about horses' behaviour 16, 149, 154–7
   about horses' physical problems 150–4
   tips for trainers 162
asymmetries 71
attention 136–7
   broad beam 141–2, 143, 144
   of horse 138

narrow-focus 142–3, 145–6
switching forms of 144–6
tips for trainers 146–7
see also concentration
auditory senses 137, 140, 145

back, horse's
   hollow/flat 24, 25, 36, 40, 53–5, 80
   lifting 24, 66
   stiffness 93
back, rider's 52, 66, 106
balance 23, 72, 160
   'uphill' 19, 20, 97
Bandler, Richard 180
basket-ball players 173–4
behind the bit 57
Belasik, Paul 27, 34, 39, 40, 50, 62, 70, 144, 163, 216, 222, 278
beliefs 148, 275–6
   about competition 166, 190–1
   see also assumptions; self-belief
bend 20–1, 76–7, 160–1
Berger, Üdo 52
Bertie 18–19, 27, 42, 160–1
body control, rider 33
body language 125, 146
breathing 140–1, 146
broad-beam attention 141–2, 143, 144, 171
'bubbles' of concentration
   bad 140–1
   good 138–40
business leaders course 128

canter
   downward transitions 111
   essence of 99–100
   judge's comments 100
Carolyn 14, 32, 86, 161, 177, 217–18
   training sessions 165, 246–53
case studies 14–15, 236–7
   Annie and *Red* 238–45
   Carolyn and *Ambrose* 246–53
   methods of working 272–5
   Roy and *Cori* 263–71
   Shane and *Ted* 254–62
cats 70, 143–4
cavalletti 155
centaurs 28, 42, 66, 234–5, 277
changes, simple 83, 111
Changing Belief Systems with NLP (Dilts) 148
chunking down 159–61
circles 20–1, 82–3, 84
Clarke, Stephen 47
classical riding 24–7
Claxton, Guy 136, 143
'cockpit' checks 132–5
collection 72, 85, 114
   judge's comments on 97–8
collective comments 105–7
commitment 128, 129
communication, rider—horse 30, 146
competence
   conscious 126, 127
   unconscious 126, 127, 144

INDEX • 285

competition 26
    aims and opportunities of 74–5
    beliefs about 166, 190–2
    as benchmark and feedback 216–17
    Elementary level 82–4
    Medium level 84–5
    Novice level 78–81, 160
    preliminary level 75–8
    showcasing your horse 218–19
    as stretch 217–18
    under-performance 165–6
    see also dressage tests
competition nerves 180–1
    effects on horse 182
    experiences of rider 181–2
    helping horse 183–4
    skills for overcoming 183, 184–8
    strategy for self-management 188–93
concentration 137–8
    bad 'bubbles' 140–1
    good 'bubbles' 138–40
consistency 131
contact 40, 54–5, 67–9
    definition 67
    improving whilst hacking 113
    judge's comments on 94
Cori (Corinthian Spirit) 53, 93, 95, 105, 133, 134, 218
    hacking 120–1
    training sessions 263–71
corners 20–1
criticism, from trainers 172
crookedness *see* straightness

de Kunffy, Charles 10, 12, 22, 26–7, 40, 67, 110, 130, 143, 144, 145, 163, 183, 193
defocusing 145, 171
difficult horse 44–5
Dilts, Robert 148
distractions 26, 44
    overcoming 138–40, 260–1
downward transitions 77, 81, 111, 217
Dressage: a guideline for riders and Judges (Niggli) 74
Dressage for the 21st Century (Belasik) 34, 50, 70
dressage
    benefits to the horse 30–1

    benefits to the rider 31–3
    purpose of 24–7
    value of 28–30
Dressage Judge's Handbook (Albrecht) 88
Dressage Principles Illuminated (de Kunffy) 22, 163, 194
dressage tests
    aims of 60–1, 74
    choosing 216–18
    Elementary 45 214–15
    from horse's perspective 196–7, 201, 212–13
    Medium 71 209-12 197, 201, 212–13
    Novice 21 197, 202–4
    Novice 24 197, 198–201
    Novice 33 197, 205–8
    'reading' 195
    visual maps 195
    see also test sheets

ears, horse's 138
elbows 40, 46, 52, 53–4
Elementary level 82–4
    dressage tests 214–15
emotions 47, 133
energy, generating/blocking 68–9
engagement 40, 94–5, 160
enjoyment, in riding 33
environment 189
Ethics and Passions of Dressage, The (de Kunffy) 10, 26–7, 143
eventing dressage 29
expert riders 144
Exploring Dressage Technique (Belasik) 27
eyes, rider's
    defocused 145, 171
    focused 145–6
    positioning 171

failures, generalization about 167–8
falling out 38, 71
falls 23
feedback
    from dressage tests 216–17
    from horse 17–18, 21, 55–6, 127–8
field, schooling in 115, 118–19
'flat' 24

flexibility 134
focus 145–6
force, use of 14
free walk 79, 113

gadgets 50–1
Gallwey, Timothy 124
garden walls, walking on 125
gates, opening/shutting 111, 120
generalizations 167–8
    constructing truthful/helpful 168–9
German National Equestrian Federation, Handbook 60, 61
goals, riding 22–3, 131–2
    ownership of 166–7
'good' riding 46

hacking 26, 32–3, 44
    progressing the training spiral 112–14
    Roy and *Cori* 120–1
    schooling movements 84, 108–11, 113, 121
half-pass 95
halt 83, 84
    essence of 101–2
    judge's comments 103
Hare Brain, Tortoise Mind (Claxton) 136, 143
harmony, mental 67
Hawk 27
head carriage
    horse 58
    see also outline
head positioning, rider 171
Herbermann, Erik 40
hind legs, 'stepping under' 56, 57, 160
hip, collapsed 18
holding hands 68
'hollowing' 24, 25, 36, 40, 53–5, 80
honesty 129
horse
    assumptions about 16, 149, 150–7
    benefits of dressage 30–1
    feedback 17–18, 127–8
    feedback to rider 55–6
    as 'happy athlete' 60–1
    as individual 27
    learning 131–2

reading of body language 125, 146
and rider's nerves 182, 183–4
state of mind 134–5
teaching new movements 80–1, 131–2
'tuning in' to 110
as your mirror 42–5
horse—rider communication 30, 146
horse—rider relationship 65–7
'how?' questions 34–5

identity 191, 192–3
imagination, use of 173–6
impulsion 69, 82–3
improving whilst hacking 113
judge's comments on 94–5
and speed 65, 69
incompetence
conscious 126, 127, 143
unconscious 126, 127
'independence,' rider's seat 31, 46
Inner Game of Tennis, The (Gallwey) 124
intentions, power of 128

Jago, Wendy 23, 33, 108
Jay 41, 55, 57, 68, 97
jockeys 193
judgement 13
judges 194, 195
indication of origin of faults 61
riders' beliefs about 166
training 88, 91, 105
judge's comments 37, 39, 92–107, 191
'above the bit' 50
'against the hand' 40
on collection 97–8
collective 105–7
on contact 94
on gaits 98–100
on halt 101–3
'hollow' 24, 25, 36, 40, 53–5, 80
'hurried'/rushing 27, 65
on lateral movements 104
on rein-back 103
on rhythm 92
on the rider 29, 47, 94, 106–7
standard phrases 88–9
on straightness 96

on suppleness 92–3
on transitions 104–5
understanding of 91
jumping 158
on lunge 117

Kimberley (dressage trainer) 29
kinesthetic senses 137, 140, 145
Kottas, Arthur 78, 115, 138, 159
Kyrklund, Kyra 166

language, use in training 137, 146–7, 273
languages, learning 16
lateral movements
Elementary level 83
introducing 80–1
judge's comments 104
teaching horse 80–1, 131–2
whilst hacking 84, 113, 121
'layers' concept 188–93
learning 16–17
by horse 131–2
sequence 126–7
leg aids 47, 106–7
teaching horse to move away from 80–1
leg yielding 81, 110–11, 161
teaching horse 81, 131–2
legs, horse's, 'stepping under' 56, 57, 160
legs, rider's 52, 56, 58
lengthening strides 19, 63–4, 79, 93, 106
Leo 140, 235
Lipizzaner 115
Lolly 18, 26, 27, 33, 47, 156
loose-schooling 115, 116–17
'Losgelassenheit' *see* suppleness
lungeing 117, 128

Marion 165, 266–7
meditative state 144
Medium level 84–5
dressage tests 197, 201, 212–13
medium strides 93, 106
memories, resourceful 169
mental experiences 169
mental harmony 67
mental rehearsal 131, 173–6
mental strategy 223–4
mentors, internal 173

metaphors, sensory 136–7, 146–7, 273
Michelangelo 60
mind, state of 132–3
mind bank 130–5
mind-body connection 65–7, 125–9
mirror effects, rider—horse 42–5
mismatch-to-match effect 59
moods
horses 134–5
rider's 132–4
music 64

narrow-beam attention 143, 145–6
nerves see competition nerves
Neuro-Linguistic Programming (NLP 34–5)
new movements, teaching horse 80–1, 131–2
Niggli, Wolfgang M 74
Nikki 115, 116–17, 159, 160
Novice level 78–81, 160
dressage tests 197, 198–208

observation, of other riders 56
Ollie 115, 116–17, 159
on the bit 50–2
on the forehand 39, 43
oneness 29–30
outline 50–2
advanced horse 58
use of gadgets 50–1

passive resistance 59, 69
patterns
judge's comments/marks 217
schooling 46–7
perfectionism 14, 110
piaffe 111
pirouettes 62, 105, 111
position of rider 38, 39–40, 46, 52–5
and defocusing 145
earning more advanced 56, 58
see also seat of rider
Preliminary level 75–8

questions, 'why' and 'how' 34–5

radio, playing around stables 157
Ransome, Arthur 16

'recreational' riding 26
Red 71, 115, 118–19, 174, 238–45
rehearsal, mental 131, 173–6
rein contact see contact
rein-back 83, 84
    essence of 103
    hacking 121
    judge's comments 103
reins
    giving and retaking 80
    lengthening 53–5, 58–9, 79
relationships 12
'relaxation' 29
rescue horses 129
resisting 40
results see test sheets
rhythm 27, 62, 63–5, 145, 160
    improving when hacking 112
    judge's comments 92
    loss of 62, 76
    'signature' 27, 63, 64
rider
    beliefs about ability 164–9
    benefits of dressage 31–3
    body control 33
    collapsed 38, 43
    control of four limbs 85
    dependency on trainer 165
    judge's comments 29, 47, 94, 106–7
    limitations 13
    looking down 43
    ownership of riding goals 166–7
    ownership of skills 275
    responsibility 16, 24
    state of mind 132–3
    straightness 70–1
    thinking like horse 187
rider—horse communication 30, 146
rider—horse relationship 65–7
Riding Towards the Light (Belasik) 27, 222, 278
routines 156
Roy 93, 95, 105, 108, 133, 134
    competition 191, 192, 218
    hacking 120–1
    position 53
    self belief 164–5
    training sessions 263–71
runners 25–6
Rural Riders 30

Russian Doll 188
Ryan, Matt 29

saddle, fitting 153–4
safety 32
Scales of Training 60–1, 160
    collection 72
    contact 67–9
    impulsion 69
    mnemonic 61
    rhythm 63–5
    straightness 70–1
    suppleness (Losgelassenheit) 65–7
school movements 73
schooling
    'cockpit' checks 132–5
    flexibility 134
    'outside the box' 112–14
    patterns 46–7
    planning sessions 135
Schooling Problems Solved with NLP (Jago) 34, 183
'Schwung' 69
seat of rider
    'driving' 106
    'independent' 31, 46
    rebalancing 77–8
self-belief 164–9
    negative 163
    tips for trainers 176–7
self-carriage, horse 19, 20, 72, 78–9, 160
self-driving 192
self-management 13, 188–93
self-talk 169–73
    critical 170
    helpful 171–3
senses, physical 136–7, 139–40, 145, 273
Shane 28, 40, 42, 138–9, 150–4, 275
    training sessions 254–62
shortening 63–4
shoulder, falling out through 38, 71
shoulder-in 83, 104
showjumpers 29
Silver Queen 108
simple changes 83, 111
singing (to horse) 64
skill, ownership of 275
slopes, use of 109, 118–19
slowing down 59, 69

Solo Schooling (Jago) 217
Spanish Riding School 30, 115
special moments 28
speed 65, 69
    see also tempo
spooky horse 44
'stepping under' 56, 57, 160
stiffness, horse 92–3
stirrup leathers, length 56, 58
straightness 70–1, 83
    horse 70, 114
    improving whilst hacking 113–14
    judge's comments on 96
    rider 70–1, 77, 83, 113–14
stretch zone 217–18
Stringer 139, 260
'submission' 55
suppleness (Losgelassenheit) 65–7
    improving whilst hacking 112–13
    judge's comments 92–3
    lateral 44, 76–7
    longitudinal 44, 76
    Preliminary level 76–7
supporters 189
suspension 69

tack fitting 153–4
Ted 40, 42, 150–4, 254–62, 275
tempo 63, 65
tension, rider's 64–5, 140–1
test sheets
    decoding specific comments 92–107
    patterns of marks/comments 217
    reading 88–91
thinking
    like horse 187
    'outside the box' 157–9
'through' 19, 20
time 51
Todd, Mark 29
tracking up 98
trainer
    belief in own skills 165
    critical comments 172
    honesty 172–3, 176
    rider dependency on 165
    riding of client's horse 272–3
trainers' tips

assumptions/beliefs 162
client's awareness/concentration 146–7
client's self-belief 176–7
training spiral 86–7
training aids 50–1
training spiral 62, 73
  and dressage judge's comments 91–107
  hacking 112–14
  Novice level 78–81
  Preliminary level 76–8
  tips for trainers 86–7
  see also Scales of Training
Training Strategies for Dressage Riders (de Kunffy) 47
transitions 19, 40
  between gaits 77–8
  canter-trot/canter-walk 111
  downward 77, 81, 111, 217
  essence of 104
  judge's comments on 104–5
  trot to halt 101–3
  within gaits 80
traps 163
travers 104
triggers 47, 169
Tristan 64, 156
trot
  essence of 99
  halt transition 101–3
  judge's comments 99
  slowing down 59
  stepping under 56, 57, 160
  transitions within gait 80
turn on forehand 80–1
turns 20–1, 76

under-performance 165–6
unwanted movements 110
'uphill' balance 19, 20, 97
Using Your Brain for a Change (Bandler) 180

V-shape (of horse's legs) 56, 57, 160

Vals 26
values 190–2, 275–6
video, mental 185
violence, physical 14
visual senses 136, 139–40, 145
visualization 185

walk 84
  essence of 98
  free 79, 113
  judge's comments 98–9
walk pirouette 105, 111
warm-up 145, 157
Wattie 36, 38, 66, 101–3
weather, internal 133–4
weight, rider's 46, 81
'why?' questions 35
wild horses 51
winning, beliefs about 191

'zone' model 217–18